CHINA BASE

County–Level Economy and Society

CHINA BASE

County–Level Economy and Society

Lixing Zou

China Development Bank Research Institute, China

World Scientific

NEW JERSEY • LONDON • SINGAPORE • BEIJING • SHANGHAI • HONG KONG • TAIPEI • CHENNAI

Published by

World Scientific Publishing Co. Pte. Ltd.
5 Toh Tuck Link, Singapore 596224
USA office: 27 Warren Street, Suite 401-402, Hackensack, NJ 07601
UK office: 57 Shelton Street, Covent Garden, London WC2H 9HE

Library of Congress Cataloging-in-Publication Data
Zou, Lixing.
China base : county-level economy and society / by Lixing Zou (China Development Bank Research Institute, Beijing, China).
pages cm
ISBN 978-9814630672
1. China--Economic conditions--2000– 2. China--Social conditions--2000– 3. Rural development--China. 4. Regional economics--China. I. Title.
HC427.95.Z6796 2015
333.3'151--dc23
2014035228

British Library Cataloguing-in-Publication Data
A catalogue record for this book is available from the British Library.

In-house Editors: Dong Lixi/Dr. Shakti Singh Solanki

Typeset by Stallion Press
Email: enquiries@stallionpress.com

Printed in Singapore by B & Jo Enterprise Pte Ltd

Dedicated to my grandparents

OVERVIEW

The whole country will be operating soundly if the prefectures and counties are well governed. County-level economy is the regional economy based in rural areas and occupies a fundamental strategic position in the national economy. Currently, Chinese rural areas are in a turbulent phase of transition, characterized by prominent conflict between urbanization and rural development, between the huge administrative system and the shortage of resources, between "small-scale production" and "big market", between the land operation right and land ownership, between "blood-transfusion" and "blood-making", and social conflicts. A new approach to coordinate urban and rural economic and social development is to **deepen the reform of the county-level administrative system, economic system and land system, speed up the construction of the market and society at the base level and enhance the overall, integrated and intrinsic dynamics of the county-level economy**. This book is of significant reference value to economic professionals, government leaders at all levels and to college students and faculties.

PREFACE

How to properly address issues concerning agriculture, countryside and farmers is a key and tough task for the reform and development of China. In the past 30-plus years, China has scored remarkable achievements in socioeconomic development, since the implementation of the reform and opening up policy, and has entered into a new phase of building a moderately prosperous society in all aspects, facilitating the socialist modernization. As the economy and society continue to prosper, some profound conflicts have also emerged and the issues concerning agriculture, countryside and farmers are the most prominent among them. Such issues have checked the socioeconomic development of China and therefore we must persevere in finding a way out and properly solve them.

Rural reform need of superstructure and economic base interaction need strategic initiative and creativity. The early reform and opening up of Fengyang Xiaogang village in Anhui province has given 18 farmer household contract responsibility systems, which is the great creation of rural reform and which vigorously promoted China's reform and development process. In the new period, China's reform has entered the phase of comprehensively deepened reform, where rural reform is particularly a difficult task, and needs new ideas, new creation and new measures. At the 18th Communist Party of China (CPC) National Congress, it's clearly pointed out that the integration of urban and rural development was the fundamental way to solve issues concerning agriculture, countryside and farmers. Efforts should be made to intensify the measures to coordinate urban and rural development, mobilize rural development, gradually narrow down the urban–rural gap and promote urban and rural prosperity. The country also should coordinate urbanization and agricultural modernization, and promote positive interaction between industrialization and urbanization with simultaneous development of industrialization, IT development, urbanization and agricultural modernization. We must continue to follow the principles of benefiting agriculture with industrial progress; city functions supporting rural development, and giving more, taking less and loosening control formula, formulate more policies to empower, benefit and enrich farmers, and allow farmers to participate in the modernization process equally and share the fruits of modernization. We must facilitate modern agricultural development, strengthen the integrated agricultural production capacity, and ensure food security and efficient supply of key agricultural commodities in the country. We must keep the focus on infrastructural construction and social undertakings development in rural areas, deepen and advance the construction of new countryside with poverty alleviation efforts, and improve the production and living conditions in rural areas, in all aspects. We must focus on increasing farmers' income and maintain the increase on a comparatively high level. We must continue to implement and improve the basic operation systems in rural areas and foster new operation entities; develop operation in various forms and of various scales and construct a new agricultural operation system that is intensive, specialized, organized and socialized. We must facilitate the improvement of the urban–rural integration system and mechanism, with focus on integrating the planning, infrastructure and public services in urban and rural areas, promote equal exchange of urban and rural elements with balanced allocation of public resources and form a new urban–rural relationship that promotes agricultural development with industrial development, rural development with urban development, mutual benefits of industry and agriculture, and urban and rural integration.

Issues concerning agriculture, countryside and farmers are development problems and need to be addressed in the course of development. But new problems will continue to emerge in this process, so the efforts to explore cannot stop. With the clear guideline, we still need to study specific issues in theory and in practice, and in particular intensify strategic and operational research on the mechanism reform and policy design. I'm glad that Dr. Zou, despite his busy schedule, has done some systematic and profound thinking on the county-level economy and society. The author is engaged in economic policy research with long-term focus on two markets, both at home and abroad, with long-term work in the policy banks. This experience has helped him in the study to have international vision, with strategic, forward-looking operability. This book is his years of work and research results, which I would like to recommend to economist, police makers and college students.

That brings us to the end of my preface.

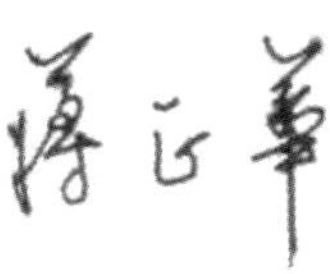

Professor Jiang Zhenhua
Former Vice Chairman of the Standing Committee
of the National People's Congress.

12 May 2014

CONTENTS

ABOUT THE AUTHOR

Dr. Zou Lixing was born in Jiangxi Province of P. R. China. As one of the "educated youths" going to the countryside in the 1970s, he was admitted by the university after the college entrance examination was recovered in China in 1978, and graduated in 1982 to work in ministries and commissions of the central government, holding a previous position as Division Chief at the research office of the State Council of China. He studied at Columbia University and American University in the US in the 1990s, and then worked in the World Bank. Since his return to China in 2003, he has been working in China Development Bank (CDB). In 2008, he was employed as a member of the World Economic Forum Global Agenda Council. Currently, he is the Vice President of the Research Institute of CDB and the Vice Chairman of China Social and Economic System Analysis Research Society. He has been involved in research on economic policies for a long time, mainly on international finance, technical economy and rural issues; he has also written research reports, drafted documents of the central government and speeches of leadership and published articles on newspaper at home and abroad. His recent publications mainly include: *Financial Empire: The US Development and*

Enlightenment published by Hunan University Press (2009 edition); *Developing Finance and Sustainable Development,* Hunan University Press (2008 edition); *Strategic Thinking on Further Promoting the Development of the Chinese–US Economic and Trade Relations* (2013, Center for International relation of United States); *China's Rise: Development-oriented Finance and Sustainable Development,* World Scientific Press (2014 edition).

INTRODUCTION

County-level economy is regional economy based in the countryside. A general approach to advance urbanization, industrialization and the coordinated economic and social development in rural areas is to deepen the reform of the county-level administrative system, economic system and land system, speed up the construction of the basic-level market and society and improve the overall integrated and intrinsic dynamics of county-level economy. Since the foundation of the People's Republic of China (PRC), in particular the implementation of the reform and opening up policy, Chinese countryside has undergone dramatic transformations and is troubled with many issues which have checked the economic development and reform of China. Chinese rural areas are in a turbulent phase of transition, characterized by prominent conflict between urbanization and rural development, between the huge administrative system and the shortage of resources, between "small-scale production" and "big market", between the land operation right and land ownership, between "blood-transfusion" and "blood-making", and social conflicts. Issues concerning agriculture, countryside and farmers in China are development problems and need to be addressed in the course of development. In the 1970s, I went to work in a poor village in an old revolutionary base area in Jiangxi and since then I have developed a special bond with the countryside and has regarded the study of rural issues as one of my top priorities. Recently, I have been able to sort out my findings in the past decades and presented them in this book.

This book consists of the following chapters:

The first chapter is devoted to the analysis of the county-level economy. Issues concerning agriculture, the countryside and the farmers are still very serious in the county-level economy due to the flaws with the dual system, the fiscal management system and the financial management system. To address these issues fundamentally, China government need to pay much attention to the development of the county-level economy, carefully develop the county-level plan, improve the county-level fiscal and financial system, establish and improve the training system for rural technicians and the basic social security system in rural areas, promote the transition of "agriculture based on the cultivated land" to "the structure paying equal attention to grain and greening", and greatly enhance the intrinsic dynamics of county-level economy.

The second chapter is devoted to the analysis of county governance. China shall deepen the reform of the county-level political and economic systems, "downsize government organs, separate government functions from enterprise management, infuse government functions with the communist spirit and conduct collaborative governance", facilitate the transformation from the county/city-level all-around government to a service government, reform the rural public administration and social service network with villages and towns as the hubs, construct a new rural system with school areas as the center and promote the steady socioeconomic development at the county level.

The third chapter is devoted to the analysis of land reform. Land is the scarcest resource and every bit of it is valuable. Idle land and hollow villages are just temporary phenomena in the course of urbanization, and they will definitely be reclaimed by future generations. Small-scale peasant economy, with the scale of about 20 to 30 mu, is a major phenomenon and trend in China in the long run. China should, at the macro-level, consider "local management of state land resources and the national land fund", and foster different market players; at the micro-level, optimize the rural land management system, form the structure consisting of "state-owned farmland, agricultural base in suburbs, rural collective land, rural construction site and household contracted land", help improve the "land-to-the-tiller" market operation mechanism, and further clarify and give play to the role of the state, the collective and farmer households in ensuring food security.

The fourth chapter analyzes land right. The focus is on the relationship between the land-use right and land ownership, in order to provide some theoretical support for the adjustment of rural land policy in the new era. The land value is the sum of values of a series of land rights. The land use right can be extracted from the bundle of land rights and is characterized by the subject, object and exclusivity of the land property relations. The land-use right can be traded, mortgaged and inherited. After clarifying the relationship between land ownership and the land-use right, China government, on the one hand, may consider setting up the national land fund in order to better reflect land ownership through the market mechanism; on the other hand, consider extending the term of the rural household land contract from 30 years to eternity and make the contract inheritable. By doing so, it's not only possible for us to tap the tremendous value resources of rural land, but also fundamentally solve the "idling" of state-owned land and promote the sound and sustainable development of urbanization and rural society.

The fifth chapter analyzes land financial market construction. Land financial market is an important part of market system. Gradually establishes and perfects the financial market, promotes the land capitalization–capital assets securitization–securities market–market standardization, improving the capacity of the government in the land market as a whole, guiding the propulsion of urbanization and new agricultural construction, realizes the intensive utilization of land resources, land and real estate market price stability, on ground, to realize the aim of sustainable utilization of land resources.

The sixth chapter analyzes the gains and losses of the cancellation of the agricultural tax. The cancellation of the agricultural tax in 2005 put an end to the thousands-of-year-long practice of paying tax for land cultivation in China, and played a certain guiding role in easing the farmers' burden, but it is difficult to fundamentally alleviate the poverty of disadvantaged farmers solely and was not good for fostering their awareness as modern rural citizens. In order to build a new socialist countryside, China needs to strengthen the education on the obligations and rights of rural citizens.

The seventh chapter discusses the following five relations in the course of urbanization: Positive interaction between urban development and industrial development, coordinated urban and rural development, mutually supportive development of new towns and old towns, rational layout of coastal areas and East and West China, and the carrying forward of the past and the present.

The eighth chapter probes into how the new household manufacturing industry supports the urbanization strategy. Urbanization needs the support of industries. And industries and urban areas are mutually supportive and dependent. The new household manufacturing industry, which emerges with the digital, intelligent information technologies, may combine traditional craft with modern technologies, original concepts with actual manufacturing, medium- and large-sized cities with widely scattered small towns, town construction with rural development, local resources with the global market, in order to provide major industrial support for the healthy development of new urbanization.

The ninth chapter focuses on the rural development plan. Only when the vast majority of farmers have reached the moderately well-off living standards can China realize the comprehensive moderately well-off society; only when the rural areas are modernized can China realize nationwide modernization. China should, according to the development trend of industrialization and urbanization, carefully develop the rural development plan and coordinate urban and rural development.

The tenth chapter analyzes the ecological control of rocky desertification. The Karst mountainous areas in Southwest China grow only rocks, no trees and are known for their ecological deterioration and large population in China. We may combine the financial and intellectual leverages, adopt the "company + finance + technology + farmers' household" operational mode and reinforce the ecological control of rocky desertification.

The eleventh chapter explores international agricultural cooperation. Strengthening international agricultural cooperation is significant for safeguarding food security in China and the world. In South America, China may focus on improving and building infrastructure for warehousing, logistics, ports and harbors and agricultural products processing, to strengthen Sino–South America strategic agricultural cooperation.

There is certain internal connection between the above chapters: To address the current major conflicts in rural areas, we emphasize the fundamental role of county economy in the socioeconomic development of China, explore the new approach to deepen the county-level political and economic reforms, analyze the relationship between land ownership and the land operation right, help improve the "land-to-the-tiller" market operation mechanism, and properly deal with the gains and losses caused by the cancellation of the agricultural tax; start from rural planning, develop a sustainable rural development strategy, and give play to the role of developmental finance in special areas (such as areas with rocky desertification, former revolutionary base areas, areas inhabited by minority nationalities, border areas and poverty-stricken areas) to facilitate local development; make full use of the domestic and international markets, strengthen international agricultural cooperation and provide necessary support to ensure food security in China.

My research is problem-oriented, and aims to provide effective solutions and reference for the modernization of China.

China's development is closely related to the land resources, land resource is the root of the "Rural, Farmer, Agriculture", the "Rural, Farmer, Agriculture" is the core of the county economy. Therefore, when I was in the research of county economy, and always carried out a land reform of the main line, I tried to have a new train of thought on land reform, promoting the development of county economy, and promoting China's sustainable development.

Here, I regard county areas as rural areas and the object of study. To study county areas is to study rural areas. County areas are mostly agricultural areas with the county town as the center and the extensive countryside as the basis, and bonded by market towns; the county level is the primary level of China's administrative system and county areas are normally viewed as rural areas in China by custom; county-level administrative areas are an integrated system with complete functions and with distinct rural characteristics, and it's helpful to design systematic policies by enlarging rural problems into county-level socioeconomic problems. Enhancing the overall, integrated and intrinsic dynamics of the county-level economy is a new approach to coordinate urban and rural economic and social growth.

Since the issues concerning agriculture, countryside and the farmers are more prominent in remote county areas than in suburban counties of medium- and large-sized cities in China; my focus is on the county economy relatively far away from medium- and large-sized cities.

Economy is inseparable from society. To enhance the role of social factors and express the feelings toward tradition and history, I tend to use the concept of rural areas here. Rural areas are rural communities consisting of market towns and neighboring villages with farmers and agriculture as the center, including the vast areas below the county-town level. Rural areas are the same with the countryside in the traditional sense.

My central argument is that: The whole country will be operating soundly if the prefectures and counties are well governed; China shall consolidate the fundamental and strategic status of county economy in the national economy. Specifically, China should deepen the reforms of the county-level administrative system, economic system and land system, facilitate the grassroots market construction and social construction, foster new operation entities, promote the integration of urban and rural planning, infrastructure and public services, advance development projects for poverty alleviation, strengthen the blood-making ability of rural areas, enhance the intrinsic dynamism of rural development, substantially improve production and living conditions in rural areas and promote county-level economic and social modernization. This strategic choice will achieve huge benefits with low cost, and thus is the general approach to advance urbanization, industrialization and the coordinated social and economic growth in rural areas. It will help not only stimulate the tremendous development potentials of county areas, but also improve the national unified market system, promote the equal exchange of urban and rural factors and balanced allocation of public resources, expand domestic production and market demands, and lay a solid foundation for the sustainable development of China. By solving the political and economic problems at the county-level, China will be able to provide precious experience and vast leeway to deepen the reform of national political and economic systems, and speed up the modernization pace of China.

The above are my humble views, some of which might be immature, to start the discussion and I'm looking forward to yours, including criticism.

Lixing Zou
May 2014

CHAPTER 1

COUNTY ECONOMY IS THE BASE OF CHINA'S MODERNIZATION

China's county economy is based on the rural regional economy. Due to the dual system, the defects of fiscal management system and financial management system, "three rural problems" in the county economy in China is still serious. This attaches great importance to the development of county economy, elaborates the county planning, perfects the county fiscal and financial system, the establishment of a basic rural security system, promotes the "land agriculture" to "the grain structure of giving attention to two or more things" transformation, vigorously promotes the endogenous dynamic of county economy, and helps to fundamentally solve the "three rural problems".

1.1. Status Quo of County Economy

County economy is the regional economy with the county town as the center and the vast countryside as the base, bonded by market towns. By the end of 2011, China had 2,853 county-level administrative areas (excluding Hong Kong Special Administrative Region, Macao Special Administrative Region and Taiwan Province); the land area in county-level administrative areas had reached about 8,682,000 square kilometers, accounting for about 90.44% of the total land in the country; the population in these areas had registered 885 million, 65.72% of the national total; the gross domestic product (GDP) in these areas had reached 24.14 trillion Yuan, 51.04% of the national GDP; the average GDP per capita in these areas had registered 27,590 Yuan, 78.43% of the national average; the general budget revenue in these areas had reached 1.32 trillion Yuan, accounting for 25.07% of the national level.[1]

"The whole country will be operating soundly if the prefectures and counties are well governed." County economy is the most fundamental political and economic unit in China and a major base for national economic development and social stability. Nationwide, county economy consists basically of agriculture, rural areas and farmers, hence consolidating and expanding county economy will play a key role in coordinating urban and rural economic and social development, fundamentally solving issues concerning agriculture, the countryside and the farmers, promoting the overall national economic development and building a moderately prosperous society in an all-round way.

Since the foundation of the PRC, in particular since the implementation of the reform and opening up policy, China's countryside has undergone profound changes, and the county economy has made considerable progress: China's agricultural products used to be in short supply for a long time and now the supply and demand are basically balanced; the integrated agriculture–industry–commerce operation mode, created by farmers in China, has made remarkable achievements in remodeling the traditional small-scale rural household operations. Like the macro trend of Chinese economy, the county economy in China has entered into the transition phase toward market-oriented economy. The agricultural mechanization level has been improved year over year, infrastructure construction such as farmland and irrigation facilities have been reinforced, and modern agricultural development represented by controlled

[1] *Source*: *Practices of China's County Economy Promoting Industry Upgrade* by the Institute of Industrial Economics of China Academy of Social Sciences and *China Statistical Yearbook 2012*. Without special note, the data in this paper are all derived from *China Statistical Yearbook* series.

environmental agriculture has been facilitated. With the development of the market-oriented economy, the change in the employment structure in rural areas, and the deepening system reforms, the farmers' income pattern has shown fundamental changes, with more and more income from market and non-agricultural sources. Transport and communications infrastructure in rural areas has also undergone dramatic changes. The nine-year compulsory education has been provided for free to rural students. The social security issues in rural areas have attracted increasing attention. But, since the county economy is based on the vast backward rural areas where traditional systems and the natural economy have deeply rooted for thousands of years, leading to the urban and rural gap in productivity, and because of the lasting influence of policies adopted by the country in the early stages of industrialization to support industrial development with agricultural resources, coupled with the deviation of policies, the county economy is at a disadvantaged and helpless position, and most counties, despite their abundant agricultural resources, have only a small scale of industrial development and a thin stream of financial revenue. The county economy is going through a hard time. In particular, since China's entry into the World Trade Organization (WTO), the shocks of international economic integration have revealed more complex and unique problems and conflicts with the county economy in multiple transitions. The issues concerning agriculture, the countryside and the farmers and more severe, in particular in the following aspects:

First, low agricultural benefits and low income for farmers. China boasts a large population but limited land. For the 260 million rural households, the land area per household is only 0.41 hectare, and the cultivated land area per household is less than 7.5 mu; it is a typical small-scale operation. What's worse, the agricultural output is limited and the price is low, so the agricultural benefits are poor. In major grain producing areas in Central and West China, the input to output ratio for grain production is nearly zero, or even negative, reducing the incentive to grow grains. The low agricultural benefits, severe regional natural disasters and uncertain market risks have made the farmers' income more unstable and vulnerable. The per capita net agricultural income for farmers was only 1,268 Yuan in 1997, and even less between 1998 and 2006, and started to increase from 2007 and reached 1,897 Yuan in 2011. In particular, in the eight major grain producing provinces in Central China (Hebei, Jilin, Heilongjiang, Anhui, Jiangxi, Henan, Hubei, and Hunan), the per capita income of farmers remained lower than the average national level for five consecutive years from 1998 to 2003, increasing by 2.73% on an average. The low income of farmers made the rural market very sluggish. The proportion of rural consumption in national consumption dropped from 31.9% in 2001 to 22.7% in 2011. The rural population accounted for nearly 70% of the national total, and the rural consumption less than 30% of the national total, severely preventing the expansion of domestic demands. Because of the low agricultural efficiency, production factors are drained, resource restraints are strengthened, food production is unstable and the supply–demand relationship is intense. From 1998 to 2010, the national cultivated land area shrank from 1,945 million mu to 1,826 million mu, close to the warning limit of arable land of 1,800 billion mu.[2] From 2000 to 2003, the grain output has fallen for four consecutive years. The situation did improve from 2004 to 2011, and by 2011, the nationwide food crops sown area had registered 110.573 million hectares, the grain output, 571,208,000 tons, and the per capita grain output, 425 kilograms. The fall of grain output and the rise of grain price increased the burden of general consumers. The first grain price fluctuation occurred in October 2003, when the grain price, mainly the price of beans, wheat and flour, increased by 20%, driving up the bean price in the international market. The second grain price fluctuation occurred in mid-March 2004. Compared with the same period in the previous year, the price of the three major grain products increased by about 50%. Specifically, the rice price increased by 60% to 70%, the wheat price, by more than 40%, and the corn price, by more than 21%. The situation improved slightly in 2005. According to the data

[2] *Source*: Speech by Cai Jiming, a Chinese People's Political Consultative Conference (CPPCC) member, at the 5th plenary session of the 11th CPPCC National Committee.

of the Food and Agriculture Organization (FAO) of the United Nations (UN), driven up by growing demands and oil price and global warming, the global food price soared by 40% in 2007; in 2011, the average value of world's major grain prices was 228, the highest since 1990. According to the estimation of UN Environment Programme (UNEP), by 2050, the agricultural output would decrease by 10 to 20%, and the rice price will increase by 30%, and the corn price will double. Hence, food security and the farmers' income are still worthy of high attention.

Second, heavy farmers' burden and rural debts. Farmers' burden is a prominent problem that has long checked rural development. Since the implementation of the reform and opening up policy, the central government has rolled out policies to ease the farmers' burden. In 2005, the State Council announced to cancel the agricultural tax, but the burden on the farmers is still heavy. The burden includes: First, administrative and institutional charges and operation service expenses undertaken by farmers, village-level organizations and farmers' cooperatives by law, and the expenses and labor borne by farmers for the village-level collective charity projects by law and regulation;[3] second, some commodity tax, medical expenses and education expenses borne by farmers in production and daily life consumption. According to the statistical results of the monitoring of burden on the farmers in a 100 counties in 30 provinces conducted by the Ministry of Agriculture, in 2011, the per capita primary education expenses for the monitored households increased by 18.1% over the previous year, and the family planning services charged 4.5% more than the previous year. Except for some developed areas in East China, the burden on the farmers in most areas exceeded the maximum level stipulated by the central government, i.e., not more than 5% of the per capita income of farmers in the previous year, and reached about 10% in reality. It's especially worthy of mentioning that

[3]According to the Ministry of Agriculture's definition of the constitution of farmers' burden, farmers' burden includes: All kinds of payment to the collective (land contract fee, collective production and housing construction fee, etc.), social burdens (fines, fees levied by local governments and the collective and administrative and institutional charges), "One Matter, One Solution" fund raising and money for labor.

the heavy burden on farmers is mainly caused by the heavy rural debts. The village- and town-level organizations are overstaffed and the village- and town-level finance has to support a large number of employees. The number of persons living on the village- and town-level finance in China is approximately nine million, with over 200 per village/town, and the number is still growing.[4] If the superstructure reforms such as the reform of village/town organizations, rural educational system reform, and county/village fiscal system reform are not thorough enough, it will be hard to realize the goal of alleviating the burden on the farmers through tax and fee policies. Statistical data show that, in 2009, among the 36 provinces, autonomous regions, municipalities directly under the central government and cities specifically designated in the state plan, 16 provinces had deficit in the summary of town/village financial statements, most of which were located in Central and West China.[5] For example, according to the survey report on the basic county/village fiscal situation in Shandong Province, by the end of 2011, the local debt in Shandong had registered 175.056 billion Yuan (excluding Qingdao), almost equivalent to the county-level public fiscal revenue in 2011. Because of the high expenditure press of local governments, it's common for them to charge, levy and raise funds arbitrarily. This is also a problem worthy of much attention.

Third, it's hard to transfer surplus rural labor force. It's a trend and a consensus that in the course of economic growth, the number of farmers must be reduced. But now it's extremely difficult to transfer surplus rural labor force in China. On one hand, the number of jobs created by township enterprises has decreased, and small towns are not attractive enough for farmers, making it difficult to transfer the rural population to urban areas and non-agricultural sectors; on the other, the employment situation in urban areas is grim, and the existence of the large number of laid-off workers objectively rejects rural labor force. Every year, many rural young and middle-aged rural residents go

[4] *Source*: Zhu Lisheng, Guo Yan. Difficulties Facing Town/Village Fiscal Operation in China and Counter measures. Data Communications. January 2006.

[5] *Source*: Chu Guoliang. Research on the County/Village Fiscal Difficulties and Counter measures in China. 27 September 2013.

to coastal provinces such as Guangdong to find jobs, but most of them find it hard to settle down in the place where they are working or become urban residents. According to the results of the sampling survey launched by the National Bureau of Statistics of China, it can be calculated that, in 2012, the number of farmer-turned workers in China reached 262.61 million, 73.4% of which were married, and among those employed outside their hometown, 58.2% were married. Nearly 80% of farmer-turned workers move on their own rather than with the whole family and their family life is still based in the countryside. They return to their hometown during vacations/holidays and busy farming season, and expect to do so when they get old, sick or lose their job. This is a special phenomenon in China. Farmer-turned workers move between urban and rural areas like a pendulum and migrant birds, leading to social problems such as "left-behind children, left-behind senior citizens and left-behind women". Such simple labor force migration costs a huge social price, at the expense of the happiness of three generations: Farmer-turned workers are not able to enjoy the family life, the left-behind parents suffer from heavy labor and mental burdens, and left-behind children have raised prominent educational, psychological and security issues. As the rural areas lose the labor force in their prime of life, villages become more and more hollow, with worrisome social security order. The farming burden is thus shifted onto women and the left-behind seniors, which further checks the modern development of agriculture.

If we compare the above issues with urban development, it won't be hard to find that the urban–rural dual structure is being consolidated. First, the absolute value of the urban–rural income gap has been growing, displaying a scissors difference. The urban–rural income difference was 210 Yuan in 1978 and grew to 14,833 Yuan in 2011. Second, the absolute value of the urban–rural consumption gap has also been widening. The urban–rural consumption difference was 195 Yuan in 1978 and increased to 9,940 Yuan in 2011, also a scissors difference. Third, the gap between urban and rural educational, health and living standards is huge. China still adopts the 2011 teachers staffing standards for primary and middle schools, and accordingly the student to teacher ratio in primary schools in cities, counties/towns and rural areas is 19:1, 21:1, and 23:1, respectively; that in middle schools is 13.5:1, 16:1 and 18:1, respectively. In 1999, in urban areas, the primary-to-secondary-school enrollment rate was 100% while that in rural areas was only 91%; the junior-high-school-to-senior-high-school enrollment rate in urban areas increased from 40% in 1985 to 55.4% in 2002, while in the same period, that in rural areas fell from 22.3% to 18.6%. Research findings of the 10th Five-Year Plan of National Educational Sciences show that, the higher the educational degree is, the wider the urban–rural gap appears: 6% of agricultural population and 21% of non-agricultural population in China are enrolled into higher-level schools; 0.8% of agricultural population and 13.2% of non-agricultural population into technical secondary schools; 0.2% of agricultural population and 11.1% of non-agricultural population into junior colleges; 0.02% of agricultural population and 5.63% of non-agricultural population into undergraduate programs; and 0.001% of agricultural population and 0.323% of non-agricultural population into postgraduate programs. In 2011, the number of health technicians per 1,000 urban residents was 7.90, while that per 1,000 rural residents, 3.19; the number of beds in medical and health institutions per 1,000 urban residents was 6.24, while that per 1,000 rural residents, 2.80; the maternal mortality rate in rural areas was 26.5 per 100,000 rural residents while that in urban areas was 25.2 per 100,000 urban residents; the mortality rate of children under five in rural areas was 19.1%, 2.7 times of that in urban areas of 7.1%; the life expectancy in urban areas was 75.2 years while that in rural areas was 69.5 years.[6] The employee pension insurance in urban and rural areas has been expanding and has basically covered all the employees, except for some individually-owned businesses and flexible employees. By 2010, the social endowment insurance coverage rate for the senior aged above 60 years in rural areas was only 34.6%, with the average monthly pension of 74 Yuan.[7] The unemployment insurance rate in urban areas has reached 71.7% while that in rural areas is almost zero.

---

[6] *Source*: UN Development Programmes (UNDP) 2005. China National Human Development Report.

[7] *Source*: www.zgxc.org.cn. 27 September 2013.

As to the subsistence security coverage rate in urban and rural areas, by the end of 2007, 22.71 million urban residents had claimed the subsistence allowance in the country, and governments at all levels had spent 27.5 billion Yuan on subsistence security, basically covering all those in need. But in rural areas, there is only the "five guarantees" system. By the end of 2011, the system has supported 5,786,200 rural residents, accounting for about 0.9% of the rural population, and the system had received 11.84 billion Yuan, while had spent 11.361 billion Yuan. In 2011, the number of rural residents participating in the new rural social endowment security was 326.435 million, and among them, 89.218 million had reached the age to claim the pension.

The hollow villages are increasing and traffic jam in cities is becoming more serious due to the urban–rural differences. As young and middle-aged labors flow and move away from the rural area, the left-behind villagers see great imbalanced age structure, social cultural structure and economic industrial layout, which gives birth to empty residences, idle land, industrial and social cultural cavities, lead to hollow villages, stagnate the development of the rural politics, economy, culture and social undertakings, and even cause them to regress. On the other hand, cities are overcrowded and have problems such as traffic jams, few job opportunities, housing shortage, polarization between the rich and the poor, deteriorated public health, environmental pollution and ecological damage. However, in the short run, the urban–rural gap will keep attracting an enormous rural population to move to cities, aggravating the phenomenon of villages being increasingly hollow. The hollower the villages and the more serious the movement of local villagers, the more congested the cities. Both just form a vicious circle and further aggravate the urban–rural dual pattern for economic, social and cultural development.

The urban–rural differences have badly hurt the rights and interests of farmers and intensified social conflicts. This issue is getting more and more serious in some aspects. For example, the rural land is expropriated at a low cost at the expense of farmers' interests, and the compensation for land requisition is often in arrears. The exchange of land for development funds and attracting investments with a low land price and even "free land" have seriously damaged farmers' interests and caused many economic and social conflicts. The situation has improved for the default of payment to farmer-turned workers. The proportion of rural workers employed outside their hometown whose salaries were in arrears fell from 4.1% in 2008 to 0.5% in 2012, and that of rural workers in construction sites was 1.5%.[8] The number of land-requisition related petitions has increased, and more farmer-turned workers have adopted extreme means to ask for their salaries. As to finance, the allocation of rural financial resources has seriously deviated from the agriculture, the countryside and the farmers. A lot of rural funds have been channeled into cities through financial institutions, making it harder for rural development. It can be said that in China, farmers are in the most difficult position, agriculture cannot solve its own problems and the poor countryside has affected the realization of a moderately well-off society in an all-round way in China.

1.2. Root Causes of Issues Concerning Agriculture, the Countryside and the Farmers

It is natural and to some extent inevitable to have the urban–rural gap in the course of economic development and resource allocation in a market-oriented way, because production factors will always flow to places with higher productivity. But besides the impacts of the universal law, there are some special institutional reasons for huge urban–rural gap in China. First, the dual system; second, the backward fiscal management system; and third, the poor financial management system. The specific analysis is as follows:

1.2.1. *The dual system: Taking too much, giving little, and stiff control*

First, the government has taken too much from farmers, and weakened the latter's ability of self-accumulation and self-development. Since the founding of the PRC, farmers have accumulated at least 1,713 trillion Yuan for national construction by

[8] *Source*: 2012 Monitoring and Investigative Report for Rural Migrant Workers.

providing capital and reducing the cost of industrialization through the scissors difference between industrial and agricultural products, and by providing abundant and cheap labor force and land resources to non-agricultural sectors. Specifically, in the 46 years from 1952 to 1997, farmers accumulated 1,264.1 billion Yuan for national industrialization through the scissors difference between industrial and agricultural products, with the average of 27.48 billion Yuan per year. The statistical data of the Ministry of Agriculture show that in 2010, farmers in the country directly borne a total of 36.355 billion Yuan of expenses, 38.63 Yuan per capita, among which, 8.792 billion Yuan was paid to the collective, 14.151 billion Yuan was paid for social burdens, and 3.412 billion Yuan paid in substitution for labor. The taxes paid by township enterprises also increased from 230.8 billion Yuan in 2001, to 313 billion Yuan in 2003, to even 968.2 billion Yuan in the first eight months of 2012.[9]

A lot of rural funds have been drained through deposits in either rural credit cooperatives: By the end of 2010, the deposit balance and the loan balance of rural credit cooperatives in the country were 8.8 trillion Yuan and 5.9 trillion Yuan, respectively, with the difference of 2.9 trillion Yuan; or postal savings: The year-end deposit balance of postal savings below the county-level registered 292.7 billion Yuan in 2000 and more than 2.65 trillion Yuan by the end of 2012.[10]

The land requisition at the low price has led to the drainage of a lot of revenue from land price difference. The government spends 10,000 to 30,000 Yuan per mu on an average on cultivated land requisition, and sells it at 150,000 Yuan to 300,000 Yuan per mu, and with about 20% of it deducted as the development cost, the government will earn a net land price difference of about 110,000 Yuan to 240,000 Yuan per mu. From 1989 to 2002, the non-agricultural construction occupied 36.894 million mu. Suppose 70% of it was expropriated from farmers, and half of it was for commercial

---

[9] *Source*: Official website of the Ministry of Agriculture (http://www.moa.gov.cn/).
[10] *Source*: chinareform.org.cn (http://www.chinareform.org.cn/) and Summary of 2012 Report on Financial Services for agriculture, the countryside and the farmers by Postal Savings Bank of China.

purposes, local governments would earn a net land price difference between 1,420.4 billion Yuan and 3,099.1 billion Yuan.

Because of their low salaries, farmer-turned workers have left most of the values they have created in urban areas. The average monthly salary of migrant workers increased from 1,340 Yuan in 2008 to 2,290 Yuan in 2012, and it is higher in East China than in Central and West China. In comparison, given that the GDP generated per migrant worker is 25,000 Yuan per year on an average, in 2012, the GDP generated by the 262.61 million migrant workers in China would surpass 6.5 trillion Yuan.

Second, the proportion of public resources allocated to rural areas is too small. The share of state revenue spent on agriculture is too small. The expenditure on agriculture, forestry and water resources is less than 10% of the total fiscal expenditure of the country (Table 1.1).

The share of national expenditure on social undertakings allocated to rural areas is too small. Among the national expenditure, the expenditure on rural education takes up less than 2% of the total educational expenditure (Table 1.2), and the expenditure on rural medical and health services, less than 40% of the total medical and health expenditure (Table 1.3).

Table 1.1: State expenditure on agriculture, forestry, and water resources (100 million Yuan).

	Total state expenditure	**Expenditure on agriculture, forestry, and water resources**	**Percentage (%)**
2007	50,091.16	3,404.7	6.8
2008	62,592.66	4,544.01	7.3
2009	76,299.93	6,720.41	8.8
2010	89,874.16	8,129.58	9.0
2011	108,930	9,890	9.1
2012	125,712	11,903	9.5

Source: The basic data is derived from the national public expenditure balance sheet of previous years, and the percentage is calculated by the author.

Table 1.2: National expenditure on education (100 million Yuan).

	Educational expenditure	Expenditure to dissolve debts of rural compulsory education	Expenditure on school building construction for rural primary and middle schools	Expenditure on teaching facilities of rural primary and middle schools	Percentage of the expenditure on rural education to total educational expenditure (%)
2010	12,550	82.78	118.16	19.53	1.8
2011	16,497.33	131.74	156.97	30.51	1.9
2012	21,242.1	38.36	167.59	44.19	1.2

Source: The basic data is derived from the national public expenditure balance sheet of previous years, and the percentage is calculated by the author.

Table 1.3: National expenditure on medical and health services (100 million Yuan).

	Medical and health expenditure	Expenditure on township health centers	Expenditure on new rural cooperative medical care	Expenditure on rural medical financial assistance	Percentage of expenditure on rural medical and health services to the total medical and health expenditure (%)
2010	4,804.18	255.09	1,041.83	78.32	28.6
2011	6,429.51	332.98	1,738.65	103.76	33.8
2012	7,245.11	457.91	2,035.1	106.16	35.9

Source: The basic data is derived from the national public expenditure balance sheet of previous years, and the percentage is calculated by the author.

The share of national expenditure on social security programs allocated to rural areas is too small. For a long time, the major sources of security in rural areas are family support and land resources. The national expenditure on rural social relief and natural disaster relief

Table 1.4: Rural social relief expenses and natural disaster relief expenses.

	Rural social relief expenses		Natural disaster relief expenses	
	Amount (10,000 Yuan)	Percentage of the total expenditure on civil undertakings (%)	Amount (10,000 Yuan)	Percentage of the total expenditure on civil undertakings (%)
2000	873,212.7	3.8	35,199,486.6	15.3
2008	3,267,531	15.2	6,098,084.0	28.4
2009	4,878,911	22.4	1,991,908.0	9.1
2010	5,796,459	21.5	2,371,831.0	8.8
2011	8,389,638	26	1,287,026.0	4

Source: *2012 China Rural Statistical Yearbook.*

is less than 30% of the total expenditure on civil undertakings (Table 1.4). From 2010 onward, national expenditure started to include the subsidies to new rural social endowment insurance fund and the expenditure on rural subsistence allowances. But the subsidies to new rural social endowment insurance fund is less than 25% of those to the social security fund and the expenditure on rural subsistence allowances did not exceed to that on urban subsistence allowances until in 2012 (Table 1.5).

Third, the administration system features urban–rural segmentation and imposes too many limits on farmer-turned workers. The strict household registration system is the major institutional guarantee for the formation and long-time existence of the urban–rural dual society. Despite the existence of a large number of rural migrant workers in urban areas, urban governments fail to include the expenditure on providing public services to these migrant workers into the government budget, but rather they charge arbitrarily, leading to a new dual structure in urban areas. Migrant workers in cities live in poor conditions with limited income and no social security, they find it hard to send their children to schools, and some of them even are discriminated against in the job market and are

Table 1.5: National expenditure on rural social security (100 million Yuan).

	State subsidies to new rural social endowment fund	Percentage of national subsidies to social security fund (%)	Expenditure on urban subsistence allowances	Expenditure on rural subsistence allowances
2010	240.09	10.4	539.53	446.59
2011	649.41	20.6	675.06	665.48
2012	932.91	24.4	666.36	698.71

Source: The basic data is derived from the national public expenditure balance sheet of previous years, and the percentage is calculated by the author.

paid less for the same job than non-migrant workers. They don't have the sense of belonging in cities. As a result, they tend to change jobs frequently, and their average duration on a job is shortened, which is bad for upgrading the industrial structure. The new-generation migrant workers have taken the dominant place. According to the floating population monitoring data of National Population and Family Planning Commission (now National Health and Family Planning Commission) in 2011, the number of farmer-turned workers born after 1980 had taken up 44.84% of the total of farmer-turned workers at working ages. **The new-generation farmer-turned workers are more and more aware of their interests and rights. If neglected, they will become more distanced from the urban life due to the long-time struggling conditions and the growing sense of unfair treatment, leading to the intensifying of the dual structure and the widening of the rich–poor gap, and even unnecessary conflicts and confrontations.** By the end of 2011, the urbanization rate in China had reached 51.27% and the rural population will quicken the pace to flow into urban areas in masses. **As the urbanization pace speeds up, we should prevent the urban–rural duality transforming into the urban duality.**

Industrial policies are more favorable for cities than for the countryside. When it's the seller's market and economic growth is mainly restrained by resources, the focus of industrial policies is to control the resource competition between township enterprises and state-owned enterprises in urban areas, and emphasize that township enterprises should obtain raw materials, process them and sell products in local areas. When it's the buyer's market and economic growth is mainly restrained by market demands, the focus of industrial policies is to control the market competition between township enterprises and state-owned enterprises in urban areas, and restrain five and fifteen kinds of heavily polluting small-scale enterprises, most of which are township enterprises.

The market regulatory policy for agricultural products leans toward the urban market rather than the rural market, and protects industrial benefits at the expense of agricultural benefits. Farmers have always borne the cost of maintaining urban social stability and the market price of agricultural products has been strictly controlled, the theoretical basis for which is that the rise of grain prices will lead to inflation.

The ownership discrimination of credit policies. In 2008, the loan balance of township enterprises registered 745.4 billion Yuan, accounting for 2.5% of the total loan balance of 30,339.5 billion Yuan, while the added value of township enterprises was 8,412.7 billion Yuan, accounting for 27.98% of the national GDP of 30,067 billion Yuan.[11] The amount of loan allocated to rural areas is not sufficient, and what's worse, the financial innovation in rural areas is restrained.

1.2.2. *High operational cost, unbalanced operation and heavy operational burden caused by the backward fiscal management system*

1.2.2.1. *High local government operational cost due to the multi-tiered government administrative system*

The government system below the provincial level consists of the provincial government, municipal/prefecture-level government, county-level government and township government. The multi-tiered government administrative system makes it convenient for counties to intercept the fund allocated by the higher-level government and drain the money

---

[11] *Sources*: chinareform.org.cn (http://www.chinareform.org.cn/) and *2009 China Statistical Yearbook*.

from the lower level, poses obstacles for the rational allocation of taxes between governments, and makes it difficult to clarify the administrative and financial powers of governments at different levels, leading to the overstaffing of government organizations, the large number of government employees and the heavy task of financial operations.

1.2.2.2. *Uneven government revenue distribution due to the poor transfer payment system*

As a governance tool, the transfer payment system is in fact a system to allocate the financial powers and it requires to, on the basis of reasonably defining the administrative power of governments at different levels, follow certain financial principles, and effectively allocate government revenue among governments at different levels, so as to match their government functions with their disposable financial resources through the top–down transfer payment system. The existing tax-sharing system fails to establish a sound transfer payment system to make up for the revenue–expenditure gap of basic-level governments caused by the mismatch between the administrative and the financial powers. This is a major reason for the financial difficulties encountered by local governments. The amount of transfer payment made by provincial governments is usually not calculated according to a standard formation, but mainly in the form of tax returns and earmarked grants calculated with a base number, and requires support fund, worsening the financial situation of basic-level governments. The transfer payment is not based on the estimation of revenue and expenditure of local government, and is highly arbitrary, affecting the utilization efficiency of the transfer payment fund.

1.2.2.3. *Heavy financial burden on local governments due to the serious mismatch between the administrative and the financial powers*

In China, the county-level financial affairs must be governed by a higher-level government, either by a provincial government or a municipal government. The power to tax is highly centralized in the central government and revenue division is led by administrative departments which have the authorization of the budget law, and legislative and supervisory departments shall not intervene. County governments in China have a very limited power to revenues, in particular the power to tax on the whole. Governments at and below the provincial level do not have the legislative power of taxation and local governments have no right to issue local government bonds. The tax-sharing system at the county-level and the revenue division of county governments are up to the higher-level governments. Since the implementation of the reform of rural taxes and fees, counties and villages have less space to increase their own financial strength. As the public fiscal system continues to improve, counties and villages will have to spend more on public security, education, health and social security, thus facing a more difficult financial situation. Township governments have too little financial power compared to their administrative power.

Governments below the provincial level haven't established a proper responsibility and financial power division mode and their financial management system is still a mess. Consequently, among provincial, municipal/prefecture and township governments, the financial power is overly centralized at the higher level, weakening the financial strength of grassroots governments on one hand, and on the other, the higher-level governments decentralize the administrative power to the lower level. As a result, the administrative power is moving downward while the financial power upward between county governments and higher-level governments. Besides guiding and promoting the economic and social development within the jurisdiction, county governments also undertake the local public services responsibilities transferred by higher-level governments, thus shouldering too many responsibilities. This phenomenon is particularly prominent at the county/village level. County/village governments are in great misery for they lack main tax sources or stable tax revenue, but have to shoulder so many responsibilities such as compulsory education, public health, infrastructure, social stability, environmental protection and administration.

What's more, the existing tax-sharing system is a dual-track system with taxes divided by either tax items or by corporate affiliations. As a result, it's frequent for higher-level governments to seize the quality resources at the county-level and the advantageous position of tax collection. If the affiliation is changed, the county government will again find itself at a disadvantage in sharing the taxes on fine resources freshly dug out at the county-level and will benefit little from new economic growth points.

1.2.3. *Household spending power overdrawn due to the urbanization's excessive dependency on "land finance"*

After the reform of the tax-sharing system, limited by the mismatch of the financial power and the administrative power of local governments, land transfer fees become a major source of fund for local governments to advance urbanization and consequently urban and township governments have become overly dependent on land finances (Table 1.6). On the one hand, land finance has driven up the housing price, enlarged the real estate bubble, and overdrew the household spending power and checked the long-term development of urbanization; on the other hand, it has formed the extensive land operation mode of "land requisition–land sales–revenue" in urban

Table 1.6: Land transfer fees nationwide from 2005 to 2012 (100 million Yuan).

	2005	2006	2007	2008	2009	2010	2011	2012
Land transfer fees	5,884	7,677	13,000	9,600	16,000	27,000	31,500	26,900
Local government revenue	15,101	18,304	23,573	28,650	32,581	35,383	52,400	61,077
Percentage of local government revenue	39	41.9	55.2	33.5	63.4	76.6	60.1	44

Source: *China Statistical Yearbook* series.

areas, wasting land resources. Statistical data show that since 2000, the urban area in China has expanded by 50% while the urban population has increased only by 26%. It means that land urbanization pace is nearly as twice fast as the population urbanization pace and the fact that the population urbanization and industrialization pace if far slower than land urbanization will threaten the sustainability of urbanization.

1.2.4. *Insufficient blood supply for county economy due to the unsound financial management system*

1.2.4.1. *The market-oriented operation of state-owned financial institutions forms the "financial repression" on rural development*

In the past decade, the financial reform and regulation in China have made certain progress in improving the overall financial management level, adapting to the development needs of market-oriented economy and effectively resolving financial risks. Now state-owned financial institutions are operating in the market-oriented way, with profit-making as their chief goal. But meanwhile, the reform of state-owned financial institutions has helped channelize the capital from underdeveloped areas to developed areas, to large cities, large enterprises and advantageous sectors.

On the one hand, because of the experiences related serious loan loss or malicious debt evasion by businesses in some underdeveloped areas, state-owned commercial banks have given their loan application approval authority to their higher level or narrowed such authority, and some of them even have become pure savings bank. The policy of depositing funds in higher-level banks within the banking system has weakened the banks' support to county economy. After the loan approval authority is concentrated at the higher level, bank branches at the county-level have no rights to grant large-amount loans, with only the rights to organize funds, to survey on and recover outstanding loans, leading to the decrease, and even negative growth of loans lent by financial institutions to county economy. Take the financial data of county areas in Yanbian (seven counties except for Yanji City) for example. By the end of July 2011, the deposit and loan balances of state-owned commercial banks stood at 20.605 billion Yuan and 6.762 billion Yuan, with the loan-deposit ratio of 32.82%, and the loan-deposit ratios of the Industry and Commerce Bank of China, Agriculture Bank of China, Bank of China, and China Construction Bank were 49.96%, 21.50%, 24.09%, and 36.91%, respectively, far below the maximum limit of 75%.[12] State-owned commercial banks have basically lost their support to local economy.

On the other hand, postal savings are playing a similar role with state-owned commercial banks in draining the capital out of underdeveloped areas, in particular county areas. With the exit of state-owned banks, postal savings banks have grown faster than rural credit cooperatives and joint-stock commercial banks; thanks to the state credit they own. Since postal savings banks only take deposits and lend no or little money, these savings are also drained from underdeveloped areas. The limited financial accumulation in underdeveloped areas is worsened by the double "blood-draining" by state-owned banks and postal savings institutions, and the obstacles to loans have formed a major bottleneck to the development of county economy.

1.2.4.2. *The management system for rural credit cooperatives is yet to be improved*

After the exit of commercial banks from the basic-level credit market, rural credit cooperatives have in fact become the main financing channel below the county-level for businesses and individuals. Take the financial data of county areas in Yanbian (seven counties except for Yanji City) for example. By the end of July 2011, the loan balance of rural credit cooperatives registered 7.391 billion Yuan, that of state-owned commercial banks, 6.762 billion Yuan, and the former took up 38.57% of the total loan balance of county-level banks.

Rural credit cooperatives are mainly engaged in "agriculture supporting" policy business and in county areas and urban–rural

[12] *Source*: Cui Chengguo, Li Xianzi. Troubles Facing County-level Banks in Supporting Local Economy. The Chinese Banker. September 2011.

integrated areas, they are obliged to provide loans to local private SMEs. Despite their important role in basic-level loans, they lack corresponding policy support from the state government. The picture of rural credit cooperatives does not look good. Because of historical reasons, the property structure and the decision-making mechanism of rural credit cooperatives have never been straightened out, checking their further development. Their staff is not professionally competent, the loan management is rough and extensive, the percentage of bad and doubtful loans is too high and there are high risks with new loans. They are not as attractive as state-owned financial institutions to deposits and thus cannot meet the huge loan demands. In early 2005, the state governments decided to deepen the reform of rural credit cooperatives. With the improving policy environment, how to change the operation mechanism and improve the management level has always been a key in this regard.

1.2.4.3. *Some policy banks fail to give full play to their role and there is financial shortage for agricultural development*

The Agricultural Development Bank of China (ADBC) has undiversified functions and fails to bring out its agriculture supporting role as a policy financial institution. ADBC, founded in 1994, has transferred businesses such as the earmarked loans for agricultural development and poverty alleviation and loans for processing and non-principal business of grain and cotton enterprises to relevant commercial banks and started to specialize in the supply and management of funds used to purchase agricultural and sideline products since March 1998. In this way, ADBC has basically become a link of national purchase of agricultural and sideline products and an institution specialized in providing grain purchase funds, rather than a policy bank representing the country to support rural development. Consequently, on the one hand, agricultural infrastructure construction in urgent need of financial input lacks financing channels and water conservancy and electricity facilities cannot be developed in a timely manner, nor can relevant industries be restructured in a timely manner; on the other hand, the government cannot give play to its supporting, guiding and regulatory roles in agricultural development, and the macro-control effect of policies is not obvious.

The "Matthew Law" here under the market mechanism is another reason for the widening gap between county economy and urban economy. In the market-oriented economy, there is a negative effect with resource allocation under the market mechanism — "the rich are getting richer and the poor are becoming poorer." Judged from the resource allocation course and effect, the market mechanism often drives market entities to concentrate their resources in projects with higher micro-economic benefits, while refuse or postpone the input into projects with higher social benefits. As a result, resources are flowing into areas with good economic benefits and out of those with poor economic benefits, making regional development even unbalanced. In the 1960s, Robert Merton, a famous sociologist, described such polarization as the "Mathew Law", which is derived from Gospel of Matthew, New Testament: "For whoever has will be given more, and they will have an abundance. Whoever does not have, even what they have will be taken from them." The Matthew Law is working in China. Take Guangdong Province for example. From the percentage of major economic indices by area in the province we can see that, from 2000 to 2011, the percentage of regional GDP, value added of industrial sectors above the designated scale and export of the western and eastern wings and mountainous areas was falling compared with the Pearl River Delta (Tables 1.7–1.9). The regional economic development was even more unbalanced than it was in the 9th Five-Year Plan period.

Table 1.7: Comparison with GDP in the Pearl River Delta.

	2000 (%)	**2006** (%)	**2007** (%)	**2008** (%)	**2009** (%)	**2010** (%)	**2011** (%)
Pearl River Delta	78.4	68.8	81.1	81.4	81.4	81.9	82.2
Eastern wing	9.9	5.8	6.5	6.7	6.9	7.0	7.0
Western wing	8.9	6.4	7.3	7.5	7.4	7.7	7.9
Mountainous areas	7.0	5.2	6.5	6.5	6.5	6.6	6.7

Table 1.8: Comparison with value added of industrial sectors above the designated scale in the Pearl River Delta.

	2000 (%)	2006 (%)	2007 (%)	2008 (%)	2009 (%)	2010 (%)	2011 (%)
Pearl River Delta	79.6	86.5	85.2	84.9	83.8	93.8	83.0
Eastern wing	4.6	3.9	1.1	1.2	5.1	6.4	6.3
Western wing	5.8	4.9	1.2	1.3	4.7	5.3	5.4
Mountainous areas	3.9	4.7	1.5	1.5	6.4	7.5	5.3

Table 1.9: Comparison with exports in the Pearl River Delta.

	2000 (%)	2006 (%)	2007 (%)	2008 (%)	2009 (%)	2010 (%)	2011 (%)
Pearl River Delta	92.2	95.6	95.9	95.8	95.2	95.3	95.2
Eastern wing	4.6	2.5	2.3	2.3	2.6	2.5	2.6
Western wing	2.1	0.8	0.8	0.8	0.9	0.8	0.9
Mountainous areas	1.1	1.0	1.0	1.1	1.3	1.3	1.3

Source: Tables 1.7–1.9 are calculated by the author according to the statistical yearbooks of Guangdong (2000–2012).

The "Matthew Law" is working in China because on the one hand, developed areas are equipped with the financial, technological and human resources for further development, with a higher return rate of production factors. When resources are allocated by the market mechanism, production factors will flow into these areas and boost local economic growth. On the contrary, the economic development in under-developed areas will be checked due to the limited inflow of production factors. On the other hand, the economic regulation and control by local governments varies greatly in terms of thinking, form, means, policy, taxation, market opening degree and even ideology. Generally speaking, the political, social and cultural conditions in underdeveloped areas are immature compared with those in developed areas; or the government has too much unrestrained power and rent-seeking acts are common for administrative organizations and officials and so are man-made "obstacles" to make profits.

1.2.5. *The urban–rural dual household registration system is unfair, and rural migrant workers in cities bear great economic and psychological burdens*

The urban–rural dual household registration system prevents rural migrant workers in cities from enjoying equal public welfare in income, social securities and education as do urban residents. At the close of 2012, the average monthly income of rural migrant workers in cities reached RMB2,290. If their cost of living were deducted, each would have an average monthly balance of RMB1,557; about 0.5% of them had wages in arrears by their employers; the percentage of old-age pension, insurance for work-related injuries, medical insurance, unemployment insurance and maternity insurance paid by the employers for the rural migrant workers in cities was 14.3%, 24%, 16.9%, 8.4%, and 6.1%, respectively. What's more, the percentage in the building industry and accommodation and catering industry was even lower.[13] Most rural migrant workers in cities choose schools that cost less and do not have any admission restrictions for their children. Such schools are weak in equipment and teaching team, laggard teaching methods and poor teaching quality. Migrant children being unable to get good education cannot change their identity as "farmers" and are unable to settle in cities when they grow up. Therefore, the existing household registration system leads to social unfairness in the short run and cures social structure in the long run. Under unfair social conditions, rural migrant workers in cities would easily feel inferior, feel like passengers in cities, lonely and feel mental imbalance. They do not have the sense of belonging or achievement, so usually feel anxious and too worried inside. Most of the aged, who are left behind, for having no children or relatives around, live in poor conditions and cannot receive timely help at emergencies, like when they are ill or during the harvest. They therefore would feel lonely and helpless. Left-behind children in rural areas, feeling no family warmth, always feel lonely and would more than often become emotionally fragile and self-abandoned, feel anxious, isolated, unconfident and

---

[13]State Statistics Bureau: *National Rural Migrant Workers in Cities Monitoring Survey Report 2012*, available at http://www.stats.gov.cn/tjfx/jdfx.

unsafe, and become pessimistic, eccentric, capricious, and selfish. Rural migrant children who follow their parents to live in the cities always feel discriminated, inferior, isolated, unsafe, estranged, uneasy and lonely. The lack of the sense of social belongings would make them depressed and extreme. Mental imbalance in farmers would easily lead to mass incidents and cause greater social harms.

1.2.6. *Policy adjustment*

The central government has noticeably reinforced the efforts in policy adjustment to address the above issues and their causes. In 1999, the central government made the scientific judgment that Chinese agriculture and rural economic development entered into a new phase; in 2000, it made the major decision about strategic restructuring of agriculture and rural economy; in 2001, it specified the increase of farmers' income as the central task of agriculture and rural work; in 2002, it developed the integrated income increase guideline of "giving more, taking less and loosening control"; in 2003, it adopted several policies to support grain production and directly subsidized grain growers. In 2004, it put forth the time table to cancel the agriculture tax, spent more efforts in tax reduction, facilitated the implementation of relevant policies, and increased the input into agricultural infrastructure. Thanks to the "one exemption and three subsidies" policy, the average farmers' income has increased by about 50 Yuan, or up 2%.

At the Central Economic Work Conference (CEWC) in December 2004, it was pointed out to coordinate urban and rural development. "We are, on the whole, at the development phase of promoting agriculture with industrial development and rural development with urban development. We should follow this trend, more active in adjusting the national income distribution pattern and supporting the development of agriculture, rural areas and farmers", and "make the determination to rationalize the national income distribution pattern, and adopt the guideline of benefiting agriculture with industrial development and urban areas supporting rural areas".

In early 2005, the State Council decided to cancel the agricultural tax, which has alleviated the burden on farmers to certain extent, but cannot fundamentally address the issues concerning agriculture, the countryside and farmers, since these issues are rooted in various aspects. Judged from the trend of modern agriculture and modern society, paying tax is a basic obligation and right of a citizen. What we want should be a tax refund and basic subsidy support mechanism for farmers with low income, rather than simple cancellation of policies. At the CEWC in December 2005, it was stressed that we should build the new socialist countryside according to the requirement of coordinating urban development.

In the *Decision of the Central Committee of the Communist Party of China (CPC) on Several Big Issues on Promoting the Reform and Development of Rural Areas* adopted at the 3rd Plenary Session of the 17th Central Committee of the CPC, it's clearly pointed out to "speed up efforts in establishing a rural financial system which integrates commercial finance, cooperative finance and policy finance and has sufficient capital, full functions, good services and safe operation and guide more credit funds and social funds to rural areas".

The *18th CPC National Congress Report* points out that, "Resolving issues relating to agriculture, rural areas and farmers is the number one priority in the Party's work, and integrating urban and rural development provides the fundamental solution to these issues".

Integrating urban and rural development is the general way of thinking to solve issues concerning agriculture, the countryside and farmers. Giving full play to the radiating function of cities will help facilitate the development of neighboring rural areas. But it is worthy of in-depth research on its effect in former revolutionary base areas, areas inhabited by minority ethnicities and remote and poverty-stricken areas. The wealth gap between county areas across the country is huge. In 2011, the per capita regional GDP of the top 100 counties was 17.55 times that of the bottom 100 counties.[14] Integrating urban and rural development can only better solve problems within a certain area around cities, and can hardly solve problems

---

[14] *Source*: Report on the County Economic Development in the Past Decade in China.

in former revolutionary base areas, areas inhabited by minority ethnicities and remote and poverty-stricken areas. The latter is far from urban areas and inconveniently located, and local villagers have long been separated from the modern society by mountains. The local educational level is low and teaching conditions are poor. Local villagers for generations have lived on simple crafts such as traditional handiwork, and have lost the employment ability needed in modern urban areas. It's still very common for local residents to live on the provisions of "Heaven". Their houses are roughly built and barely decorated, and the infrastructure is extremely backward, with only water wells and shelters. There is almost no medical and health organization. It's common for local people to treat minor diseases with folk prescriptions and resign themselves to the fate in case of serious illness. The roads and bridges are too bumpy for vehicles, and the only way out of the villages is by foot. The traditional and closed ways of production and living and ways of thinking are deeply rooted in local villagers, will take a lot of time and funds for change, and cannot be done overnight by local governments alone. These areas will become more and more closed and poorer in the long run, since the local governments have no funds or capacity to make a change, and there is no urban support nearby they can rely on.

1.3. Way of Thinking to Strengthen the Economic and Social Development at the County-Level

1.3.1. *Firmly build up the fundamental status of county economy in the course of China's modernization*

County economy is the basic unit of national economy and the bearing point and foothold to improve people's livelihood in China, thus irreplaceable in Chinese economic growth. In the early days of the implementation of the reform and opening up policy, rural reform and township enterprises tremendously stimulated the economic growth in China. County areas are the main battlefields of agricultural development in China, and the basis to safeguard national food security, and county industry is the major carrier of Chinese industry. In the new era, in the course of building a moderately well-off society in an all-round way and vigorously advancing modernization in China, by vigorously developing county economy and improving the intrinsic dynamism of county economy, we will effectively incorporate urban–rural issues, agricultural issues and non-agricultural issues, farmers' issues and citizens' issues into regional development, help promote the coordinated development of urbanization and agricultural modernization, develop the positive interaction between industrialization and urbanization, and form a new industry–agriculture–urban–rural relationship that promotes agricultural development with industrial development, boosts rural development with urban development, benefits industry and agriculture mutually, and integrates urban and rural developments. So to speak, adjusting the development approach and resource allocation at the county-level is a new way of thinking to advance industrialization, urbanization and agricultural modernization and solve issues concerning agriculture, the countryside and the farmers, and will help root out fundamental problems encountered in the economic and social development of China, and overcome the weaknesses in the course of modernization.

1.3.2. *Carefully develop and improve the county economic and rural development plan*

First, we shall combine the county economic development plan with the master plan for national economic and social development, with the urban plan, township plan and industrial plan; take not only urbanization development but also rural development into account, with the focus on rural infrastructure construction, specialty industries and social livelihood undertakings, and guarantee the fine quality of rural construction with reasonable standards. Secondly, in light of the natural resources of a county area, we shall formulate the regional functional zoning plans within the county area, may specify the national functional zoning plan, further clarify areas for optimized development, priority development, limited development and prohibited development, and further specify their respective scope, development objective, development direction and development principles.

Thirdly, according to the development phase of county economy, we shall carefully develop and improve the medium- and long-term development plans for county economy and the rural development plan, seek truth from facts, combine the economic plan outline with specific plans in light of the reality, plan major events with significant influence in a feasible way to highlight the characteristics, build pillar industries to support county economic development, channelize investments, and concentrate all resources to change the status quo characterized by "weak agricultural development, small industrial scale and little financial strength". Fourthly, we shall follow the requirements of the concept of modern countryside and rural construction, carefully develop and improve the rural development plan, continue to advance residence construction for farmers with support infrastructure construction and environmental protection, realize the harmony between Man and Nature, and create a healthy and safe living environment for rural residents. We shall construct infrastructure networks such as roads and electricity to fully dig out and utilize all sorts of rural resources, and promote the sustainable development of county economy.

1.3.3. *Set up a mechanism to coordinate urban–rural development*

The key to coordinating urban–rural development is to coordinate policies and measures, break the urban–rural dual system, remove institutional obstacles checking the agricultural and rural development, adjust the allocation of public resources and increase the input into agriculture and rural areas. We shall, first coordinate urban–rural industrial policies and protect the rights to equal development in rural areas; secondly, coordinate urban–rural employment and realize the free flow of labor force; thirdly, coordinate urban–rural public-welfare undertakings and assume the government's responsibilities in rural public-welfare undertakings; fourthly, coordinate urban–rural social security, and extend the social security system to rural areas; fifthly, coordinate fiscal and financial resources, and promote the balanced allocation of public resources. Governments at all levels are the main coordinators. Not exclusive of the role of the market mechanism, we shall emphasize the dominant role of government, give full play to the central government and local governments, rationally allocate resources, promote coordinated urban–rural development and guarantee the realization of a moderately well-off society in rural areas by 2020. We shall combine "blood transfusion" with "blood making" to strengthen the intrinsic economic dynamism in former revolutionary base areas, areas inhabited by minority ethnicities and remote and poverty-stricken areas, and gradually develop their capacity for self-development.

1.3.4. *Set up and improve the county-level public finance system*

It's a major function of public finance to promote county economic development. The central government and provincial governments should bear the corresponding economic cost for the reform of rural systems and gradually include rural educational, health, cultural, infrastructure construction and social security aspects into government expenditure. The government should also clearly define the expenditure responsibilities of the higher-level government, county (municipal) and township governments, rationally adjust the expenditure scope and the income scope, clarify the income attribution, strengthen the efforts in finance transfer payment, and establish rules and systems to regulate and manage the transfer payment fund. We shall set up and improve the public finance system with matched financial and administrative powers, and improve local governments' ability and level of providing public products and services; strengthen the agriculture-supporting role of policy banks and development banks, and increase the financial input into agriculture, the countryside and farmers; improve the rural credit environment, guide commercial banks and postal savings institutions to lend to township enterprises, or restructure the branches of these financial institutions at the county-level into local community banks, give play to the advantage of community banks being close to clients, and improve county-level financial services. We shall also deepen the reform of rural credit cooperatives, clarify the property relations, reinforce the restraint mechanism, improve the balance sheet, and reform the organizational structure and management mode in light of local situations; launch policy insurance business, set up the cultivation/aquaculture risk fund or fraternity, and set up and improve the multi-tiered and multi-form credit guarantee system; straighten out the capital relationship between policy banks, development banks, commercial banks, postal savings institutions and rural credit cooperatives, and support them with non-banking financial institutions such as insurance companies to form a positive mechanism for the cycling of rural capital.

1.3.5. *Set up and improve the rural technician training system and the basic social security system*

The government shall set up county-level vocational colleges, vigorously train technical workers needed by the market and with local characteristics, and facilitate the transition of the rural population and the human resources, to provide distinct technical talents for local development, and qualified technicians for urbanization and industrialization. The government shall also set up the rural subsistence security system in an all-round way, accurately define the objects and scope of support, and rationally raise funds; develop the multi-type and multi-tiered medical security system, or may set up the cooperative medical fund, give the priority to establishing major disease insurance for farmers with a county (or township) as the unit, and encourage the development of commercial medical insurance in areas where conditions allow; set up and improve the rural social endowment system at a varying levels according to the varying economic development levels; set up a stable fund-raising mechanism for the rural social security and expand the funding channels. With the establishment of the public finance system, the central government and provincial governments should be given corresponding play, to gradually establish and improve the lasting mechanism for rural social security.

1.3.6. *Promote the transition of "agriculture based on the cultivated land" to "the structure paying equal attention to grain and greening"*[15]

From 1985 to 2012, the per capita grain consumption fell while the per capita animal foodstuff consumption rose year by year in China. In the future, the per capita consumption of animal products in China will continue to grow rapidly, and as a result, the feed demand will increase drastically, threatening the national food security. Therefore, paying equal attention to "grain and greening" should be the general direction of future agricultural development. The agricultural system adapting to the food structure in China is no longer "agriculture based on the cultivated land", but is and should be "the structure paying equal attention to grain and greening" and valuing "grassland agriculture". By "grassland agriculture", we mean to introduce forage grass (including forage plants) herbivorous livestock into the agricultural system, plan the cultivated and non-cultivated land in a unified manner, and value the development of forage industry. On the cultivated land we should grow forage together with grain, or with forest, with vegetables, with cotton, or with tobacco and to fully realize the production potentials of all sorts of agricultural land by employing technologies such as forage-and-crop rotation. The implementation of the grassland agriculture system can help save the cultivated land and water resources, protect ecological security, and extend the industrial chain. The "grassland agriculture" is a new agricultural system that pays equal attention to ecology and production, grains and forage, adapts to the times and the needs of urban–rural coordination, and is suitable for global economic integration and a key part of the implementation of the "five in one" concept raised at the 18th CPC National congress.

1.3.7. *Inherit, carry forward and develop rural cultures*

Rural cultures refer to the cultural accumulation formed by farmers in their daily life and under the influence of special natural and

[15]This viewpoint is developed at the guidance of Professor Ren Jizhou, academician of the China Academy of Sciences and China Academy of Social Sciences.

geological environments, economic characteristics, political structure and ideology. Some outstanding rural cultures have been deeply rooted in the mind and behaviors of farmers, penetrated into every aspect of rural life, present in every link of agricultural production and are precious cultural legacies. In the course of modernization, we shall not only inherit and carry forward traditional outstanding rural cultures, but also make innovations and inject continuous vitality and nutrition into rural cultures; not only keep the characteristics of rural cultures, but also learn from and absorb alien cultures and urban cultures, so that rural cultures will gain endless vitality and energy, and realize development and innovation in the course of confrontation and integration, maintenance and transformation, creating a cultural atmosphere for the economic and social development at the county-level and lay the cultural foundation for rural modernization.

1.4. Conclusions

County economy is the basis of national economy and an integrated economic system with full functions. In the 21st century, the county economy, with county towns as the center and the rural areas and the base bonded by market towns, occupies an immovable fundamental status in the modernization course of China. Rural development needs the guidance of urbanization and urbanization construction needs rural support. With the development of urbanization, a large part of the rural population will move into county towns and market towns, but the extensive countryside will still be the major living place for farmers in China. As the infrastructure conditions such as roads and electricity and living conditions improve in rural areas, there will definitely be urban residents who choose to return to the countryside. The land and other resources in China are extremely precious and every bit of them needs to be rationally utilized and protected. The gap between rural and urban residents should be narrowing.

The county economy is confronted with a lot of problems and challenges. The issues concerning agriculture, the countryside and the farmers are particularly severe in China's county economy due to the flaws with the dual system, fiscal management system and financial management system. For example, as far as agriculture is concerned, farmers and herdsmen lack new growth points, the cultivation structure is not reasonable, the restructuring is not in place, agricultural production is disconnected with market demands, and rural migrant workers still contribute a large portion of income to rural households; the conflict between "small-scale production" and "big market" is prominent, and there is no effective channel to obtain market information due to extensive operation, leading to blind production, chaotic circulation, poor sales and the failure of output increase to generate more income. The processing level of agricultural and livestock products is low and in many places, industry is separated from agriculture and husbandry in the course of development: Agriculture and husbandry provide no raw materials for industrial development, while industry fails to support agriculture and husbandry effectively. There are no leading enterprises with strong impetus and the trade market for agricultural and livestock products are not maturely developed. The report of the 18th CPC National Congress points out that, "It's the top priority of the CPC to solve issues concerning agriculture, the countryside and the farmers and integrating urban and rural development is the fundamental approach to solve these issues". A new approach to coordinate urban and rural economic and social development is to develop the county economy and enhance its intrinsic development dynamics.

In the new era, it's necessary to firmly establish the fundamental status of county economy in the course of China's modernization, carefully develop and improve the county economic and rural development plans, deepen the reform of county-level political and economic systems, set up the mechanism coordinating urban and rural development, form and improve the county-level public finance system, financial system, and the rural technician training system and social security system, promote the transition from "cultivated-land based agriculture" to "the structure paying equal attention to grain and greening", inherit, carry forward and reform the rural culture, and stimulate the overall development of the national economy and the all-round construction of a moderately prosperous society.

CHAPTER 2

TO STRENGTHEN THE BUILDING OF COUNTY GOVERNANCE CAPACITIES

County governance is the basis of national governance. Based on a profound analysis of the plight of county governance in China and the reasons for such plight, this chapter actively explores new ways of strengthening the building of county governance capacities like deepening county political and economic reforms, "streamlining government organs, separating economy from politics, adhering to the Communist Party of China (CPC)'s leadership and implementing collaborative governance", speeding up the transformation of all-round county (city) government into service-oriented government, innovating the rural public management and social service network centering on towns and townships, building a school district-centered new-type rural mechanism and promoting stable economic and social development in counties.

County governance is the basis of national governance, and a weak link in national governance as well. It is made up of county (city)-, town and township- and village-level governance, constituting the basic system of national governance. A country will be stable if its foundation is stable; a country will be developed if its foundation is developed. Following the trends of the times, adapting to the changing situation, inheriting excellent traditions and actively exploring new ways of building better county governance capacities is of great significance to the lasting stability and sustainable development of the country.

2.1. Status Quo of County Governance

2.1.1. *Connotation of county governance*

County governance means comprehensive administration through the county political system, operational mechanism and management system. Counties here refer to regions covering the county, local townships (towns) and villages and centering on the county seat. Governance here mainly means adjusting the administrative framework, functions and systems following the requirements of modern governments at the basic level. County governance involves the geography and size of population and has comparatively completed administrative functions. It is at the interface of the state and the society, and plays a transitional role in the national political and economic systems, not only comprehensively reflecting the operation of and changes in the entire system, but also demonstrating the interactions between the state and the society in a concentrated way. In the transition from the planned economy to the market economy, from agricultural civilization to industrial civilization and from a traditional society to a modern society, county governance, as a superstructure, has specific and profound influences on the development of counties in terms of policies, economy, society and culture. Main manifestations are: First, the capabilities and role of the county government; second, institutional facilities and working efficiency; and third, the development of the basic-level democracy.

County governance involves hierarchical relations between higher level governments and the county government, and horizontal relations between the county and other regions, as well. In various relations, the county government, as a party concerned, exercises its power and has a foundation status. If the functions of the county government are not improved, simply "strengthening the county government by giving it more power" would increase the risk that government power harms public interests while strengthening the autonomy of the county government. If the county governance capacities are not improved, counties will surely lack inner vitality as an important component of the big market. Therefore, our research focuses on restructuring, institutional adjustments and capacity building within the county government and highlights the ways of building a regional mechanism that adapts to the national conditions of China and modernization and sees interactions among the governments at the county, town and township and village level, and of building better county governance capacities. In county governance, the functions and contents of governance at the three levels, are different.

County (city) governance capacities shall be built mainly in the following seven aspects: First, increasing legal awareness and improving the county government capability for law-based administration; second, advocating a common spirit and improving the capability for moral-based administration; third, making plans in advance to improve the planning and implementation capability; fourth, enhancing public services to improve the capability for providing public products and services; fifth, adhering to the market orientation and improving the county government's capacity for selecting better governance tools and its working efficiency; sixth, enhancing security awareness and improving the county government's capacity for maintaining local security and social stability, and resisting risks and settling public crises; and seventh, increasing the governance transparency to fight against corruption and encourage honest and clean administration.

Efforts at the level of the township government should focus on social administration, including the capacity of managing the local society, solving matters that the village-level organization has difficulty in solving or can hardly solve, and providing public services to facilitate the development of local society and economy.

For village-level organizations, priority is given to villagers' autonomy, including the capacity of leading the villagers to get rich, solving "matters that individual households have difficulty in solving and can hardly solve", and protecting the local ecology and historic properties. As a matter of fact, the basic-level governance capacities involve many other aspects. This paper focuses on exploring the basic-level autonomy, activeness and initiatives and analyzing the inner vitality at the basic level from the angle of sustained social and economic development.

During the 1980s, China applied the household contract responsibility system in its rural areas, which greatly released its farmers' enthusiasm in farming and their initiative, enormously promoted the reforms and development of various industries in China, and laid a solid foundation for the rapid development of China for nearly 30 years. It will have immeasurable influences on the stable and healthy development of China in the 21st century to, in the new era, start with counties at the grassroots level to deepen county-level political and economic restructuring, explore new modes of county governance that meet national modernization requirements and have local characteristics and functions, promote the building of county governance system and capabilities, speed up building and improving the political and economic foundation for the immediate interests of the local people, mobilize the activeness and creativeness of the vast cadres and strengthen grassroots governance capacities.

2.1.2. *Evolution of county governance*

In the 5,000-year-long development of Chinese civilization, China has carried out extensive explorations of and accumulated valuable experience in county governance. In more than 2,000 years of evolution since the Spring and Autumn and Warring States periods, county organizational systems have formed relatively independent geographic entities in such fields as politics, economy, society and culture, and demonstrated the functions of the national political system in a comparatively concentrated way. County governance has always been the foundation for ruling a country.

Since the Qin Dynasty, "imperial power had been extended to the lowest level of counties", and county-level administration had been the most basic administrative organization in China. Autonomy was adopted below the level of counties. In ancient China, "township" was by no means a part of the administrative organization of state power, but a voluntary social organization very similar to the state administrative organization. Township organization along with the village system and Baojia registration system (a tithing system adopted in ancient China) formed a rural governance system integrating political, military and educational functions, forming a whole set of rural management systems. In the rural management system, big families, squires and local celebrities held important positions. There was a set of relatively independent "clan power" in villages. Therefore, there were actually two mutually associated and relatively independent "imperial power" and "clan power" systems in the rural area, of which "imperial power" controlled the rural area in a special form of entrustment and had more cultural symbolizations; and "clan power" had practical jurisdiction and governance rights and formed the "squire autonomy".

At the turn of the Qing Dynasty and the Republic of China, there was a mass movement for local autonomy across China. Liang Qichao said, "To take local autonomy as the foundation of country building is a true understanding of the essence of politics and meets the urgent demand of China now"; Sun Yat-sen pointed out, "Local autonomy is the plinth of a country. A weak plinth will lead to national instability." For national salvation and modernization, "local autonomy"[1] was tried at the county level, and efforts were made to establish basic-level organizations in the rural society, extend formal state power to inside the rural society, renew the division and coding of the rural areas, break the isolated autonomous village community and form the mode of "rural administration" that met the then conditions.

In the early days of the People's Republic of China (PRC), to speed up national industrialization, the Central Government of China betook itself to fundamental social, economic and political reforms, applied its

[1] In 1928, the then Nationalist Government issued *County Organization Act*, launched "county autonomy", and made local autonomy the foundation of political construction. Since "it not yet meets the conditions for autonomy, but it forcefully implements autonomy" (Liang Shuming), "county autonomy" finally became a carnival for landlords and squires. After Kuomintang retreated to Taiwan, it learned lessons and issued, in 1950, in Taiwan Province, China, *Outline of Implementing Local Autonomy in the Counties and Cities in Taiwan Province*, which promoted the transformation of the political system and democracy in Taiwan.

experience in politics in the revolutionary period to social and economic development, penetrated "Party affairs" to the concrete work of organizing counties, townships and villages, and formed the mode of county administration featuring "integration of politics and economy". In particular, in townships and villages, from 1958 to 1983, it adopted collective economy with people's communes as the mainstay. The three-tier management of people's communes, namely "commune, brigade and production team" management, was very similar to the vertical management of "battalion, company and platoon" in the army. The mode played a certain role in promoting the construction of the national industrialization system and village infrastructure. However, it almost deprived farmers of their autonomy, greatly depressed farmers' enthusiasm and initiative, restricted the development of the forces of production and led to low production efficiency in the rural areas. Farmers lived in poverty and were not allowed to change their household registration, which contributed to the forming of the dual urban–rural social structure and further widened the urban–rural gap.

After China launched the reform and opening up, the household contract responsibility system was widely adopted across China, farmers became ever more passionate and enthusiastic, the efficiency of agricultural production improved greatly, and the rural area ushered in a new period of development. In December 1982, the Fifth Plenary Session of the Fifth National People's Congress (NPC) passed the provisions of Article 95 of the new Constitution, namely, "People's congresses and people's governments are established in provinces, municipalities directly under the Central Government, counties, cities, municipal districts, townships, nationality townships and towns." In October 1983, according to the provision, the CPC Central Committee and the State Council of China issued *Notice on Implementing Separation of Politics and Society and Setting up Township Governments*, and the town and township political structure was restored in villages across China. In November 1987, the 23rd session of the Sixth NPC Standing Committee passed *Organic Law of Villagers Committees* (*Trial*). The above law has been enforced on a trial basis since 1 June 1988, to establish villagers' committees across China, hoping to change the practice of direct orders for and intervention with village affairs and transform the government's functions to adapt to administrative adjustments in the new era and allow the villagers to solve their own affairs. It was a correct idea. However, unsupported and hardly deepened, the reform failed to form interactions among counties (cities), towns, townships and villages; in addition, inconsistency and poor overall effect of the reform led to many new problems and contradictions.

2.1.3. *Plight of county governance and the reasons*

In recent years, the Central Government along with people's governments at different levels have set great store by developing county economy and society. In particular, priority is given to issues concerning agriculture, countryside and farmers. The Central Government issues No. 1 Document every year to stress the importance of such issues, and launches relevant policies. Despite the stable development of county economy and society, many severe problems still exist. The most prominent one is the lack of inner vigor of basic-level organizations and the masses in counties, townships and villages. As the effects of the rural policy launched in the early days of the reform and opening up have been gradually released and no longer existed, county economy sees a weakening sustainability; and county governance is weakened. In the system where cities govern counties, city governments usually deduct and intercept resources by capitalizing their administrative supremacy over counties, leading to the phenomenon of "cities feed on counties" and restricting county development. In the construction of new socialist countryside, China has cancelled agricultural taxes, and more and more resources are running into villages, but the conflicts of social management remain sharp and "the relations between cadres and the masses", "social stability" and "the burden on farmers" are still hot social issues. Social disorder is rapidly growing, with frequent events of people venting their anger and mass events "where there are no direct conflicts of interest" occur frequently, evolve rapidly and involve drastic behaviors and interwoven conflicts that are difficult to be dealt with, causing crises of government governance. Mafia-like and criminal forces grow continuously and basic morals bankrupt in some regions; individuals dig "wells of the sulks" and families dig "weirs of sulks", and ordinary villagers find it more and more difficult to control their fate. Under the goal of building a harmonious society, it has become carte blanche to "solve internal contradictions with the Renminbi (RMB)", however money cannot buy lasting stability. Reasons are as follows:

First, social and economic transformation in China is a long-term and arduous task. It is also a long-term and arduous task to increase farmers' income, adjust the agricultural structure and reform the system for managing the rural society. It is difficult to fundamentally solve the problems with one or several policies in a certain period. Progressive supporting policies and scientific and rational top design are needed, so is constant effort to address problems and difficulties.

Second, rural and urban development is unbalanced, with obviously laggard rural economic and social development, severely lagging infrastructure construction and public utilities for education, culture, hygiene and social relief in most villages, and lack of living subsistence for some farmers.

Third, there are too many local government agencies and bureaucracy is rampant. County-level administrative system has five sets of leadership, namely the CPC committee, the government, people's congress, the Chinese People's Political Consultative Conference (CPPCC) and discipline inspection department, causing Parkinson's "organ diseases". They erode government credit, and cause high administrative costs and inefficiency of public resources. Inefficient in and half-hearted about their work, they even abuse power, fail to their duties, play favoritism and commit irregularities. Some government organs and civil servants consider only their own rights and interests, but never take into consideration the interests of the masses or the overall situation of social and economic development.

Fourth, the secretary of a county CPC committee, as a local government leader, has too much power and plays a decisive role in not only selecting and appointing cadres, but also making decisions on major projects. To supervise such power, "higher authorities are too far to reach, lower departments may feel risky to do so, and organs at the same level have difficulty to do that, discipline inspection departments can only take soft actions, while it is always late to rely on judicial departments".

Fifth, some organizations at the basic level are slack, and do not have due fighting capacity and organizational strength; such organizations have lost people's trust which is also the foundation for their work due to corruptive or bad behaviors of some cadres; some villages see a severe loss of basic norms and lack of standard or bottom line for right and wrong, as traditional norms inside of clans and villages have vanished while new law-based norms are yet to develop; as a result, the evil triumphs over the virtuous; to better accomplish tasks assigned by higher authorities, some irresponsible town and township leaders employ ruthless and wicked villagers obedient only to them, and nibble together with them the interests of the village.

Sixth, since the abolition of the agricultural tax, collective economy has been further weakened, so has the basic-level organizations, worsening the "disunity" where farming households, even individuals are the basic units; against the background of growing market-based countryside, most villages do not have effective intermediaries and mechanisms to connect the farmers with the big market outside, leading to failure to effectively connect household operations with the big market.

Seventh, there is no effective mechanism for coordinating rural operation. In the direct interactions between higher level governments and the farmers and in building the interest relationship between the government and the farmers, authority of the local government and construction of basic-level organizations in villages are ignored.

Eighth, the management functions of townships and villages are unclear. Some township documents conflict with *Organic Law of Villagers Committees*; some township leaders "violate the law by following orders", and strengthen administrative intervention with and control of village-level organizations, especially villagers committees, in order to accomplish the tasks and indicators assigned by higher authorities. Most selections of the villagers committee members become a mere formality, and cannot proceed in strict accordance with the law.

Ninth, some regions do not follow principles when carrying out local governance, and lack the mechanism for educating people with struggles and that for seeking solidarity through criticizing. They fail to adequately educate and guide the farmers as there is no process of combating the minority and educating the majority.

Tenth, there are not enough in-depth investigations and studies. Media reports and the petition system are too simplified and superficial. Some false information or one-sided information is spread *via* short messages and the Internet. Superior leaders are always the right ones and cadres at the basic level are mostly the wrong ones. Under the "veto by one vote" system for basic-level cadres, more abnormal conflicts shift up, leading to more severe contradiction between cadres and the masses at the basic level.

In line with the above, the current county governance in China embodies not only the elements of traditional ruling by officials, but also the styles of the army during the revolutionary period, being incommensurable with the requirements of real party politics, the market economy, as well as democracy and the rule of law. County governance is the weakest link in national governance. County political system has potential serious crises. It seems to be normal on the surface, but actually has increasingly sharp conflicts of all sorts which are on the verge of being triggered, and may even cause massive economic and social crises and violent social unrests, and even endanger national stability and development.

2.1.4. *Thought on county governance*

The thought on reforming county economic and social management and political governance in China is: To build the county services-based political, economic and social administration systems against the big background of advancing urbanization, agricultural mechanization, industrialization and modernization in the 21st century, on the basis of abiding by orders of the country and the Central Government, for the immediate interests of the local masses and for the need to develop modernized county economy and society. In terms of politics, it is to set the principle of county government autonomy, and bring forth new ideas on the local electoral system and encourage the county government to be responsible for higher level authorities and county residents, and mainly for the latter. In terms of the organization, it is to "streamline government organs, separate political affairs and economy, combine the CPC with politics, adhere to the CPC leadership in political affairs and stress social participation and collaborative governance", give full play to the initiative and advantages of the CPC, the government, the market and the society, and maximize public interests in county governance. In terms of institution, it is to build a county governance mechanism where counties (cities) are the centers of local administration, town and townships serve the society and villages (natural villages) are the foundation of autonomy, and to build a people's will-based new-type relationship between modern county government and the citizens in China. In terms of functions, it is to strengthen and promote the county (city) government-centered public management and social service functions, bring forth new ideas on the public management and social service network with town and townships as hubs (support), build village-level organizations with vitality, effectively push forward and accelerate the process of "democratizing, streamlining, socializing and making service-oriented" county governance, creating conditions for stable development of county economy and society.

To make it more convenient to do researches or launch trials, counties here mainly refer to county (city)-level administrative divisions that are closely linked to the vast rural areas. They do not include county-level districts that make a city. The following are discussions at three levels.

2.2. Thoughts on the Reform of the County (City) Government System

2.2.1. *To promote the transformation from versatile government to service-oriented government*

The versatile county (city) government shall be transformed into service-oriented one, to become a planning, coordinating and servicing authority instead of the authority. The government shall do things that the market cannot do, reduce its direct intervention with economic affairs, strengthen its management and responsibility for public affairs, including development planning, economic regulation, market supervision, environmental protection, social management and public services, protect the disadvantageous and promote social equity.

In the years of reform and opening up where economic construction was the priority, it was by no means that county governments did not manage the economy. The problem is that the government carried out administration most as the revolutionary government did. Revolutionary governments showed a strong sense of official and made arbitrary decisions in politics; mobilized the masses to get involved in rush production and ignored economic laws; and the CPC leaders intervened with concrete economic affairs, causing blur separation of political administration and economic activities. Such governments carried forward the elements in the revolutionary years, and played an important role in the years of war and the transitional period. It is understandable that they presented some problems in economic construction and social development. However, they can hardly adapt to the rules of economic and social development in the long period of modernization. Therefore, the government must adapt itself to cater to the political, economic and social development in the period of modernization, and systematically reform itself, in terms of concepts, structure, institutions, functions and methods, etc. As an overall category, government transformation is neither to repair the existing government management system nor to adjust government functions in the general sense, but to build modern county (city) governments that have gone through systematic reforms and adapted to social and economic transformation.

The main feature of modern county (city) governments is that they are built on the basis of the will of the people, represent the fundamental interests of the people, properly exercise public power and perform government functions. In the new period of social and economic development, one of their important responsibility is to manage public affairs, including development planning, market development, social management and public services. Therefore, it is necessary to build a political eco-environment that helps county (city) governments to display their functions.

2.2.2. *To strengthen the construction of county political ecology*

In the report to the 18th CPC National Congress, it was proposed to "actively develop inner-Party democracy and strengthen Party creativity". Inner-Party democracy is the lifeline of the Party. To promote people's democracy with inner-Party democracy is the focal idea of the construction of county political ecology. The basic thought would be: To push forward the construction of county democracy by strengthening the building of inner-Party democracy, change making decisions for the people into mobilizing the people to make their own decisions, advance extensive and multi-layer institutionalization of deliberative democracy, bring forth new ideas on the decision-making mechanism with wide participation by the masses, optimize the allocation of county power and resources, improve the county governance structure, keep a balanced power structure, change county-level political functions and bring forth new ideas on the mechanism for county governments to serve the people, ameliorate the overall functions of the county government system, ensure the cooperation, checks and balances of county government organization systems, smoothen the channels for public opinion and give full play to the role of social supervision.

Firstly, try decentralization of democracy within the Party. To expand the powers the plenary session of the county Party committee, changes the traditional leadership by the standing committee of the Party committee into new-type democratic leadership within the Party; the county Party committee has only the difference nomination right in major matters like staff appointment and removal, and the plenary session of the county Party committee makes the final decision by secret ballot to prevent, at the institutional level, the discretion on major issues of a few or one person as much as possible.

Secondly, try permanent tenure of county-level Party representatives. To give Party members more power, change the pure leadership of Party committee over Party cadres into common leadership over Party cadres by Party members together, and Party representatives of a predetermined number may sign jointly to launch the procedures for removing any member of the Party committee, any member of the standing committee of the Party committee and the secretary of the Party committee; and to give full play to the sense of responsibility and the role as supervisors of all Party members at institutional level.

Thirdly, try democratic selection in county-level Party organizations. To establish an inner-Party electoral system, change the "top–down" system for nominating important candidates by the Party committee into the "bottom–up" campaign system; to recommend excellent Party members to hold important positions in the Party and the government by developing and implementing the county Party organization campaign regulations; to ensure interactions between advanced organizations and excellent talents at the institutional level and provide the most proper talents for county governance.

Fourthly, try the county (city) head responsibility system. To build a basic-level democratic governance mechanism; winner in the campaign within county Party committee shall serve as the secretary of county Party committee and the first head of the government to undertake the political responsibility for realizing the awareness and interests of citizens in districts under their jurisdiction on behalf of the Party; to create conditions for the county Party committee to recommend a candidate for the direct election of the county (city) government together with candidates recommended by other social organizations; to establish the political authorizing and responsibility system, and allow candidates who fail in the election to participate in people's congress. Candidates must be locals (living in the area for certain years and being familiar with local conditions) and able to solve local affairs in the interest of local people. Streamlined and highly-efficient government organization shall be established, consisting mainly of the county (city) government and county people's congress. The co-location system of government departments and the CPC organization shall be established in accordance with the principle of "combination of Party and political affairs and separation of politics and economy", for example, the education, sports, broadcasting and TV, press and publication departments share the work place with the publicity department, and the Civil Affairs Bureau units with the United Front Work Department as one. The government shall be separated from market intermediaries, for example, institutions and market intermediaries can handle supportive, technical and service affairs, giving full play to the decisive role of the market in resource allocation. General selection shall be organized for representatives to county people's congress, and members of the standing committee of the people's congress shall be full time. County residents exercise the rights to deal with county issues as county masters, directly remove incompetent officials, examine and approve local development planning, determine local rules and supervise the work of the county government. The CPPCC county committee, as part of the delegations to people's congress, shall take part in the work of people's congress actively. Efforts should be made to build and improve a publicity and hearing system, make public Party affairs, political affairs and social affairs open in the county, give full play to the role of free media in the county, listen to public opinions extensively and ensure people's right to know, right to participate in, right to express their opinions and right to supervise over major issues concerning people's livelihood, focus on training citizenship in the people, set up the concepts of democracy and the rule of law to lay a political foundation for sustained development of the county economy.

2.3. Thoughts on Reforming Township Government System

2.3.1. *Town and townships are an important guarantee for social security*

Town and township governments face the farmers directly in most cases. They should let farmers, as relatively independent market players, solve problems in their own capability, and handle those beyond their capabilities. They mainly administer villages where there are many problems "things that cannot be settled or are hard to be handled by a single household", even "by one or two villages." In the process of economic and social transformation, Chinese rural areas see severe contradictions between rapid growing demand for rural public products and services on the one hand and serious shortage of such products and common services on the other. The priority task of the town and township governments is to settle such contradictions. If such contradictions could be timely settled locally, they may be trivialized, otherwise they will become disasters and have great impacts on the overall situation.

2.3.2. *To strengthen the social management and service functions of town and township governments*

To fulfill the social management and public service functions of the county (city) government in local town and townships, it is necessary for a country to maintain a competent and efficient township administrative structure, properly address issues concerning agriculture, villages and farmers, promote economic development, increase farmers' income, intensify public services, strive to ameliorate people's livelihood, push forward basic-level democracy and promote rural construction. To reduce the burden on farmers, build service-oriented governments and improve the capability of township governments for performing their responsibilities, it is necessary to increase financial input and ensure working expenses. Township administrative agencies shall receive support from government finance as community-based organizations in cities, and wholeheartedly provide administrative services for local people. To develop new engine for the development of county economy, certain adjustments may be made to the layout of townships (except small prefectures and townships emerging to meet the need of rural trade) according to the level and trends of industrialization in townships, especially according to the situations and trends of local pillar industries and industrial development, and based on county planning for social and economic development. Such adjustments may be dividing large townships into small ones, or concentrating relatively small townships, or setting county-controlled cities to promote urbanization and improve the efficiency of administrative management. To lower the cost of elections at the basic level, town and township governments may be set as branches of county (city) governments, of which the major leaders are appointed directly by the county government (the head of large towns and townships can be elected directly) and receive supervision of the local people and higher level authorities. To better display the role of town and township governments as firewalls in the state, it is necessary to strengthen the construction of their important public institutions,[2] encourage individuals and collectives to provide services for socialized public projects, build a network of basic social security and public service that covers all districts under the jurisdiction of local town and townships, give play to the radioactive role of town and townships in villages, and provide public services for promoting agricultural technologies, animal and plant disease control, quality detection of agricultural products and other urgent public services. To integrate resources and improve service efficiency, it is necessary to perfect the ways of classified reforms of township institutions and supporting measures, focus on setting up the township administrative service center, the agriculture service center and the social management service center to provide one-stop convenience services for farmers. To enhance the sense of responsibility in important town and township institutions and improve their technologies and services, ameliorate the quality of public services, it is necessary to allocate a certain percentage of government funds for agriculture and villages, to strengthen the building of important township institutions, intensify trainings of practitioners and consolidate and develop the team of rural technicians. When handling public affairs, we should never make the farmers feel any burden to receive public services nor expect rural technicians to do well with an empty stomach. Proper increase of input in this regard may have a multiplier

[2] "Seven stations and eight offices": "Seven stations" refer to Agricultural Machinery Station, Rural Economy Station, Agricultural Technology Station, Culture Station, Water Resource Station, Animal Husbandry Station and Epidemic Prevention Station; "eight offices" refer to Police Office, Taxation Office, Civil Affairs Office, Office of Finance, Land Management Office, Forest Management Office, Post Office, Savings Office, Health Office, Firefighting Office, and Land Exchange Office.

effect. To ensure effective use of public resources, it is necessary to build a sound and transparent financial system, fairly and reasonably use public resources, receive social supervision, avoid under-the-counter operations and promote finance to truly reflect the essence of being public.

2.3.3. *Town and township governments function as hubs*

Town and township governments play a special role in county governance. Though county (city) governments and township governments are leaders and the led, township governments, as political power at the basic level, have to undertake indicators and tasks of higher authorities on the one hand and exercise independent administrative service functions over township affairs on the other. In particular, they have to be responsible for a great deal of issues concerning local social management and services. Although township governments instruct and provide service to governance, they will have to be held liable for any problems in village governance. Higher level authorities usually implement "three vetoes by one vote" on township leaders. Therefore, the work to be done by township governments is the hardest of all. Speeding up the reform of county governance and fundamentally combing the county–township–village management mode helps relieve the pressures on township governments, improve the functions of township governments as hubs, and further consolidate power at the basic level.

Specific measures include: First, to link villagers committees with county and township people's congresses. County and township people's congresses are state organs at the county and township levels, and the main form adopted by local people to exercise their democratic rights as masters. Head and deputy head of the villagers committee who are elected *via* village autonomy shall naturally become village representatives at the county and township people's congresses, which changes the power completely "outside the system" into certain power "within the system". With the organizational binding force exerted by the people's congress on delegates to the people's congress (i.e., members of the villagers committee), villagers committee and county and township governments may have good and favorable interactions.

Secondly, in the process of thoroughly implementing *Organic Law of Villagers Committees*, regulations on the guidance of the work of villagers committees by township governments shall be further developed or improved to prevent two harmful tendencies of village governance: "Affiliated administration" and "excessive administration".

Thirdly, the political performance assessment indicators at the county, township and village levels shall be reformed. Consultation with the villagers committee should be conducted and villagers' opinions should be widely collected on the basis of the local realities and by considering opinions and demands of local cadres and masses, especially those concerning the villagers committee.

Fourthly, efforts should be made to intensify publicity and education, train the concept of modern democracy, the awareness of law and the spirit of contract of cadres and masses at the basic level, improve their quality and consolidate the mass foundation for good governance.

2.4. Thoughts on Reforming Village Governance

Administrative villages are at the same level with natural villages, both being at the most basic level in the rural area in China and in the Chinese society. Village governance is an important content of social construction. Considering the basic situation in rural areas and the trend of social development in China, it is necessary to actively explore new ideas on reforming village governance. Main contents of the reform include: In terms of the governance area, school districts will replace the traditional scope of jurisdiction of villages–natural villages; in terms of governance talents, it is necessary to give full play to the role of CPC members and talented people living in the rural area; in terms of mode of governance, modern legal concepts and excellent traditions and norms shall be combined; and in terms of governance structure, the basic-level political organizations should be organically integrated with economic development.

2.4.1. *To adjust administrative villages–natural villages (teams) according to school districts*

The administrative village–natural village pattern in China is a result of natural conditions and historical evolution, and has made important contribution to national prosperity and the glorious history of China. With constant developments of industrialization and urbanization, rural population, the living conditions and means of work of rural residents will see further changes. Whatever changes they are, the Chinese people will never change their cultivation of and attention to children. Chinese villages have an earnest desire for a great thought and method to improve rural education, so as to allow rural children to share the fruits of modernization like urban children do. Therefore, when thinking about restructuring the basic-level social management system in rural China, I proposed to adjust the administrative village–natural village (team) pattern to make it more convenient for primary and middle school students to receive education. In the foreseeable future, even if China becomes as modernized as the developed countries, permanent population in administrative villages–natural villages will keep accounting for 20–35% of the total Chinese population. Besides, given the natural and special association between the rural and urban areas in China, the gap between them will be reduced gradually, dual-direction flow of people will become frequent, and villages will remain places having a flourishing population, and that is for sure and could be foretold. In the meantime, a considerable part of the rural population will move to live in cities, some even in big and medium-sized cities, or nearby counties and townships. Under this irreversible trend, it is necessary to properly integrate multiple resources in villages and adjust the traditional administrative village–natural village (team) pattern. To select ideal villages (or sites), full consideration shall be given to ensure the scope of student sources and students' safety and convenience, gathering educational resources, improving teaching conditions and strengthening the construction of central primary schools (and middle schools, if applicable), and reasonably planning the construction of rural, traffic and power infrastructure around schools. Construction in the above two aspects and policy orientation may promote some villages to gather together naturally, and promote the adjustment of contiguous stretches of land, relatively intensive operation of the rural economy and relatively concentrated and effective management of the rural society so that a rural administrative structure that echoes modernization in China will be formed on the basis of inheritance.

2.4.2. *To give play to the role of excellent rural party members and talented people*

For thousands of years, in the vast areas where the state contacts its people, rural talented people have been playing an important role. They represent not only the state, but also the farmers. They themselves are farmers or their ancestors were farmers. Being naturally associated with the rural society, they are not only bridges but also the buffer zone between the state and farmers, and are an important informal backbone force in the rural society. In the Chinese history, villagers have always had autonomy. In the new period, such advantage is very possibly inherited and carried forward and rural talented people may greatly play their role. It is an important way of strengthening village governance.

Rural talented people here involve outstanding rural Party members, local people with high morals and wisdom, teachers in local schools, and those with local origin who live elsewhere but pay great attention to their hometowns. Such people may be retired cadres or cadres who work elsewhere, teachers, technicians, and entrepreneurs, etc. If we develop a policy which prohibits active cadres in government organs and other active staff to do part-time jobs, but allows the above people to do part-time jobs in village-level activities in their hometown, we could surely make them a great power in the building of a modern rural society. They have feelings for their hometowns, and the knowledge and capability of living and working in the modern society. As long as they are permitted, they would be very glad to do something for their hometown. Modern traffic and communication technologies and rhythms of life and work in the rural and urban areas are making the urban and rural areas closer and closer, creating conditions for the wanderers to serve their hometown. Recently, staff of the State Council Leading Group Office of Poverty Alleviation and Development made investigations in Xiongwu Village in Baoan Town, and Yewu Village, Shigutang Town, Qingyuan City, Guangdong, and they happened to coincide with my proposal at this point.[3] Therefore, such proposal has an important practical foundation. The power of such people is closely aligned with local folks, and that may give birth to endogenous forces in rural areas in China for stable development and accelerate the process of modernization in rural China.

2.4.3. *To explore organic combination of basic-level political organizations and economic development*

At the village level, the rural core is generally a central village plus several natural villages (teams), or a bigger village with hundreds or thousands of residents. To govern areas of such a size, we may consider building two parallel organizations: One is the school board where the central school is the heart, and head of the school, head of the village and part-time board members, totally three to five in number, are appointed by the local department of education in the hope of integrating resources in all aspects, strengthening traditional culture, modern

[3]According to the investigations made by Cao Hongmin, Jie Ping and Su Juan from the State Council Leading Group Office of Poverty Alleviation and Development in Xiongwu Village, Baoan Town, Lianzhou and Yewu Village, Shigutang Town, Yingde, Qingyuan City, Guangdong Province in 2013, the council members in Xiongwu Village do not only include local farmers, but also the security captain of Foshan Municipal Public Security Bureau and the head of audit management office of Lianzhou Municipal People's Court who do not work locally. The introduction of such external power has changed the internal management structure, helped and supported daily village management and decision-making on village affairs, expanded the village's social sources to a great extent, and strengthened the effect of village governance. Over the past several decades, more than 160 residents in Xiongwu Village have moved out and settled in many places in Guangdong; some have even moved and settled abroad. Local villagers maintain the ancestral homes of these people to arouse their feelings to the hometown, tactfully keep root contact with them, and constantly consolidate the village's social resources. "Lost rituals have to be found in the folks." The innovative social assistance to the poor in Xiongwu Village is greatly vital.

civilization and moral guidance, starting with children and teaching them knowledge following the general rules while carrying forward local culture, building the sense of law and morals in children, teaching them modern civilization, knowledge and technologies to lay a solid foundation for sustainable rural development. When central rural schools are completed, rural families will also be willing to send their children to rural schools to receive traditional cultural education.

The other is the villagers committee focusing on peaceful content living and working, environmental protection and cultural relics maintenance. The villagers committee is elected democratically by the villagers according to the *Organic Law of Villagers Committees*, and gives full play to the role of villagers' political power. Its members may be local villagers or people with local origin and willing to come back to do something for their hometown. They may also be village officials who are undergraduates and other staff designated by the township government. They are mainly responsible for village planning, development and safety; managing and operating collective resources in the village, leading the villagers to get rich, trying to solve "matters that cannot be done or cannot be done well" by one family, insisting on production and operation as well as the village management. For a fairly long period, the villagers committee plays dual roles between townships and villagers: It has to be responsible for townships and for local villagers. Therefore, remuneration for local village cadres is mainly from income of collective operation or family operation, and certain subsidies may be got from the township government; part-time staff may get a certain amount of money from collective income as their remuneration. Remuneration for staff or village officials who are university graduates designated by the township government may be solved by the county (city) and township governments. With these two organizations, villagers' autonomy has an organizational guarantee.

2.4.4. *To always combine modern legal concepts with excellent traditional norms*

The fundamental way is to educate the villagers. Villagers are plural. They are a group made up of many individual farming households.

To educate farmers is to help them realize their interests as a whole, their long-term interests and fundamental interests and to prevent a small number of villains from harming the interests of the whole village and villagers' common feelings. It is necessary to adhere to legal education, and to find solutions to contradictions from traditions. A mechanism for solidarity *via* criticism and that for education *via* struggles should be established. Village rules and regulations may be developed and principles followed. On issues of right and wrong, no one shall be a goody-goody. The illegal and criminal behaviors by a few people can never be connived. The right thing to do is to crack down upon the illegal and criminal minority, educate the majority, encourage healthy tendency, stifle perverse trends, and create a harmonious, stable and developing environment in the rural area. At the occasion of special celebrations in the village or by creating new rural activities and rural signs, village rules and regulations may be improved and bettered, the rural cultural atmosphere where traditions are combined with modernization may be strengthened and common sense may be enhanced to push village governance to the path of modernization.

It is a major systematic project to reform county (city), town and township and village governance in China, which will have great impacts on the sustainable development of the nation. The day that the reform of county governance succeeds will be surely the moment that China becomes a prosperous and strong country. Beautiful villages, beautiful towns and beautiful county economy make a beautiful China.

2.5. Village Vicissitudes and Reforms

China is in an era of great reforms, and witnesses great changes of its townships and greater changes of its villages. Changes in villages are more than just changes in their outlook. They are changes of the rural society. The rural society is transforming from clan folks society (acquaintances society) to family residence society (semi-acquaintances society); and small family-cored relationship of residing as visitors is gradually transforming into the clan-cored folks relationship. The transformation presents six features.

First, village residents become strange. Villages are open; the relationship between traditional and mutually-cutoff rural groups, lineage, clans and families becomes diluted; residents of the rural society do not trust or rely on one another easily like they did before; the household contract responsibility system makes rural families more independent and villagers less contacted; more farmers go to work in cities and seldom live in their hometown; villagers become unfamiliar with each other, and homesickness and relationship between villagers have been weakened.

Second, villages do not have main labor forces. A great number of young and middle-aged villagers leave their hometown and work elsewhere. There are not enough main labor forces in the villages, but the old, the weak, women and children. The rural society is not independent and becomes more attached to the urban society. It is more and more difficult for villages to maintain their basic life and production with internal forces, and the traditional self-sufficient family farming cannot be continued.

Third, villages become hollow. Many rural residents have moved out. Some village houses are occupied by fewer people or become unoccupied. Some migrant workers who return to their hometown choose to build new houses around the traditional houses, not at their original homestead. Villages become emptier and emptier.

Fourth, rural economy is diversified. Villagers begin to have different jobs, incomes, connections, hobbies, demands and habits, which are quite different from the traditional rural economic society.

Fifth, rural culture is disappearing. Fewer and fewer traditional handicrafts, customs and memories are passed down. It is more and more difficult for the society and individuals to find villages to be the hometown or find village customs; local consensus has gradually disappeared, and traditional norms are more and more depreciated. Villagers are less connected by interests, and have a weakening emotional attachment or sense of belonging to the rural society; they do not feel uneasy for not knowing their parents' personality or village customs. Villagers and those working elsewhere lose the sense of subject to the village, hold that village prosperity or declining has nothing to do with them and their personal achievements have nothing to do with the villages. Their concept of the origin becomes increasingly weak, and the basic ways and theories of communicating with people in the rural society have witnessed great changes.

Sixth, the rural society is depressed. Many traditional residences have been dissolved and grown with weeds. Rural population has decreased and more and more people are leaving the rural area. Rural disorderliness is becoming more and more serious.

In the great reforms in China, in the transitional period of a traditional society and in the rapid development of urbanization and industrialization, it is unavoidable that the rural society witnesses major vicissitudes. However, such vicissitudes are not terminal. When seeing a dramatically changing rural China and the historical process of major vicissitudes since the birth of villages in China, we sigh and have a stronger sense of responsibility. To achieve overall modernization and the great rejuvenation of the Chinese nation, we may learn from others, and imagine, lead and depict the blueprint of vicissitudes in rural China in the 21st century.

Chinese villages in the 21st century will by no means be what they are like today. Now Chinese villages are going through the transitional period with great reforms in China. With deepened and advanced modernization, delicate planning, institutional innovation, original concepts and coordinated development, Chinese villages will present a great vision where the traditional and the modern are combined.

Rural economy with famous brands. Priority is given for displaying local advantage in resources, making the best use of local resources, developing and maintaining brand products and winning market with famous brands.

Rural culture with distinct features. Excellent factors in historical traditions are carried forward and a characteristic cultural life is created for not only self-entertainment, but also attracting the outside world.

Rural society with law and order and legal principles. National laws are deeply embedded into the rural society; villages display citizenship and public morals; local regulations and rules that do not conflict with the law will similarly have some influences on the villagers; villagers follow not only local consensus, but also national legal consensus; and the entire rural area has access to relatively symmetric social information.

Rural environment favorable for living. Rural population is decreased; rural environment is quiet and natural; rural sanitation is fundamentally improved and villages have an intensive atmosphere, and become more livable.

The above vision will by no means appear naturally. Proper measures must be taken. First, it is necessary to develop delicate plans for rural development when developing county economy; second, it is necessary to make overall planning and build a rural security system when adjusting the dual urban–rural structure, and foster and advocate civilized concepts in the vicissitudes of the rural society; third, in the wave of urbanization, it is necessary to improve governance capacities and promote coordinated urban and rural development.

2.6. Summary

Counties (cities) in China may have millions of population and cover tens of thousands of square kilometers, as populous and large as a country. Or they might be like a "small sparrow having all the vital organs", as they have complete social patterns and characteristics, except military and diplomatic functions. "Stable counties make the country stable, and chaotic counties make the country chaotic." County economy is the greatest livelihood economy, as well as the foundation of stable social development on the whole. County (city) governments are not only bridges to connect cities with villages, but play an important role in connecting the power of the Central Government with local governance. In particular, in economic and social transition, county governance is directly related to lasting stability of the state.

To strengthen the building of county governance capacities, priority shall be given to well solving local concerns, mobilizing the inner vitality of the basic-level organizations, and improving the sustainability of county economy and society. County governance is not to separate from the big market. Under the conditions of the market economy, it is unnecessary or impossible to block necessary links among the markets. To strengthen county governance is to improve the strategic position of county economy in the big market and give better play to the basic role of county economy. County governance is not to block the association with higher level administrative organs, but to clarify the administrative responsibilities of different levels, better carry out national development strategies and create conditions for achieving modernization in an all-round manner.

At the Third Plenary Session of the 18th CPC National Congress, it was proposed to "modernize the national governance system and capabilities". The building of county governance capabilities is the basis for modernizing the national governance system and capabilities, demonstrating the strategic meaning of political restructuring. The key to build county governance capabilities is to deepen county political reform which is a basic project for building socialist democratic politics. When economy is developed to a certain level, the awareness of participating in the discussion of political issues and of being masters gets further strengthened. To follow the trend and deepen county government reform is a move that adapts to the development need of the market economy and public administration in the new era. It helps satisfy growing public demands for good governance and public products and meets the development trends of the era. County government, including its cadres and the masses under its leadership, is relatively easy to manage. It is a better strategic choice to make county political reform as a breakthrough point to deepen reforms. It shall demonstrate the principle of "from the easy to the difficult, from the top to the bottom, in a proper scale, and with trials". Although it may cause major changes locally to reform county governance, reform of county governance is unlikely to greatly impact the stable situation nationwide. To launch political restructuring at the county level, the Central Government has strong initiative and controllability. For example, it may build and improve a central auditing system and people's court system that are completely independent of the local governments, maintain the control of the local governments by the Central Government, and truly place the activities of people's governments at different levels under the law. Follow the principle of "unifying rights and responsibilities and shifting down the center of gravity", the functions and responsibilities of the county governments may be expanded, and some of the provincial and municipal economic and social management rights may be transferred to county governments, which could not only improve the autonomy of county governance, but also promote national administrative efficiency and create conditions for deepening reforms in an all-round manner. The experience in county autonomy in Taiwan, China is referable. Chinese theorists and practitioners have done a lot of studies in this regard. On the whole, based on trials, the conditions for building county political ecology are met. It is entirely possible to achieve transformation of the county governments, ameliorate governance and service capabilities and strengthen the inner vitality of county economy and society based on the development of market economy. It is easy to adjust some other conditions like the county leaders voidance system, as long as we have determination. It is very necessary for the central, provincial and municipal leading departments to take the chance, launch trials and put the building of county governance capabilities on the agenda before timely advancing it. It is an issue concerning the lasting stability of the country.

CHAPTER 3

FURTHER IMPROVE THE MECHANISM TO ENSURE "LAND TO THE TILLER"

"Land to the Tiller" is the basic condition to social and economic development. Peasant economy on a moderate scale may be an important phenomenon and trend which will exist in China for a long time. On the macro level, we need to take into consideration the "classified management of land and National Land Fund" and cultivate diversified market players; on the micro level we should optimize the rural land management system, and form a structure consisting of "state-owned farmland, agricultural and sideline product bases near the cities, rural collective land, rural public land and household-run land so as to improve the market operational mechanism for "Land to the Tiller" and further clarify the status of and give full play to the role of the nation, the communities and rural households in food security.

Land reform is the most difficult reform. China's New Democracy Revolution in the 20th century started from land reform, and so did its reform and opening up campaign. Its effect is obvious, yet the underlying difficulties are quite a few. "Land to the Tiller" is the basic appeal of the human society, and also an important principle of social and economic development. "Land is the base of the world", as stated in *Xunzi*, and the subsistence of human being and social development is impossible without land. Arable land in China is in shorter supply than in any other countries. During China's modernization in the 21st century, whether the issue of arable land can be properly addressed not only influences the development of China, but also is pivotal to its subsistence. It is an important strategic project, therefore, to actively explore the methods to improve the mechanism to ensure "Land to the Tiller".

3.1. Severity of the Land Issue

3.1.1. *Land is the scarce strategic resource*

With the development of human society, the shortage of land resource caused by population increase and economic development is becoming more pronounced. In particular, the arable land per capita is on the decline due to the large-scale industrialization, too fast population increase and the serious encroachment by non-agricultural uses. According to a research report of the World Bank, the arable land per capita in the world declined from 0.56 hectare in 1950 to 0.236 hectare in 1996, and that in China dropped from 0.182 hectare in 1950 to 0.087 hectare in 2008. Pursuant to a study by the Commission for Integrated Survey of Natural Resources, Chinese Academy of Sciences, based on the advanced technological level in agriculture at present, the maximum productive capacity of grain in China should be approximately 830 billion kilograms, yet the actual average productive capacity from 2002 to 2012 is approximately 571 billion kilograms, only approximately 410 kilograms per capita (including that for industrial use and for fodder). Over recent years, 75% of soybean has to be imported. In a word, arable land is a global strategic resource, and it is especially important in China.

3.1.2. *Dilemma of the arable land in China*

Let's analyze the dilemma and trend in use of arable land in China from the three aspects: Agriculture, farmer and rural areas. China now has the peasant economy featuring per capita land of 1 mu and 3 fen (approximately 863 square meters) and no more than 10 mu (approximately 6,667 square meters) per household. Land contracted by rural households is not only of a small scale, but also fragmented; most rural households earn income from generational division of labor for agriculture and non-agricultural sectors. As the ownership of land is placed idle, the land-use right not steady, the land disposition right crippled, the land income right limited and the land policy not matching, the land for agricultural use is extensively operated with low efficiency, and much arable land is left idle as some farmers who worked in town still occupy arable land; on the other hand, the above factors led to great deficiency in scale operation with serious waste of land resources. Because of historical reasons and the reality, during the economic transformation of China, the average area for operation per household in rural areas of China in the 21st century will remain approximately 20–30 mu without big reform in policy, and scale economy in agriculture is impossible. Peasant economy will probably remain in China in the long run. The most distinguished feature in agriculture in China is the peasant economy with not too much arable land per household among rural labor force. They enjoy the right, expectation, joy and reward from their labor with the periodic agricultural production.

For farmers in China, "those who are afraid of being starved will be starved to death, and those who aren't, won't"; most young migrant workers are caught in the dilemma of "no prospects going out to work and no meaning staying at home". Given the reality, an intergenerational division of labor was formed without a better way out: The adults go to the urban areas to work while the aged, women and children are left behind, nicknamed as "993860 force". Quite a number of farmers work both as workers and farmers. They go home to help during the one or two months of peak season for agriculture, and work in the urban areas during other months. Quite a few migrant workers who have settled in the cities have their income partially from the land, and take their land as a leeway when they go back to their hometown should they fail to stay in the city any longer.

Rural areas in China are on a serious decline. The social structure is mainly formed by the aged, women and the children, and only few adults who act as the major labor force. Their collective action is lack of power, and those issues "hard to be done well and hard to be done at all" by one household mostly are hardly solved by present village committees and primary-level organizations. Village committees are mostly multi-functional form of structures in the village without the qualification or ability to allocate resources as a legal person. Due to the large number of villagers working outside, huge difference in villagers' ideas and income, and divorcing of villagers with the villager economically and socially, enough people cannot be found to attend the collective decision making, making it hard to take coordinated collective actions. After the agricultural tax was cancelled, the village collective retreats from agricultural production affairs, and village cadres are more and more distant from rural households, and the collective irrigation systems accelerated their disassembly in most villages.

3.1.3. *Argument on rural land*

Rural economy and rural society in China have lasted for over thousands of years, and they used to formulate the backbone of Chinese economy and society, making significant contribution to civilization. Among the huge waves of modernization and in the era of major transformation, rural economy and rural society face grim challenges. The traditional villages are disappearing and its gap with the city is becoming wider and wider. Facing such reality, it is a big question lingering on many people's mind that how to improve the mechanism of "Land to the Tiller", to let farmers live a decent life and allow the villages to experience a "nirvana". There are also many opinions, all with positive attitude. Yet objectively speaking, we haven't found an ultimate solution to the problem.

Among the current debates, there are mainly two camps of views. One proposes the distribution of land ownership. Those holding this opinion believe that farmers should own not only the land-use right, but also the land ownership, and that only by doing so can "Land to the Tiller" be realized, and the farmers' drive be mobilized. In fact, it is not the case. Tillers' land does not necessarily be their own. It can be rented or obtained through other forms. The initiative of the tiller has something to do with the ownership of land, but it is not necessary that tillers' enthusiasm can surely be boosted with the land ownership. Some scholars have proved from the angle of property right that private ownership of land will impair the peasants' interest and will strengthen the resistance and rejection towards public policy-making.

Another is flexible land-use right. People holding this view propose to break the pattern that the land-use right remain unchanged for 30 years, believing that flexible land-use right can solve the issue concerning "Land to the Tiller". It is not this case either. Without corresponding institutional guarantee and reasonable market mechanism, the problem cannot be solved for sure even with certain flexibility with the term of land-use right. In the 1980s, the term of the first round of land contract of farmers was 15 years. From the 1990s, the second round was for a secured term of 30 years as the 3rd Plenary Session of 12th Communist Party of China (CPC) Central Committee further raised that the existing land contract should be kept unchanged. Being unchanged is conducive to the foundation of stability of the society and the stability of the rural society. Rural area is a major part of the Chinese society. Rural population is large, and farmers in the city are linked to the rural area in countless ways. Land back home allows farmers more room for maneuver and achieving a sense of affiliation. During its fast development, China's stability as an agricultural country can maintain the stability of the foundation of the fast economic development, which serves as a stabilizer and reservoir for China's modernization. The disadvantage of being unchanged is that the stable land contract relationship mismatches the changes and development of the rural population. A large amount of migrant workers still have the right for land contract and operation, yet farmers engaged in rural production in rural areas do not have enough land. It is hard for farmers to reach the moderate scale of operation of 30 mu, and it is highly inconvenient to farm on scattered land under the existing policy.

To address the issue of "Land to the Tiller", we should start from details with a holistic view while employing innovative mechanisms. With deep love to my fellow country folks, I attempt to probe into some new ideas as I reflect and compare, and do whatever I can to address issues concerning the agriculture, the countryside and the farmers.

3.2. Improvement of National Land Management Structure and System

According to the Constitution of People's Republic of China (PRC), land resources belong to the people, and the representative of land ownership is the State Council. Yet as far as the actual situation of the use of land in China is concerned, the direct allocator of the land in China are the local governments of various levels, only through which the State Council can exercise its function. To a great extent, therefore, "state-owned" is in fact "local government-owned", and the principal status of the country as the owner of land is became void. The result is, on the one hand, local governments use as much land as they can without cherishing it as that land belongs to the country; on the other, the interest of the whole country is replaced by local interest, which impaired the interest of the country from land use and the macro-control ability of the central government, and influenced the country's potential in sustainable development.

How to improve such a situation? I hereby propose two ideas for structural optimization. One is classified management of the land, and the other is classified management of arable land. In this section, I will mainly discuss the former.

An ideal design of classified management of land is, based on factors including national strategies, population trend and industrial prospects, to clearly distribute the long-term right for using construction land (land for transfer) of the country to four levels with appropriate proportion in the form of administrative ordinance of the State Council: For country's use, for provincial governments' use, for municipal governments' use and for county governments' use. These lands are parallel resources which can be transferred to a certain extent in the market. This design has three major benefits. First, it materializes the status of a portion of territory, allows more parties to exercise their initiatives and stresses the managerial responsibility and initiatives of local government on construction land. Second, it clearly defines the construction land resources for various regions, which helps local governments improve medium- and long-term development planning, make reasonable use of the limited construction land and promote local economic and social development according to local conditions. Third, it establishes a number of subjects of the land ownership, which is beneficial for nurturing the land market and circulation mechanism on a macro scale, strengthen the control of central government and help improve the sustainable development of economy and society.

Because of the above benefits, some countries have implemented similar mechanism of classified management of land since long. For example, the US exercises diversified land ownership with both public and private owners. Private land accounts for 51%, state and state government owned land 47%, and Indian reservation 2%. Land of the federal government mainly comprises of land of the federal government and authorities stationed in various states, counties and cities as well as military land, etc. Governments of states, counties and cities own their land respectively. Ownership, land-use right and beneficial interests in the land of the federal state, county and city are independent from each other without arbitrary expropriation or transfer. In cases of necessity, land must be obtained by compensation by purchase and sale or rental. There are variety of modes of ownership within the federal-owned land of 3,084,000 square meters: Bureau of Land Management controls 60%, Bureau of Forestry 24% while Department of Homeland Security, Bureau of Reclamation, National Park Service and Water and Power Resources Service, the remaining 16%. Disputes over land ownership are subject to the court, and the government no longer assumes the arbitrary role.[1]

As land ownership belongs to different parties, one could purchase from other parties when its land is not enough. In 2004, state

[1]Zou Li-xing (2009). *Lessons from Developments of US: Mechanism of Finance Imperialism*, p. 303. Hunan University Press.

and local governments of the United States spent US$1.5 billion on purchasing land development right.[2] In the States, approximately 2 million acre of arable land is protected as one needs to purchase its exploration right.

The above classified management of land, however, is hard to put in use in China. The first reason is that China is not well prepared either in ideology or regulations for diversified land ownership, and it takes a long time to reach the basic consensus on the new idea of classified management of land. Secondly, the measurement and negotiations over division proportion of the construction land of the central and local governments is an arduous gaming process involving significant political wisdom. Thirdly, the reform in land management mechanism is closely connected with the reforms in political mechanism, administrative management and other deep-seated reforms, and it needs global design, coordination and cooperation and action as the circumstances require. Fourthly, functional planning of the territory should be done not only on the national level, but more importantly, on provincial and county levels. Four categories, namely, optimized development, key development, limited development and prohibited development, should be clearly defined, and so are their respective scopes, development periods, development directions and exploration principles. This is a fundamental project whose success provides a more solid basis of technology and policy for land administration.

Despite the above difficulties, we may well start the in-depth research and initiate pilot projects in certain areas. At the same time, we may actively explore ways for improvement under present situation. For example, we may consider establishing National Land Fund for regulation and control. In the principle of "guided by the government, operated in the market and managed by the experts" and developing along institutional innovation and sustainable development, we establish the system of National Land Fund by incorporating the income from land into Central Land Fund and Provincial and Municipal Land

---

[2]Ding Cheng-ri (2007). The transferable development rights in the USA and its implications to arable land conservation in China. China Agricultural and Economic Information Network [16 April 2007].

Fund for regulation and control by certain proportions before including it into local fiscal revenue. As an important macro-control, it will facilitate the coordinated urban and rural development. As I have elaborated on National Land Fund for regulation and control in Chapter 5: Land Financial Market Construction, I will save the details here.

3.3. Improvement of Rural Land Management Structure and System

Arable land and rural construction land is the most precious land for production and life among all kinds, which directly concerns the subsistence of the nation and the stability of the country. This kind of land, not only is the key guarantee for agricultural growth, but also has become an important tool for Chinese urbanization and rapid industrialization. It is concerned with land income of various parties and its distribution, and is regarded as the "fuse" for social conflicts and disputes over interests, thus it is the epitome of issues concerning agriculture, countryside and farmers of China. Land for cultivation per capita in China is already far below the world average, yet the limited arable land must feed the present population of over 1.3 billion and more in the future. It is, therefore, a major strategy which entails the initiative from various parties. After summarizing the present institution and the actual situation, I hereby propose a new idea of classified management of arable land.

The basic idea of classified management of arable land is: Dividing the arable land and construction land in the rural areas all over China roughly into three types. The first is land for large-scale farms, including the agricultural and sideline product bases near the cities. This kind of land belongs to the country, occupying approximately 35% of the total area of arable land. For example, large-scale farms on provincial level can make effective use of the intensive operational advantages and give full play to the pivotal function as a national barn with their natural conditions and historical factors. The second is rural collective land and public land in the villages. It belongs to local communities, taking up around 5–10%. In particular, public-owned arable land is mainly operated by way of corporate farm, which facilitates the exercise of intensive operational advantages by taking up collective productive tasks hard to be fulfilled by one single family. It can also centralize the land left behind by or rented from migrant workers and make good use of the land resource. This kind of collective agriculture plays an important role in adjusting the balance in provision.

Public land in the villages include collective construction land, experimental land or vegetable plot for rural schools (school land), embankment for local rivers and the barren land near lakes and mountains. Public land in the villages is common in history. Professor Fei Hsiao-Tung recorded in detail the actual situations of the public land in the villages as he observed in *Earthbound China: A Study of Rural Economy in Yunnan*. Mr. Tang Zhiqing in his "*A Study of Rural Society and Economy Modern Shandong*" mentioned that "in the 16th century, the proportion of the official and public land in Shandong was as follows: Approximately 9.2% of the arable land in the province was *tuntian* (military agro-colonies used mainly in border regions to supply the army garrisoned there), 27.2% official land and 13.6% public land. The total of official and public land was 50% and private land 50%." It shows that a certain portion of public land is nothing new in China. In the industrialized China, maintaining a certain amount of public land is very likely to be an important approach in improving rural land mechanism. We can allot one or two mu of vegetable field to rural schools and organize the students to grow vegetables or melons. It can not only cultivate the industrious spirit of the students, but also add fresh vegetables to the lunch tables in rural schools and improve the school condition.

The third is household-operated land and homestead. Whether to maintain the present land contract system or to further implement the reform on land ownership, household-operated land will remain the feature of Chinese rural economy for a long time to come. With changing conditions, a portion of household-operated land may be transferred under the operation of clans and professional farmers, and forming three modes of family operations for the land. Though clan operation and professional farmers operate a larger area of land than a single family, they can hardly reach the extent and effect of scale operation, so in essence it has not changed the characteristics of family operators. As a result, generally speaking, household-operated land will remain a large proportion in the rural land structure in China, approximately 55%. With the migration of rural population and the employment of various policies, the typical phenomenon of "1 mu and 3 fen per capita and no more than 10 mu per family" may be improved to be "3–4 mu per capita and 20–30 mu per family". Even with that level, it still remains the peasant economy, or moderate peasant economy. Peasant economy in China will remain for a long term, which is attributable to three reasons. First, peasants have ingrained affection to the land and it can hardly be disposed of. According to the data of Department of Rural Economic System and Management, Ministry of Agriculture, at the end of 2007, the area under circulation was 5.2% of the area of contracted cultivated land. This is a very low figure. Situations in Taiwan can illustrate this point too. In the 1950s, Taiwan successfully implemented the mechanism of "Land to the Tiller", which greatly stimulated the enthusiasm of the peasants, and the annual growth rate in rural production reached 5.2%. From 1962 to 2000, Taiwan further initiated two land reforms, both aiming at expansion of operations but with limited effect: Only 7.84% of peasants gave up land ownership.[3] Secondly, peasant economy is very tenacious. In nature it values lineage and inherence, which epitomize the combination of social and natural reproduction. To some extent, land is what the peasants rely on, the basis to the development of peasants' families and the foundation of the peasants to establish their career and themselves in the society. As a result, it is the peasants' instinct to safeguard their land and peasant economy. Quite a few of migrant workers, when find life in the city is getting difficult, can well go back to their villages and feed themselves by being engaged in agriculture. Peasant economy, therefore, plays a very important role as a stabilizer and reservoir in China's modernization. Thirdly, it is obvious that the "transaction cost" of mobilizing internal labor such as relatives is relatively low in peasant economy, even for family farms

---

[3]Gao Xing-Song (1999). Peasant economy and the development of Taiwan agriculture. Collected Papers of Taiwan Research.

or professional farmers. Peasant economy is not only an important force in food supply, but also provides peasants with opportunities to employment and income.

With the progress of urbanization and industrialization, quite a few farmers go into town as workers or merchants, so back in their hometown the mode of "part-time farming" is formed. This mode of livelihood continued to safeguard the connection between farmers and the subjects to agricultural labor. At the same time, the need and information brought back by the home-coming migrant workers enhanced the connection between peasants and the consumption market of agricultural products. Peasant economy, mainly relying on labor input and small-scale agricultural machinery, is usually intensive cultivation with strong adoptive ability to the market, and is ecologically more advantageous than modern agriculture which adopts scale operation. Peasant economy, therefore, is the important foundation to Chinese modernization.

Figure 3.1 is a summary to the above classified management of arable land.

Figure 3.1: Classified management of arable land.

Optimizing rural land management structure and mechanism based on the actual conditions of villages in China and the development rules in agriculture is conducive to further exercising the role of the country, the community and peasants' families in the food security of China, for sustaining the stability of the villages and for protecting the peasants' benefit. The country should strongly support the development of state-owned large-scale farms and the agricultural and sideline product bases near cities and scale economy to provide support for food security. Local governments should appropriately guide the development of collective agriculture and support the construction of rural infrastructure such as water conservancy and road to leverage and adjust food security. The people should strongly support the improvement of household-operated land mechanism and fully exercise the fundamental role of peasant economy in food security.

3.4. Establishment of the Market Operational Mechanism of "Land to the Tiller"

With the progress in industrialization and urbanization, rural areas in China are bound to generate the impetus and need for the circulation of cultivated land based on household-operation. Private ownership or land ownership of other forms should be equipped with corresponding market mechanism to guarantee normal operation of the land in circulation. We attempt to design a market especially for circulation of the arable land, which will facilitate the land transfer from those who do not farm, and help realize "Land to the Tiller".

This market will develop around the location of county government. The county government will lead to establish rural land cooperatives and connect each village and villages under its jurisdiction, track the use of rural land and guide the rural land transfer. It will also exercise the administrative function on rural land ownership endowed by county government and provide services to the transfer of rural land. This market is for rural land transfer, especially that of arable land, and it does not allow private corporate enterprises to go directly into the agricultural production, and other companies or individuals not engaged in agricultural production are not allowed to enter this market either. The undertaker of the transferred rural land cannot change the use of the land.

This market has complementary institutional guarantees. For example, there is "Administrative Measures on Registration and Measurement of Land Transfer" to regulate the procedures, form, term and certificate of land transfer. There are different regulatory measures for different forms of land transfer including subcontracting, transferring, exchanging, renting and buying shares. For short-term substitute farming, no procedures are required. There is also "Administrative Measures on the Fees of Land Transfer", under which land transfer between families and relatives can be waived of the transfer fee subject to the wish of the farmers involved. The subtracting fee, rent and transfer fee should be negotiated and determined by the parties involved, and the interest from the transfer belongs to the contractor which any organization or individual should not hold back or withhold. Moreover, there is "Reward and Punishment of Transfer and Use of Land" to encourage rural land transfer through bypassing and reasonable use of the transferred land. Relevant compensation policies have been formulated to encourage land transfer to farming experts, and punish improper land transfers and change of land use.

This market also has a set of external interactive mechanisms. For example, to encourage the migrant workers to give up their land rent during the transfer so as to reduce the burden of the renters, we may consider the policy of "social security replacing the rent". The social security fund for migrant workers will be paid by national finance, and in return, the transferred arable land will not be charged with rent. The implementation of this policy may encourage the transfer and concentration of rural arable land.

Rural land cooperatives are service institutions for the welfare of local villages, farmers and agriculture. They are platforms for the transfer of operational rights of rural land for farmers and other major market players under the guidance of the local governments. Their aims are to fully exercise the fundamental supporting role of the market to rural land, offer services to the regulated transfer of the operational rights of rural land, facilitate the moderate scale operation and reasonable use of land and support the sustainable development of rural economy. Their major responsibilities are publicizing and implementing national and regional laws, regulations and policies, etc., concerning rural land and formulating the regulations and plans for the transfer of operational rights of rural land; initiating the transaction of operational rights of rural land and provide guidance to the execution of transfer contracts; coordinating the relationship between farmers, village organizations and enterprises during the transfer and transaction of the operational rights of rural land and safeguarding the rightful interests of both parties in the transaction; examining the parties involved in the transactions of the operational rights of rural land and their terms, and being responsible for collecting and settling the transfer information, conducting market research, establishing clients' portfolio and registration, mainly responsible for market administration such as providing service guide, releasing information and notifying the public, etc.

At present, the condition for establishing this kind of market is relatively mature, which is mainly shown through the new policy of "allowing paid transfer of land-use right abiding by the law" after the 30 years of contract period as regulated by the central government in 1993. That is the most important policy condition. Land-use right can be transferred, which to some extent granted the farmers the entitlement of interests of the land ownership.

Land transfer to some extent has the basis in practice, and is being accelerated. The land of some migrant workers is mostly ploughed by their parents. If their parents are too old or weak to carry out agricultural production, the migrant workers would subcontract it to their friends, relatives or neighbors with a symbolic rent. Such phenomenon will be more common. Of course, in general, the proportion of the arable land in transfer is not high, and the development in various places is not balanced. Most land transfers does not facilitate the operation by villages, and very little is used for planting grain, cotton and other staple crops in the transferred arable land which has realized the scale operation. According to the investigation done by the Department of Rural Economic System and Management, Ministry of Agriculture, only 6.4% of the land transferred on a large scale to

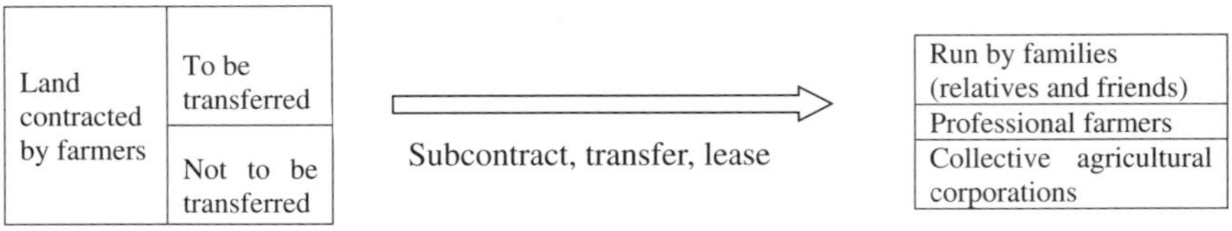

Figure 3.2: Strategies and forms of land transfer in the market mechanism.

the enterprises or proprietors is used for planting grains. One important reason is the immature market for land transfer in rural areas. It prompts us to work more on the establishment of market mechanism. The combined effect of the market mechanism and other corresponding policies may accelerate the normal effective transfer of the rural land and support the sustainable development of agricultural production. Figure 3.2 summarizes the strategies and forms of land transfer in the market mechanism.

In the future, when farmers undertake land through contracting, one portion will remain in the present form of peasant economy, occupying an important status in the land structure in rural areas, while another portion will be transferred in various forms subject to the actual situation.

Transferred to relatives and friends. To farmers, this provides the most relief, the strongest sense of security and the most ease at heart, as the land ownership remains intact according to the law and for relatives and the farmers themselves, and that leaves room for migrant workers who will be supported by relatives when they are back home. This kind of transfer, therefore, is driven by inherent impetus, and therefore relatively reasonable. Against this background, if guided scientifically, the land may become a family farm, which will serve as an important force in the modern operational mode of farms.

Transferred to professional farmers. This is the government's preference, which can both better exercise the technical advantages of the professional farmers, and facilitate the formation of scale operation. Yet during the land transfer transaction, one needs sound judgment and encouraging policies. There may be some land being transferred to professional farmers, but it cannot be many, for in the eyes of the farmers, this mode cannot provide them with sufficient sense of security, and it is not as assuring as transferring the land to their relatives and friends.

Transferred to collective agricultural corporations. A portion of land may be transferred to the community, and be re-allocated by the community either as the public land of the community or for establishing the collective agricultural corporation and become an important part of the land structure in the rural areas.

The household, clan and professional farmer who operates land, and the collective and the state who own the land are all parallel parties in the classified farmland ownership, and constitute the foundation for China's agricultural economy. This new pattern fully takes into consideration the actual situation of the farmers, and is conducive to solve the practical issues in the transfer of rural land, to evade the problem of arable land being deserted, and to sustain the stability of the rural area, and promotes the sustainable development of the agricultural society.

3.5. Case Study: Land Reform in Taiwan

3.5.1. *Background*

Taiwan shares the same root with the mainland of China. Despite the political and economic differences, they are very similar in terms of their dense population, shortage of arable land resources and the background of difficulties in rural areas. To ease the predicament in the rural areas, Taiwan carried out the First Land Reform, the Second Land Reform, Food Stabilization Fund, Community Renewal, and Rural Rejuvenation Plan. The construction model in rural Taiwan offers an excellent reference to the rural construction in the mainland.

3.5.2. *Land reform in Taiwan*

In the 1950s, the First Land Reform featured: "Rent Reduction to 37.5%", "Sale of Public Land", "Land to the Tiller". The government purchased land and entrusted the farmers with it, and made it compulsory that the rent shall not exceed 37.5% of the total harvest of the main crop. These land policies greatly improved the tenant farmers' life and stabilized the agricultural situation in Taiwan.

In the 1970s, Taiwan initiated the Second Land Reform and re-divided the arable land to integrate small plots of land and encourage collective operations by establishing collectives in vegetables, flowers, forestry, carps, livestock, sugarcane and Chinese olive. Thus without changing the land ownership, the operational scale of the farms was enlarged and the issue of low efficiency in scale operation in agriculture by individual families addressed. These efforts created conditions for professional and mechanized operations as an enterprise.

In 1974, Taiwan established the Food Stabilization Fund to stabilize the price of crops, encourage production and safeguard the farmers' benefit. The Farmers' Association in Taiwan played an important role in information exchange, quality control, market development, training and education, etc., and became an important bridge between the farmers' and the enterprises, and the enterprises and the government.

From 1980s to 1990s, Taiwan started the Community Renewal, encouraging the residents to participate in constructions concerning community environment, industry and culture, etc., in a creative manner so as to build a harmonious rural society.

In the 21st century, Taiwan launched the Rural Rejuvenation Plan. Centering on present rural communities, the plan attached importance for nurturing distinctive industry in the rural areas, ecological restoration and revitalization and recycling of special landscapes by way of voluntary participation of the farmers under the guidance of the government to reach multiple goals in the long run. This campaign contributed to the recycling efforts in rural areas and improved the living conditions of the residents.

3.5.3. *Features of rural construction in Taiwan*

First, land ownership is clearly defined and was reached by stages. In the transformation from traditional agriculture to modern agriculture, corresponding land ownership was adopted to concentrate the ownership of land and long-term land-use right to facilitate the agricultural production on a large scale in the form of enterprises with a certain level of mechanization and modernization. Second, the channels of capital are diversified. A relatively mature financial system was established in the region of Taiwan. Besides the financial support from the government, there are many other channels to raise funds for rural development. For example, the provident fund system establishes a community fund through collecting a certain proportion of income from non-agricultural operators (such as those running guesthouses or those engaged in tourism) to provide for public expenditure and for caring for the disadvantaged groups in the community. Third, the infrastructure system is established and improved, including water supply and water recycling facilities, sewage processors and garbage recycling facilities, facilities for reserving the space of traditional culture and network and information infrastructure, etc. Fourth, industries with distinctive features are developed. Based on the features of rural communities, they support the development of processing industry for featured products and recreational agriculture to encourage the development of affiliating industries of agriculture. It raises the comprehensive competitiveness of rural communities and their attraction to employment. Fifth, brands of products are promoted. In business philosophy, a batch of agricultural products were developed and nurtured and a team of leading agricultural enterprises was cultivated. The transformation of growth pattern in agriculture was thus expedited and the overall quality and economic effectiveness greatly enhanced.

3.6. Summary

Based on an in-depth analysis to the predicament of arable land in China, this article actively explores the safeguarding mechanism of "Land to the Tiller". Arable land is a strategic resource which we seriously lack, and China has no reason to ignore any piece of arable land. During urbanization and industrialization, there was decline in Chinese rural areas, some remote villages disappeared and some arable land was laid deserted. This is temporary phenomenon in China's modernization process, and in the future, people will ultimately use all arable land as they can because arable land is really too precious. At present, the pressing task of the officials should be consolidating and improving the mechanism and the market of "Land to the Tiller", not only for ensuring land for those who really want to farm, but also for creating conditions for the construction of modern countryside in the 21st century.

It is impossible that the modern society is comprised of only farmers, but farmers there must be. Farmers in any society are the most important laborers. The main structure of agricultural development changes with the social progress and technological development. In a long period to come, rural arable land may be roughly classified into five categories with respective five production players: Large-scale farms (state-owned), agricultural and sideline product bases near the cities (collective), rural collective land (collective), rural public land (collective), household-run land (household). In the 21st century, the average operational scale per household in most rural area of China is approximately 20–30 mu, making large-scale agriculture economy barely possible.

To address the lasting peasant economy in China, and properly concentrate and effectively use the precious arable land resources, it is necessary to establish a market operation mechanism of "Land to the Tiller" where the government interacts with the market. This mechanism, on the macro level, may require the optimization of national land management institution, and grant the parties relevant to the land with a certain level of national authorization. It may be a hard nut to crack and may not be able to be implemented recently, yet we may test it in pilot projects. In the long run, it may be a meaningful conception. On the micro level, we need to optimize rural land management structure. There is certain foundation for its implementation, and we should accelerate its progress. In practice, we need to establish a National Land Fund supported by the government as an important leverage of the government to regulate and control the land. On the one hand, the Fund collects a portion of revenue from the land for long-term balance and development, on the other hand, it guides the regulated operations of the land transaction market all over the country.

The adjustment of national land management structure and rural land management structure is conducive to the establishment of major players in agricultural production, National Land Fund at the central level and local land transaction markets contribute to the formation of a unified market network all over the country, and new markets and new players are helpful for improving the operational mechanism of "Land to the Tiller".

CHAPTER 4

LAND RIGHTS RELATIONSHIP ANALYSIS*

This chapter focuses on the relationship between the right to use land and land ownership and aims to provide some theoretical support for adjusting the rural land policy in a new period of time. Land value is the sum of the values of a series of land rights. The right to use land could be stripped out of the bundle of land rights. It has the subject and object of right in rem and is exclusive. The right to use land may be traded, mortgaged or inherited. On the basis of clarifying the relationship between the right to use land and land ownership, efforts may be made to set up a national land fund to better demonstrate land ownership *via* the market mechanism on the one hand; and to extend the current duration of the rural land household contracting period from 30 years to permanent and make land inheritable on the other. It may not only explore the huge value of rural land resources, but fundamentally solve the problem of state-owned land "being placed idle" and promote urbanization and healthy and sustained rural development.

Since China adopted the reform and opening up policy, it has entered the historical period of rapid economic development and accelerated urbanization when land, besides being a key guarantee for agricultural

*This chapter was written in November 2007 and was revised a little recently.

growth, becomes an important tool in rapid urbanization and high-speed industrialization in China. It is important to financing and fiscal growth and stability of the local government, thus is regarded as the "fuse" that may trigger social conflicts and disputes over rights and interests and is a concentrated manifestation of issues concerning agriculture, the countryside and the farmers in China. It has become the core of sustainable social and economic development and an insurmountable topic in China to ensure about 1.8 billion mu of farmland, about 400 million mu of rural land for construction, 30,000 administratively designated towns and market towns and 3 million villages, as well as the abundance and development of 750 million rural population. Along with the fast urbanization and industrialization in the recent 30 years, Chinese urban population has reached 580 million now and the urbanization rate of China is over 45%. In the next 12 years, about 300 million farmers will move from villages and towns to cities, being the biggest concentrated urban transformation in human history and the most magnificent social change in the modern world. There are enormous hidden dangers behind the rapid economic growth in China: Extensive expansion of the land for construction, serious waste of farmland resources, unreasonable structure and pattern of land use, the prominent conflict between people and land; less intensive land use caused by urbanization, loss of state-owned assets, excessive burdens on land finance, hardly effective regulation policies, and huge potential fiscal and financial risks in the land financial market. Therefore, to transform the traditional modes of economic development and land management is crucial for deepening reform and development, and it is the strategic foundation for the lasting development of China.

To solve the above problem, it is a must to analyze the mechanism for the formation of land property rights, and propose a new set of principles, thoughts and mechanisms concerning macro management of land finance, both in theory and practice.

4.1. On Land Ownership

From the perspective of current land property characteristics in China, the biggest characteristic of the Chinese land system would be the separation of the land ownership from the land-use right. Land in urban China is owned by the state; collective land belongs to the collective; and they may be delivered to specific land users by way of granting or contraction within a certain period, and such land users obtain the right to use the land for a certain number of years by paying a certain amount of money for it. In terms of the practices of land use in China, "being state-owned" has actually become "being owned by the local governments", "being collective-owned" has actually become "being owned by the county/township governments"; the status of the state or the collective as the land owner has been virtualized in reality; farmers cannot make decisions over their land, the land-use right cannot circulate reasonably, and their land contract and management rights are not well guaranteed.

Land, as a kind of real estate, has been regarded as one of the biggest values since the ancient times. The value of land, from the perspective of law, is the value of land rights, or the sum of values of a series of land rights. Each concrete land right has a corresponding subject, and has a different economic purpose. Therefore, the understanding of the right in rem shall be a process that goes from simple to complicated, from "whole" to "parts", and involves many players. It is inevitable in economic development and social progress.

4.1.1. *From the mechanism for the formation of land ownership*

The forms of land ownership are closely related to different stages of the formation of land property, and the formation of land property has four stages,[1] namely the stage of undeveloped land, land development stage, the stage of land lease and selling (land lease and transfer) and that of realty formation, operation and maintenance. Before land is developed, the subject of land rights is the subject of land ownership, that is, the state or farmers as a collective. At this time, the

[1] It may also be regarded as having three stages: Land lease and selling, in the strict sense, is a point in time, and an important node to realize the usufruct of land development right and the transformation of land development right to land-use right, that is, the most crucial place in the establishment of land development right.

subject of land rights is demonstrated in the single form of ownership, and the subject is the state or farmers as a collective.

At the land development stage, after forming construction conditions, land rights are expressed as local governments' right to develop and manage land, and the corresponding subject shall be decided accordingly: If such land is rented, the state shall be holding land rights; if it is sold, the land user shall be holding land rights; if there are buildings or fixtures on such land, realty-related equities shall be subject to concrete situations following the principle of consistent building property rights and land property rights: if the land is rented by the state, the state shall be holding rights to such realty, and its behavior of renting such buildings or fixtures falls into the bundle of land-use right; if such land is sold, the land user shall be holding rights to such realty, and the behaviors, of the land user, of disposing, possessing, profiting from and mortgaging such realty fall into the bundle of land-use right.

Till the stage of realty formation, operation and maintenance, land rights are manifested in multiple forms, as the case may be. If realty-related equities belong to the state, the behaviors of selling, mortgaging, disposing of and profiting from such realty shall fall into the bundle of rights held by the state; if realty-related equities are privately held, the behaviors of selling, mortgaging, disposing of and profiting from such realty shall fall into the bundle of rights held by the individual(s) concerned.

At the first, third and fourth stages of the formation of land property, corresponding land rights, either state-owned land rights, rights to the collectively-owned land by farmers, or land-use right, land lease right, etc., are all rights in rem in nature, and they are the rights to freely possess, utilize, profit from and mortgage land, etc. However, at the second stage of the formation of land property, land development right is not a right in rem in nature, but executive power over land enjoyed by the local government within the area under its jurisdiction. According to *Real Rights Law of the People's Republic of China* and relevant legal provisions, rights in rem are the basic property rights, and the premise for creditor's rights. The land administration, management and development rights enjoyed by local governments which are not rights in rem in nature cannot form the basis of creditor's rights, let alone a series of financial innovations on rights in rem. Therefore, it is a must to consider how to include land development by local governments into the scope of the right in rem so as to solve a series of financial problems in the process of land development at the second stage of the formation of land property.

After being clarified, state land ownership shall be further materialized. For example, at different stages of land property rights, the rights that are part of state land ownership may be stripped out and made into assets or capital, and then *via* a kind of innovative (financial) institutional arrangement, state rights over land at different stages during the existence of land property rights are solidified into products that can circulate, namely land financial products. As land is transformed from a resource to capital, there is the trend that strengthens logical evolution of land system innovations into the management of land financial assets, that is, to strengthen institutional innovations on the management of land resources by managing land resource assets, which may combine the land market and the financial market more closely and make it possible to establish a perfect land finance system. For example, efforts may be made to establish a land fund to help demonstrate the value of state land ownership; in addition, effective use of such a set of market-oriented value system of state land ownership will play a positive role in the land and real estate markets which are seeing yet-to-be-satisfying macro control.

4.1.2. *From the rent theory*

In China, the state owns land, differential rent I shall all belong to the state, while differential rent II shall go to land users within the deadline of land selling or that of land lease. As the forming of differential rent is attributed to urban governments' financial investment in the infrastructure construction, which ameliorates the regional environment of urban land, namely, convenient local traffic and better infrastructure and public facilities, most differential rent shall belong to local governments.[2] Therefore, by separating state land ownership from land-use right, efforts may be made to try to separate state land ownership from the land development right enjoyed by local governments, to separate central from local interests in land, so as to form the three-layered land right relationship involving the Central Government, local government and developer. That is, the state, as the land owner, enjoys the right to demand absolute rent; local governments, as land developers, enjoy the right to demand differential rent I; and land developers, as the land builder, shall enjoy the right to demand part of differential rent II. Therefore, it is conducive for realizing state land ownership economically *via* financial innovation to form a central land fund which demonstrates the land ownership of the Central Government by capitalized future absolute rent, and the local land fund based on future capitalized differential rent I demonstrating local land ownership, and future capitalized differential rent II demonstrating mainly the local land development right. More importantly, it helps the state strengthen substantial contents of state land ownership by way of capitalizing rent; solve the problem that state land ownership exists only in name, i.e., return on state-owned land assets runs off outside the institutional system; establish a land assets and capital operation and transfer system, achieve nationwide distribution of income, balanced economic development in different regions and coordinated urban–rural development.

4.1.3. *From the process of formation of land value*

Land presents two basic forms of value before and after it is put into the market, namely the development value and the market value. Specifically, before it is put into the market, land experiences two stages, i.e., the state of being undeveloped and the process from undeveloped land to developed and usable land, or the development of "uncultivated land" into "cultivated land", during which the subject of land rights has to correspond to that of land ownership, or the

---

[2] Bi Bao-de (2006). *Land Economics*, 5th Ed. China Renmin University Press. pp. 341, 344.

state. After it is put into the market, land also experiences two stages, namely land lease or selling and realty maintenance and operation, during which land rights are demonstrated as more than just land ownership, but composite rights involving land ownership, land-use right and many other land rights. Below is an analysis of the forms and rights of land before and after it is put into the market.

4.2. The Forms and Rights of Land Before and After it is Put into the Market

4.2.1. *The forms and rights of land before it is put into the market*

4.2.1.1. *Undeveloped land and its property right*

Generally speaking, unused land does not have any market value. However, due to the finiteness and scarcity of land resources, unused land that can reach certain standards of land for construction in the future is expected to appreciate in value. That is because when the supply of new construction land cannot meet the growing demand for land, there will be an implicit demand for the undeveloped land in the suburbs. Once such undeveloped land is allowed to be used for the purpose of construction in the master plan for land use and urban planning, the demand for such land will surely grow due to the change in its purpose, and then the unused land will have a market price under the market mechanism. Such a market price could be understood as the price of such land for its changed purpose. Since the state is the subject of rights to the undeveloped land in reality, the price of the undeveloped land is the right price of such land. That the state transforms the unused land into construction land by planning can also be understood as the state sets land development right as the land owner. If anyone intends to change the purpose of such land, he/she/it has to purchase the land development right from the government. The government of course could get a sum of money income by selling the right to develop such land. Now China has not set any land development right, restricts the change of land purpose only by its master plan for land use and overall urban planning, and

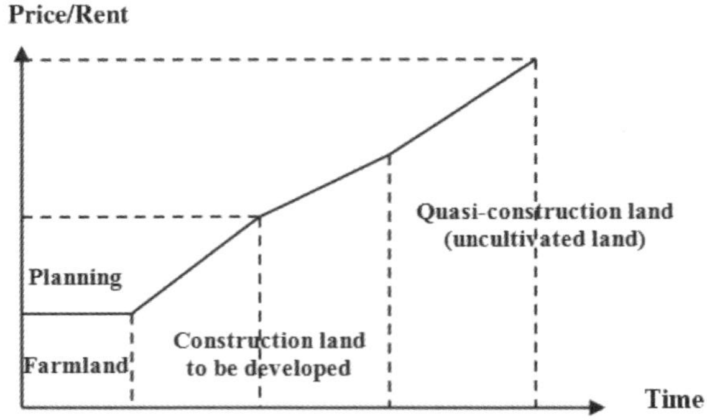

Figure 4.1: Planning implementation and changes in land price.

applies a strict system for managing and restricting land purpose. However, due to the absence of state land ownership, local governments actually play the role of the land owner. Driven by their own interest mechanisms like developing local economy, increasing local gross domestic product (GDP), manifesting their political performance, the current local governments more than often swap capital with land, and that is the most inexpensive and riskless way. Figure 4.1 shows and also explains why the master plan for land use and urban planning are always products of the "will of leading officials", and why the effects of carrying forward strict system for managing and restricting the change of land purpose are often unsatisfactory.

Therefore, it is necessary to set land development right to unused land for the purpose of protecting the ownership of such land. Land users must purchase land development right from the state if they intend to change the purpose of such land under the premise that it is permitted by the master plan for land development and overall urban planning. The state may establish a public welfare and special land development fund, with the income it gets from selling such land development right, for the purpose of protecting basic farmland, sorting out farmland and supporting rural economic development. Such public welfare land development fund could be made a source of capital for land fund, or one of the sub funds of land fund. Land development fund is a capital pool that contains national revenue of selling land development right to local land users, and a sub-fund of the central land fund as well. Under the overall arrangements of the land fund, land development fund is mainly invested in supporting the development of land and infrastructure construction in underdeveloped areas, and in supporting local economic development in poor areas in such forms as small group loans or production loans to farmers. It is not for profit, but for public welfare in nature. It is a tool of the land fund to realize regional equality by transferring financial resources.

The ownership of rural collective land which is at the same time potential construction land belongs to the farmers as a collective. According to the current land acquisition policy, the government has to pay, to the farmers concerned, such fees as land compensation, resettlement fees and compensation for attachments to or green crops on the land, but no revenue from land appreciation after farmland becomes construction land, if it intends to acquire land from the collective of farmers. The revenue from the appreciation of farmland after it is changed into construction land is made up of two parts, namely revenue from social land appreciation, thanks to the implementation of government planning and regional environmental effects; and that from the application of investment in land brought about by buildings or fixtures built by land users; for the first part, according to the principle "all the application be turned in", revenue from appreciation shall belong to the state; for the second part, based on the analysis of rent theory, the collective of farmers, as the land owner, shall have the right to enjoy part of the revenue from the appreciation of land investment. Therefore, the land acquisition policy at the present stage does not conform to farmers' interests, or national interests.

To solve the problem, China may start with peeling off the bundle of land rights, set land development right against the land that is potential construction land as the land owner, and finally separate land development right from land ownership *via* financial innovations. By social fundraising, the state may establish a land acquisition fund, on the basis of part of the revenue from social land appreciation that belongs to the state, to pay compensation fees to the farmers losing farmland (the collective of farmers) by installment and continuously. The sum of cash flows becomes the price for farmers' land development right. In so doing, China may establish a mechanism for realizing the principle "all the appreciation shall be turned in" in a more reasonable way, i.e., it may absorb social capital and give rewards and realize public interest by way of establishing funds. What's more, with such a mechanism, it could solve such problems as the rights of farmers losing farmland cannot be guaranteed; compensation fees are not in place; as well as a series of problems that are easily caused by lump-sum monetary compensation, and could provide a set of stable and lasting approaches for the farmers to get financial support.

4.2.1.2. *Forms and rights of land from "uncultivated land" to "cultivated land"*

The process from "uncultivated land" to "cultivated land" is an important stage for the appreciation of land value. The process is the so-called primary development of land, during which land may be sold or leased for land acquisition, demolition and the construction of municipal facilities like "three connections and one leveling" (which assures that a construction site is connected to water and electric power supplies and roads, and that the ground is leveled before a project begins) so as to get revenue from the land appreciation. At this stage, the status of the state as the subject of land ownership is demonstrated as land development right and usufruct. In practice, local governments have actually become the subject of land development. Specifically speaking, local governments carry out land acquisition, demolition, consolidation, development and reserve *via* local land reserve agencies, tender, auction or list land that meets the conditions for selling, collect land premium in a lump sum and realize part of land usufruct.

In the process, land development right experiences the dual entrustment-agency structure of state-local governments-land reserve agencies under the local governments. Because of the gaming mechanism between the central government and local governments, where both do not work with each other, land development right under state land ownership exists only in name, and is held by local governments that are motivated by their own interests. The latter entrusts their subsidiary land reserve agencies to organize land development.

Such translocation of land development right in practice leads to defects in at least four aspects: First, that the local governments get into market behaviors as civil subjects,[3] is in itself suspected of getting engaged in market behaviors for the best interests with land administrative monopoly; second, such a behavior weakens the status of the state as the terminal land owner, as well as the state's capability of macro control of the land market; third, although local governments realize the right to get revenue from the appreciation of land in its development by collecting lump-sum land premium to some extent, they, at the same time, lose the usufruct of land as a scarce resource in the future (or the call option to the appreciation of land in the future); besides, the collection of huge amounts of lump-sum land premium not only increases the financial cost of land users, but also increases the motive of the land users to impute the burden to the consumers.[4]

If an effective institutional design could be made to demonstrate the status of the state as the land owner in land development, i.e., to materialize and valuate the land development right under the state land ownership, and put into practice through the central land fund, the above problem may be solved. The central government raises great amounts of capital by selling the land development right, forms a capital pool as a source of the central land regulation fund, and then invests such capital in buying the land fund equity or securities in

[3]Land reserve agencies are institutional organizations instead of enterprises under the local governments, yet they operate urban land assets following the principle of profit maximization, play a fuzzy role and have fuzzy functions.

[4]The current high prices for housing serve as a pointed illustration. The fact seems to prove that clever realty developers are proficient in playing two magic cubes, namely land and capital in the current situation of the stock market: They raise money by going public and then buy land with the money they have raised by going public, achieve land trading against higher and higher prices, which then pushes forward the increase in the cost of land trading on the whole and causes the phenomenon that the prices for housing keep growing all the way and are more and more difficult to be regulated.

developed areas so as to launch concrete open market operations of land, i.e., to sell part of the equity or securities when prices on the land market grow so as to ease the pressure of demand; and to buy some of the equity or securities of land fund in developed areas when land prices decline so as to ensure balanced supply and demand.

To exercise land usufruct is a claim of the central government for the appreciation of land after "uncultivated land" is developed into "cultivated land". Seen from the past practical experience, local governments, as the agent of the central government, get some revenue equivalent to land usufruct by selling land in a lump sum, but at the same time, they lose the call option of land in the future. The central government may sign an agreement with local governments to have the latter retain part of land usufruct and involve that into the orbit of local finance. However, for the part that may generate revenue from market appreciation in the future, both may agree that the central government will share such revenue that contains slightly higher risks. Then, with innovative financial tools or the power of the financial market, the central government may also securitize such parts of possible future earnings to form a major source of central land fund and become an important force on the land market.

4.2.2. *The forms and rights of land after it is put into the market*

4.2.2.1. *At the stage of land lease or selling*

After "uncultivated land" is developed into "cultivated land", local governments sell the land-use right to the land user for a certain period in a lump sum. As the agent of land ownership, local governments get earnings by selling land-use right; and land users may build houses or other fixtures on the sold land, and then sell, lease, mortgage or get profit from such houses or fixtures. At this stage, corresponding subjects of the rights in the bundle of land rights are diversified, and each of the subjects of land rights shall share the profits brought about by such rights successively.

In reality, after getting revenue from selling land usufruct in a lump sum, the local governments realize the economic benefits that they intend to realize as actual land owner, and land users can also realize the economic benefits they intend to realize after selling, leasing and mortgaging land. **The land-use right obtained by the latter is independent of land ownership and basically has all the powers and functions of land ownership in a certain period. Therefore, after land-use right is sold, the role of the state as the land owner has actually and totally virtualized. Apart from mandatory administrative means, it is very unlikely to get involved in the control of such part of land with economic means.** But such part of land that goes into the market is the bulk of the urban land in stock. If an effective institutional design could be made to enable the state to play a role as the land owner, it may solve the problem of growing land and housing prices in China now.

It is proved that, the "tender, auction and listing" of land in China now plays a role in fueling the prices on the realty market. Land users (developers), as one side in the gaming, could buy and store land with less equity fund and at ultra-realistically high prices by paying land premium through installment or in batch, getting loans on mortgage in the early stage, under the circumstance that the current financial system and land selling system are to be perfected, grabbing the earnings from land appreciation that should have been for the public. In recent years, China has been tightening its land and financial policies, and a great number of listed realty companies in China made use of the rich financial channels and convenient financial conditions to partake in the tender, auction and listing of land on the open market almost "at all costs", one-sidedly contributing to high land prices and soaring realty prices. Financing for hoarding land, frequent "prime lots" and bubble of the housing prices makes it impossible to carry out macro-control policies.[5] It should contribute to solving the above problem to consider improving the lump-sum

---

[5]According to the data of the National Bureau of Statistics of China, the current year capital source of the realty developers during January 2009 and August 2009 was very close to RMB3.4 trillion, up 34% year on year, of which RMB738.4 billion was domestic loans, up 46%.

land selling system, renting or selling, for short periods, land that is featured with prominent location advantages and high and stable earnings like land for business, the service industry, entertainment and leisure to enterprises for the latter's use by collecting annual rental or land revenue by installment.

To collect annual rental or land premium by installment actually strengthens the status of the state as the land owner and weakens the status of enterprises as land users. This is because, collecting annual rental or land premium by installment actually realizes the state's rental power under its land ownership; secondly, to sell land rights by realizing the rental right weakens enterprises' land-use right in disguise and highlights the status of the state as the land lessor, and enables the state to carry out effective macro control by collecting land rental as the land owner. The ways of selling or leasing land may be decided flexibly and accordingly by the land purpose and specific regional conditions and the reality. For land that is highly profitable like land for business and the service industry, since it is expected to bring back high earnings in the future, annual rental system or the collection of revenue from selling land by installment may be adopted; for land that is expected to bring back secondary earnings like land for the purpose of industry or warehousing, etc., and land for ordinary residences, may be sold to give operational enterprises or residents stable land ownership. As for land for commerce and the service industry in downtown areas, to separate lease from land ownership and replace land-use right with it will strengthen state control over land. That is also an important link in innovating on the land financial system. The annual land rental or revenue from selling land which is paid by installment is the foundation for capitalizing land assets. Packaging such part of expected, stable and continuous flow of land rental and making it into tools that could circulate in the financial market not only forms one of the most important capital sources for the central land fund, but is very significant to the state to control the market for urban land in stock with economic or financial means.

4.2.2.2. *At the stage of realty maintenance or operation*

After the buildings or fixtures built on the land are sold, the subject of land rights and that of realty rights shall be decided accordingly. If land is sold and obtained, after the buildings or fixtures built on it are sold, the subject of land rights and that of the real estate rights are consistent. For such part of land and its realty which has entered the market, the state enjoys urban land ownership in name, but as mentioned above, its status as the land owner has been totally and completely virtualized. Except mandatory administrative means, it is impossible to carry out macro control over such part of land with economic means, and rely on self-control under the market mechanism; if land is leased and obtained, the subjects of land rights are multiple. The state, as the lessor, enjoys the right to lease and get revenue from leasing land in the bundle of land rights; the lessee has all the rights to such realty as contracted in the agreed duration, and is dutiful to pay rental to the lessor, namely the state, on a regular basis. Therefore, the state could somewhat control such part of land and the realty on such land in theory.

Take the construction of affordable and low-cost housing for example. Under the current system, the original intention to build affordable housing goes against the reality. Due to a general rise of the prices for housing in over popular regions, land is allotted and transferred for free to build affordable housing. However, pushed by the market, the prices for affordable housing are growing fast to a level so high that families with medium and low incomes cannot afford them. The problem can also be solved by the integration of land with finance: When the prices for housing go significantly beyond ordinary residents' purchasing capacity, the state allots some land for the construction of lodgings or low-rent housing as the land owner, and then rents them out to the urban population with medium- or low-income to ease the difficulty in getting housed or buying houses of the urban residents, especially those with medium- and low-incomes. Specifically speaking, the state commissions the land development for constructing low-cost housing to realty developers, while registering residents who need to rent houses and asking them to pay rents in advance, lease the low-cost housing to them after it is completed, and pays the rent from the residents in advance to the realty developers as the latter's investment profit. In the process, developers do not have any right to the land or realty, and play the sole function to accept the land development right under national commission, build realty on such land and help the state make the realty leasable. In the process, the state may consider designing or making use of land financial products that are based on lease right. For example, it may establish some agency similar to Federal National Mortgage Association in nature, gather together the rent that registered residents promise to pay within the lease term to form a realty rent pool in the future, properly securitize it, sell it to the securities market, pay the future rent income to the investors as their equity income, and spend funds raised on building low-cost housing, meeting the demand for loans of people who need to rent houses and repairing, maintaining and upgrading low-cost housing so as to try to stabilize the high realty prices in the market and ease the conflict caused by residents' high demand for housing.

The state is unable any more to control or intervene with realty where land ownership and property rights have become one. Hence such part of realty has to be reasonably distributed by the market mechanism to maximize the value of the land assets. That is to say, the financial market may be capitalized to design a series of financial tools for circulation and trading on the basis of realty rights according to the demands of different realty rights holders, like issuing MBS, ABS, REITS, CMBS, etc., to realize an effective operation of values of mature realty.

To make the above ideas highly operable, and to enable the land-use right of the local governments, agricultural companies and farmers to circulate reasonably, we must also analyze the operability of usufruct-based land-use right.

4.3. The Operability of Setting Usufruct-Based Land-Use Right

Real property right in rem refers to the right that realty rights subject enjoys to directly control realty and exclude others' interference into it. The representative of land ownership in China is the Chinese State Council. However, those that directly control land are local governments at different levels, agricultural companies and farmers. Theoretically, in the first and second stages of the formation of land property, land property right is manifested as single land ownership or land-use right, land management right. In reality, the usufruct of land ownership at the central government level is not fully demonstrated, being not right nor proper; the land-use right and land management right enjoyed by local governments, agricultural companies and farmers are land usufruct in nature, but without the name of land usufruct, thus are not right nor proper. Therefore, it is very necessary to "correctly and properly decide the position" of land-use right under the premise that local governments at different levels, agricultural companies and farmers actually enjoy the right to directly control land, i.e., to separate land-use right from the bundle of land property rights, and form a legal right that is different from the state land ownership in nature, but is somewhat usufruct to counteract any third party or any party. It will not only be conducive to manifesting and strengthening the economic contents and interests demand of the state land ownership, but more beneficial for local governments at different levels, agricultural companies and farmers to engage in operational activities that are good for land development and use based on their land-use right; and for the financial institutions to launch a series of financial innovations, which is not only very significant, but also highly operable. Therefore, land used by local governments at different levels, agricultural companies and farmers actually possesses the features of the subject of land usufruct.

The land used by local governments at different levels, agricultural companies and farmers also possesses the features of the object of land usufruct. Right in rem refers to the right to dominate particular and independent objects. Objects of the right in rem shall be concrete and special things so that the obligees could clarify the objects and scope that they dominate. Land in the local administrative areas is under direct control of the local governments, thus local governments have the right to directly control it: Before land is developed, direct control by the local governments is manifested as the latter's right to regulate land purpose and approve land for construction; when land is under development, local governments' direct control is manifested as primary land development right; after land is developed, local governments' direct control is manifested as the right to sell the developed land. Similarly, agricultural companies and farmers enjoy the right to directly control the land within their scope of operation to some extent. Therefore, in terms of the forms of actual land occupation and control, land controlled by local governments, agricultural companies and farmers undoubtedly possesses the features of object of land usufruct.

The land-use right enjoyed by local governments, agricultural companies and farmers is also exclusive. The right in rem is exclusive. There cannot be a number of incompatible rights in rem over the same thing; the right in rem already set can exclude other rights in rem over the same thing. Local governments, agricultural companies and farmers not only monopolize the land within their scope of operation, but according to the current relevant regulations on land management and reserve, primary land development is carried out by the local governments, agricultural companies and farmers, and right to use the developed land is also monopolistic and exclusive, providing an important condition for the transformation of the land-use right to the right in rem.

The land-use right enjoyed by local governments, agricultural companies and farmers possesses the feature of directly enjoying the benefits. One important feature of the right in rem is that its subject enjoys the right to enjoy all the benefits on the basis of it. For real property, usufruct holder could get benefits from the value in use of the real property, and the obligator of the real rights for security enjoys the right to mortgage the real property. Local governments, agricultural companies and farmers may openly sell their land on the market, get some profits from it, and that conforms to the income features of right in rem; whereas seen from the financing methods of land, local governments, agricultural companies and farmers actually enjoy the right to mortgage land, i.e., they may seek financing from the bank by taking the value in use and appreciation value of land as the guarantee. That is to say, the land-use right enjoyed by local governments, agricultural companies and farmers also possesses the features of usufruct and real rights for security, and that forms an important factor in the preparation for the transformation of the land-use right into the right in rem that is different from land ownership.

The direct control over land by local governments, agricultural companies and farmers is open. According to the civil law system, a right in rem becomes effective only after it is registered. After being made public, the right in rem has all the rights to counteract all the third parties. The current system for selling and trading land in China possesses such characteristics. Local governments, agricultural companies and farmers clearly involve the land to be traded into the master plan for land use and urban planning. Land that does not conform to the master plan for land use and urban planning cannot be involved in the scope of land acquisition, development, consolidation and selling. Therefore, the land-use right held by local governments, agricultural companies and farmers is certain and public in the society, which also provides a favorable factor for the transformation of land-use right into the right in rem.

The land-use right under the direct control of the local governments, agricultural companies and farmers is antagonistic. Another important characteristic of the right in rem is that the rights enjoyed by the holder of the right in rem counteract all uncertain parties. In the current process of developing, reserving and selling land, the local governments, agricultural companies and farmers are the subjects of a series of procedures; more importantly, land, once it is qualified for being sold, will be tendered, auctioned and listed openly in the market. Although the scope is not certain, once a land rights contract is signed with the land user, the latter would get land-use right which has to be made public before becoming effective as a right in rem and form all rights to counteract all the third parties.[6] Therefore, the land-use right enjoyed by the local governments, agricultural companies and farmers clearly possesses the right to counteract all the third parties.

4.4. Methods and Steps to Set Usufruct-Based Land-Use Right

4.4.1. *Setting*

China now applies land ownership under the central leadership system, i.e., the PRC is the sole land owner, and the Chinese State Council is

[6] Different from antagonism which is claim in nature, and formed by the creditor and the debtor by signing a contract and reaching an agreement on consensus.

the representative of state land ownership. However, the Chinese Central Government, as the land owner, may grant the right to exercise land ownership to local governments, agricultural companies and farmers. An important content of such a right is to realize the right to develop and use the land directly under their control by local governments, agricultural companies and farmers. To avoid any conflict with the state land ownership, ensures the value and value appreciation of state-owned land assets, highlights the economic contents of the state land ownership; and to guide local governments, agricultural companies and farmers to reasonably develop and utilize land, measures may also be taken to separate the land-use right enjoyed by local governments, agricultural companies and farmers from the bundle of land property rights to form a land usufruct under the state land ownership and confirm and finally set it by legislation.

4.4.2. *Registration*

According to Article 9 of Chapter 2 of Part One of the *Real Right Law of the People's Republic of China*, "Until it is registered in accordance with law, the creation, alteration, alienation or termination of the real right of a realty shall come into effect; unless it is otherwise prescribed by any law, it shall have no effect if it is not registered in accordance with law" and Article 17 of Chapter 2 of Part One of the *Real Right Law of the People's Republic of China*, "The realty ownership certificate shall be the evidence for the holder's ownership of a realty. The items recorded in the realty ownership certificate shall accord with those recorded in the realty register; unless it is proved that there is anything wrong in the realty register, the one recorded therein shall prevail in the case of any inconsistency." The right to use land under the direct control of local governments, agricultural companies and farmers may be registered at the government land registration agency for further confirmation. In the meantime, considering that local land management department is actually a functional department of the local government, it is suggested to register the above land-use right at the Ministry of Land and Resources of the People's Republic of China and report it to the State Council for record to avoid relevancy influences.

4.4.3. *Acquisition*

The acquisition of the land-use right which is the right in rem in nature is an important step to smoothly realize the land management right and land-use right by local governments, agricultural companies and farmers. The central government is the one that sets land development right for land reserve agencies, land development enterprises, agricultural companies and farmers. To get land-use right, land reserve agencies or land development enterprises may select qualified developers as the trustors of land-use right *via* government bidding and commission, or select appropriate land-use principals by commission through the market, and then register and announce it. The government or relevant management department may issue the certificate for land-use right to qualified land-use principals, and form the acquisition of land development right and land-use right as land usufructs.

4.4.4. *Loss*

Local governments, agricultural companies and farmers will lose the land-use right after they successfully sign the land-use right contract with new land users through the open market, and new land users pay the remuneration for the assignment of the land-use right and obtain the certificate for selling land-use right. At this point, the land-use right enjoyed by the new land users successfully replaces the original land-use right, terminates the original land-use right and leads to the revocation of it by the land management department in the government.

4.5. Utility Analysis of the Specific Use of the Land-Use Right as a Right in Rem

4.5.1. *It provides a legal basis for land development*

In the primary market for land development, local governments mortgage the ownership of undeveloped land for bank loans so as to finance for land development and reserve projects. However, according to relevant articles of the *Chinese Constitution* and *Law of the People's Republic of China on Land Administration*, local governments are not qualified land owners, thus it is legally groundless for local land reserve institutions or authorized developers to mortgage land to be developed for financing. In line with the above, land development right and land-use right have actually had a series of basic features of right in rem. To make them right in rem and then to mortgage land to be developed or usable land for bank loans conforms to its right to possess, dispose of, profit from and mortgage as one of usufructs. Therefore, if, on the basis of land ownership, debtor–creditor relationship or agency relationship could be established with other civil subjects in the market so that all stakeholders could profit from right relationships of all sorts derived from such right in rem, it promotes full and effective use of such right in rem.

4.5.2. *It provides a legal basis for innovating on the land financial system*

Land is a scarce resource, and for the enormous magnitude of its value and its property of being uneasy to circulate, it is hard to split its value and value in use, and that does not go with the trend of making effective use of things that's highlighted by the market economy. China has a big population but less farmland, and the Chinese economy is growing quickly. Land therefore becomes a precious resource and wealth. So it has to not only use land resources in a scientific, reasonable and intensive way, but make use of natural increase of land value to speed up the flow and use of land value so as to create even greater value and value in use (social wealth). Finance is a tool to achieve optimal allocation of scarce resources at different stages and times and in different places by credit and currency, etc., under the mechanism where market allocates resources. As far as the manifestations of land property at different stages are concerned, land developers and realty operators and managers have huge demands for capital, thus they need to achieve full mutual penetration and integration of land assets and finance in an all-round manner and from different angles, with the help of financial tools and the market, to create greater values. The current land economic system relies too much on bank loans, which then gathers a great number of risks and the revenue from land appreciation runs off in vain. Therefore, it is the urgent priority to establish a "land assets-assets capitalization → capital securitization → securities marketization → market standardization" system on the revenue from land appreciation and it is even more imminent to speed up the integration of land assets and direct financial market. Finance is actually virtual trading of rights. It is featured by achieving the obligees' and obligators' different economic purposes by forming contractual rights and obligations above some right in rem. Take the above example of making land ownership a right in rem, suppose local governments set land development right and land-use right and are allowed to deliver them to land reserve agencies, land development companies or other qualified primary developers by way of authorization, entrustment or bidding, the trustee could take the entrusted land development right and land-use right as a kind of asset and their valuations as the basis to issue bonds, trust products and other financing instruments to the investors on the basis of the future revenue from land development right and land-use right. Investors could share the interest on the revenue from land appreciation after the undeveloped concerned land has been developed and used to the level of "cultivated land", and the trustee may raise capital for development and construction at a lower cost and in a shorter time. That improves the efficiency of land development and use, and effectively disperses market risks in the form of marketizing the revenue from land appreciation.

4.5.3. *It plans the market for selling land*

Land is the commodity with the biggest value in the current Chinese market economic system. Now, China has nearly 10 billion square meters of township and village houses, nearly 400 million mu of collective land for construction, 1.827 billion of arable land, 177 million mu of gardens, 3.542 billion mu of forestland and 3.929 billion mu of grassland. Together, they are worth at least more than RMB100 trillion in the market value. After opening up the financing channel of the realty system by mortgages, guarantees, etc., there would be at least a credit demand of RMB5–6 trillion. If land, especially farmers' land is capitalized, it would better solve the problem of capital accumulation for the construction of villages and townships in China, promote the development of the economic system that's dominated by domestic demands, and ensure that the Chinese economy would climb to the historical peak.

4.6. Summary

Land issues must be solved in order to realize urbanization, the core of which is to correctly handle the relationship between land ownership and land-use right. Studies of the innovations of the Chinese land financial system analyze the entire process of formation of land property at the national level, adhere to the direction of "land assets-assets capitalization → capital securitization → securities marketization → market standardization", theoretically certify corresponding rights to land, after state ownership has been stripped out, at different stages of land development and use, and further clarify the feasibility of the property boundaries of the central government, local governments, agricultural companies and farmers. On the basis of clarifying the relationship between land ownership and land-use right, China may consider establishing a national land fund to better demonstrate land ownership *via* the market mechanism on the one hand; and extending the current 30 years of the contracting period of rural land to permanent and make it inheritable on the other. It not only helps explore the enormous value resources of rural land, but may possibly solve the problem of state-owned land "being placed idle" fundamentally, and promote the healthy and sustained development of urbanization and the rural society. It is crucial to establish three mechanisms: The mechanism for the state to regulate local governments with land ownership; the "territory management" mechanism for local governments to form orderly operation and intensive development when the state makes use of the tool of land economy; and the mechanism for selling the value of land rights enjoyed by farmers. Policies may be issued to ensure permanent contracting of rural land by rural households, a national land regulation fund may be established to, by the market-oriented operations and regulation of the value of state land ownership, reasonably guide and well adjust urban and rural construction, increase the self-cycling and growth of land capital, and achieve sustainable use of land and the harmonious and balanced urban and rural economic development.

CHAPTER 5

LAND FINANCIAL MARKET CONSTRUCTION

Land financial market is an important part of market system. Gradually established and perfected, the financial market, promotes the "land capitalization → capital assets securitization → securities market-market standardization", improving the capacity of the government in the land market as a whole, guiding the propulsion of urbanization and new agricultural construction, realizes the intensive utilization of land resources, land and real estate market price stability, to ground, to realize the aim of sustainable utilization of land resources.

Land finance is a form of finance that generally refers to the behaviors of fund raising, circulation and settlement concerning land development, improvement and operation, i.e., to obtain capital financing with land as the credit guarantee. Land finance falls into two categories, namely, urban land finance and rural land finance, with the latter always being the core issue concerned by all countries, and meanwhile, the key to the market-oriented reform of China's land financial system. As the product of market economy, land finance is an important component of the financial industry. In a number of developed countries and regions, land finance occupies a higher proportion in the total credit of financial institutions, whereas in China, it is still a new subject. After over thirty years of reform and opening up, China has initially established the socialist market system. The marketization of production factors have become an inevitable trend, which objectively requires the establishment of corresponding land financial market, so as to promote the healthy development of China's real estate industry, and in the meantime, optimize agricultural land resources allocation, as well as create favorable conditions for urbanization and agricultural modernization through land circulation.

5.1. Evolution of Land Financial System

5.1.1. *Review of the reform of urban land circulation system*

The urban land circulation system has gone through three stages since the reform and opening up over 30 years ago.

5.1.1.1. *From free allocation to paid use*

In the era of planned economy, a single administrative allocation system of land was adopted in urban areas in China, featuring complete denial of the product attributes of land, entire withdrawal of land from circulation, the free and indefinite use of fixed urban land, the transformation of rural land to urban land *via* land expropriation, allocation of land resources in accordance with administrative organizations and means, hidden land revenue, and serious loss of land revenue.

After the reform and opening up was launched, the gradually deepening economic reform has called for urgent reform of the urban land system. In 1980, the State Council promulgated the Provisional Regulations concerning use of land for construction by joint ventures, stipulating joint ventures shall pay fees for the land used by them, including land newly requisitioned and the sites of the original enterprises, and specifying the standards for site use fees. In 1981, Guangdong Province promulgated the Provisional Regulations governing land in Shenzhen Special Economic Zone (SEZ), which stipulates the term of use and fee standards of different types of lands for three types of foreign-funded enterprises. Afterwards, relevant laws and regulations were developed in Shanghai, Guangzhou and other cities to collect land-use fees from three types of foreign-funded enterprises.

5.1.1.2. *The establishment and gradual improvement of urban land market*

At the initial stage the urban land paid use system was adopted, the limited amount of land transactions stopped land prices from being formed under the market mechanism without interference. In order to gradually standardize the urban land market, in 1989, the State Administration for land uses issued Regulations for gradation and classification on urban land (trial), which sets up the uniform principles, methods and procedures for urban land gradation and classification, promoting the classification, gradation and assessment of urban land. China suffered a huge loss of state-owned land assets prior to 2001 due to the agreement-based paid land transfer as the mainstay, arbitrary price, opaque information, and lack of market competition. To improve the market-based land allocation, the State Council formulated the Notice of strengthening the administration of state-owned land assets in May 2001, which establishes the bidding, auction and quotation system for commercially used land. According to the notice, land-use rights bidding and auction shall be vigorously practiced nationwide in line with the principle of market economy, with a view to ensure the openness, fairness and justice of land-use rights transaction. The supply of state-owned construction land must be open to the public, unless it relates to the security of the state and is required to be kept secret. After the release of supply plan concerning land for commercial and other purposes, bidding and auction shall be organized by land administration authorities according to law for land with two or more intentional users. The bidding and auction activities for state-owned land-use right must be done in an open manner. In July 2001, the Ministry of Land and Resources issued the Notice on rectifying and standardizing the land market, which emphasizes on improving the land market system: First, to establish the system controlling the total amount of the construction land; second, to establish the centralized supply system of urban construction land; third, to establish the open transaction system of the land-use right; fourth, to establish benchmark land price regular updating and releasing system; fifth, to establish the land registration and query system; sixth, to establish the collective decision-making system. In October 2001, the Ministry of Land and Resources issued the Directory of land allocation, which specifies the scope of allocated land, and that the land exclusive of the scope should be paid when used.

In May 2002, the Ministry of Land and Resources issued the Provisions on the transfer of state-owned land-use right by bidding, auction and quotation, which clarifies that the land for such commercial purposes as business, tourism, entertainment and commercial residence must be transferred through bidding, auction and quotation. In October 2004, the State Council issued the Decision on deepening reforms and tightening land management, which specifies that investment must not be attracted by illegally squeezing down prices; moreover, land for industrial use, in addition to the land required to be transferred in the form of bidding, auction and quotation pursuant to existing provisions, should also be transferred in these modes, aiming at promoting market-based allocation of land resources.

In August 2006, the Ministry of Land and Resources issued the Rules on the transfer of state-owned land-use right by bidding, auction and quotation and Rules on the agreement-based transfer of state-owned land-use right, which clearly define the six kinds of lands that must be transferred by bidding, auction and quotation and the five kinds of lands that can be transferred on the basis of the agreement, and specify the scope and detailed procedures of the transfer of the two types of lands, and establish the coordinated decision-making and price dispute resolution mechanism regarding state-owned land transfer. In December 2006, the National Standards for the minimum transfer prices of land for industrial purposes was introduced. In response to different social and economic development levels, land resources as well as benchmark land prices in varied regions, the Standards adopt an integrated evaluation method, i.e., to divide the lands into 15 grades with the benchmark prices ranging from 60 Yuan to 840 Yuan per square meter. As emphasized by the Ministry of Land and Resources in the notice, the industrial land-use right must be transferred at the lowest price for such lands through bidding, auction and quotation.

In September 2007, the Ministry of Land and Resources issued Provisions on the assignment of state-owned construction land-use right through bidding, auction and quotation, which mainly deals with the legal basis, scope and principles for bidding, auction and quotation, the development and release of the transfer plan and scheme, the formulation and releasing of documents concerning the bidding, auction and quotation, releasing of procedures and results, the payment of land transfer fees, and the grant of certificates for state-owned construction land-use rights, and relevant legal liability. This Provision marks a substantial and significant progress in China's land market system development.

5.1.1.3. *Creation of urban land reserve system*

The land reserve system is an urban land management system and operation mechanism. In this system, the government purchases the land ownership or use right according to law under the market system to make preparation and reserve for land development as per the land-use master plan and the urban planning, with a view to supply urban construction land or regulation demands for such land. In cooperation with corporate restructuring, in 1996, the first land reserve institution of China, the Shanghai Land Development Center was set up in Shanghai, in order to revitalize urban reserve land assets, optimize allocation of land resources, and facilitate the government's control over the land market. Commissioned by the municipal government, the center serves as a public institution dealing with land acquisition, reserve, and transfer. Since then, land reserve institutions have been set up in Hangzhou, Xiamen, Nanjing, Qingdao, Guangzhou, Zhengzhou and other cities in succession. In April 2001, the State Council promulgated the Notice on strengthening the administration of state-owned land assets, which requires capable local governments to purchase and reserve construction land on a trial basis, with a view to enhance the government's ability to regulate land market. The people's government of the municipalities and counties can set aside part of the land revenue for land purchase, and financial institutions shall provide credit support according to the law. Afterwards, land reserve institutions were set up in most cities to practice land reserve system. Despite the active role land reserve system played in promoting the development of local economy, there is still a long way to go before establishing a nationwide controllable land market, which calls for intense efforts to push forward the reform in this regard.

5.1.2. *Review of the reform of rural land circulation system*

Since the reform and opening up, the rural land circulation system has undergone prohibition, permission and control uplifting and the change of attitude from being obscure to explicit encouragement, with the amendment to the Constitution in 1988 as the symbol.

5.1.2.1. *Land transfer was officially prohibited*

Land transfer was prohibited institutionally from the beginning of reform and opening up till 1988. In the early years of 1980s, land transfers in some areas were basically hidden and illegal as they were the spontaneous behaviors of farmers without policies and system support. It was clearly stipulated in Provision 4 of Article 10 of the 1982 Constitution that "no organization or individual may appropriate, buy, sell or lease land or otherwise engage in the transfer of land by unlawful means". Meanwhile, it was stipulated in Article 80 of General Principles of the Civil Law that "land may not be sold, leased, mortgaged or transferred by any other means." In 1986, the Supreme People's Court stipulated in the judicial interpretation of Opinions on the trial of the case of the disputes arising from the land contract in rural areas that the contract will be invalid in case the contract-undertaking party subcontracts or transfers the contract to other parties without the consent of the party that lets the contract. During this period, rural land transfer was strictly prohibited.

5.1.2.2. *The prohibition on land transfer was lifted*

In 1984, the Communist Party of China (CPC) Central Committee released the Circular on rural work, known as Document No. 1 in the year, which firstly relaxed policies regarding rural land transfer by stipulating "during the contract period, members who ask to reduce the land they contract or to stop contracting land due to their inability to farm or their engagement in other businesses can subcontract the land to others with the agreement of the collective." And in April 1988, the 1st Session of the 7th National People's Congress (NPC) made amendments to the Constitution, which really recognized the legitimacy of rural land transfer. It was clearly stipulated in Provision 4 of Article 10 that "no organization or individual may appropriate, buy, sell or otherwise engage in the transfer of land by unlawful means. The right to the use of land may be transferred according to law." After the adoption of the amendment, the circulation of the land-use right was recognized in Constitution, from then on, the land that was originally prohibited from lease could be circulated in line with the regulations of law. Whereas, the circulation was limited to means of subcontract and other forms of circulation like transfer or lease were still prohibited. According to the Decision on several issues regarding the establishment of the socialist market economic system, adopted at the 3rd Plenary Session of the 14th CPC Central Committee in 1993, "while upholding the collective ownership of land, the state extended land contract period, and allowed the inheritance of right to operate the contracted land with developmental production projects, as well as the paid transfer of the land-use right in accordance with law". On 30 December 1994, the Ministry of Agriculture made further instructions on rural land transfer in Opinions on stabilizing and improving land contract relations, and required that "while adhering to the collective ownership of land and maintaining the use of the land for agricultural purposes, the state shall protect the legitimate rights and interests of the contract-undertaking party to subcontract, transfer and exchange the land or invest in the land during the contract period". In 2001, the CPC Central Committee clearly stated in Document No. 18, the Notice on the circulation of rural households' right to the use of contracted land, that it was the objective requirement of agricultural development to allow the reasonable circulation of the land-use right. It was stipulated in the report at the 16th CPC National Congress in 2002 that "wherever conditions permit, the transfer of the contractual right of land can be carried out according to law and on a voluntary and compensatory basis so as to develop scale operation step by step." Land transfer was then legitimized.

5.1.2.3. *Land transfer is standardized*

Law of the People's Republic of China on the Contracting of Rural Land has been effective since 1 March 2003, which stipulated that "right to operate the contracted land obtained through the contracting by households may in accordance with the law be circulated by means of subcontract, lease, exchange, or transfer or by other means". The law presents some constraints on the principles of land circulation, and has laid a legal foundation for the practice of land transfer, symbolizing the formal establishment of the circulation system of rural land contracted management right. On 1 March 2005, the Ministry of Agriculture implemented Measures for the administration of circulation of rural land contracted management right, which provided clearer and more specific regulations in policies and systems on the transfer mode, the signing of transfer contract, as well as the management of land transfer. In addition, due to the uneven economic development and significantly different regional conditions, many places have formulated their own land transfer systems according to local realities.

5.1.2.4. *Breakthroughs have been made in policy*

The New Property Law passed in 2007 is significant in protecting farmers' land-use right, and many issues concerning rural land property rights have been discussed, which intrigued the prospects for the reform of rural land circulation system. Land circulation became the core issue of debate at the 3rd Plenary Session of the 17th Central Committee of the CPC in 2008. It was put forward again in the

Document No. 1 of the CPC Central Committee in 2010 that rural land circulation market should be established. New breakthroughs have been made in rural land since then. The Decision on major issues concerning comprehensively deepening reforms adopted in November 2013 further stressed the need to build a coordinated urban and rural construction land market. Under the premise that it conforms to planning and the control of land-use, the sale, leasing and demutualization of rural, collectively owned construction land for commercial purposes is allowed, and the land is granted the equal rights with state-owned land to come to the market and be priced with the same standards. Special emphasis was given to the protection of farmers' usufruct rights of homestead, the improvement of the homestead system in rural areas, carry out a pilot program in some areas to steadily push forward the mortgage, guarantee, as well as transfer of farmers' homestead property rights and discover other channels for improving farmers' income. It was also emphasized that a rural property-rights trading market should be established so that the rural property transfer transaction will be operated in an open, fair and standard manner.

5.2. Reasons to Promote the Marketization of Land Finance

First, the current real estate market has become a core issue that plagues the steady economic growth in China. On the one hand, China's economy still needs the real estate industry to function as a pillar industry to some extent, on the other hand, the problems in the real estate industry, such as excessively high price and non-standard transactions, still seriously affect social harmony and stability and people's well-being. So far, a lot of policies regulating the real estate market have been adopted but they only deal partially the problems, rather than solve them permanently. In this regard, I believe the fundamental reason lies in local governments' excessive reliance on land revenue in absence of sustainable sources of resources, which radically gave birth to the inner impulse to raise the prices of houses. Therefore, people name this kind of funding operation mode of local governments as "land finance." For example, statistics show that in 2009 the land market transactions nationwide were extremely active, with the urban land-transferring fees of the top 20 cities reaching 801.9 billion Yuan, an increase of 160%. In most cities, urban land-transferring fees accounted for 30% to 45% of local fiscal revenue. As another example, according to 2009 year-end inventory of land-transferring fees by China Index Research Institute, the land transfer fees totaled 1.5 trillion Yuan, accounting for 4.4% of the gross domestic product (GDP) and 23% of the national fiscal revenue, which was, in fact, a conservative estimate. In the fiscal revenues of quite a number of local governments, land-transferring fees accounted for a surprisingly large portion, with some reaching 60%. In order to reduce the local governments' impulse of developing "land finance" and permanently solve the basic contradiction in real estate market, I believe the governments should vigorously promote the market-oriented reform of land financial market and the fiscal and taxation system, to provide diverse fund sources for local urban construction through the innovation of land finance.

Second, rural land circulation and development are confronted with a number of problems, with lack of effective land market as the crux, which resulted in the failure of market-based land pricing during the land circulation and development. Moreover, the implicit asymmetric information and the substantial interests in this regard gave birth to corruptive practices like government failure and rent-seeking behaviors. Therefore, developing land finance and allowing the mortgage of the land-use right as a property can help to raise more funds and provide strong financial drive for the development and improvement of land market. Land finance is expected to become the intermediary agent where land can integrate with other production factors like labor and funds to promote land circulation, with a view to optimize the allocation of land resources, achieving the scale management of land, and improving the efficiency of land resources. So from that point of view, to develop land finance and support the development and improvement of land market is the fundamental solution to current problems in land circulation and development.

Third, the public finance can hardly meet the demand of urbanization for the large amount of fund, while in terms of market-oriented financing, farmers and small- and medium-sized enterprises (SMEs) face widespread problems, such as difficulty in mortgage and guarantee, the imperfect risk diversification mechanism and lack of special guarantee fund or institution. Hence, to establish and improve the land financial system and raise funds *via* mortgaging the transferred land in urbanization is significant in solving the lasting severe shortage of credit to agriculture, rural areas and SMEs. At the same time, as the building of urban facilities involves a long period of construction and payback of the investment, and features high risks, their fund demands can hardly be met by ordinary commercial loans. Therefore, it is particularly important to give full play to land as a financial tool in raising fund and to broaden the land financing channels, while promoting the conservative and intensive use of land by building the fund raising platform *via* the land financial system.

Fourth, currently, instable fiscal strength and excessive reliance on finance of the local government increase risks to local public finance and the financial system. Such problems can be attributed to the incomplete and non-standard land financial system to a large extent. The under-developed land financial system resulted in the unitary mode of land financing, and the superposition of credit and market risks. The imperfectness of the land financial system is also manifested by the absence of regulatory system, which showcases that to some extent many land financial activities at present are "semi-legal". For example, land reserve institutions nationwide take a loan from bank with the reserved land and ask local government to provide credit guarantee. Meanwhile, some land reserve centers are directly involved in land development as primary and secondary developers, which cause enormous controversy. These controversial behaviors result from the lack of regulations and supervision in land finance. In response to these problems, the establishment of a sound financial system is needed, particularly relevant laws and regulations and the regulatory system, to ensure the compliance and orderly and effective operation of the land financial market.

Fifth, the financial reform brings about new opportunities for the development of land finance. Problems like how to make good use of valuable land resources, how to cultivate and improve the land market, how to do a good job in and provide financial support for land acquisition and reserve, and how to do a good job in the maintenance and appreciation of value, and income distribution of the state-owned land assets, are more of a deepened financial issues than an economic one for a developing country like China. It is learned from foreign experience that land finance is an important part in the national land and financial system of Western developed countries, which plays a significant role in the rational allocation of land resources and the development of agricultural economy.

5.3. Inspirations from the Marketization of Land Finance in Foreign Countries

Land financial system is generally implemented in Western developed countries, with that of Germany as the most representative. As early as the 18th century, Germany began to implement land mortgage credit system, in which rural land was mortgaged to avail farmers of capital financing, help them to develop agricultural production, purchase farmland, and get involved in rural construction, and help government to promote agricultural policies. The securitization of the mortgaged land is the topmost feature of German land financial system. With the necessary support from the government in terms of policy, law and funding, farmers in Germany at that time, who were willing to obtain loans with their land as the collateral, were expected to form cooperatives which can issue land securities with the land as guarantee in exchange of funds. Five inspirations can be drawn from the practices of the developed countries.

First, land financial system is a long-term credit system, as well as a basic state policy to support agricultural production, rural development, and the improvement of material living conditions of farmers.

Second, the systems are established by private enterprises with the support from the governments. The inherent characteristics of agricultural production barred general businesses and financial enterprises from involving in this kind of industry, generating poor profits. Therefore, no matter it is in Germany which developed at the earliest stage, America which developed later, or newly emerging economies, it is often the government that provided strong support through preferential policies, legal protection and fund allocation from the establishment of institutions to the fund supply, so that long-term and preferential funds can be provided for the development of rural economy.

Third, the issuance of land financial securities is the core to maintain the normal functioning of land financial system. Most countries make the utmost of land as the high-value property; issue an enormous sum of securities with land as collateral, raise large amount of funds, in support of the development of land finance and agricultural production.

Fourth, cooperative is the important primary organization of the land financial system. It is usually the case that the costs to borrow money in rural areas are high due to the higher cost in credit management in terms of time, labor and funds, which result from the small quantity, scattered spatial distribution, and complex procedures of these loans. In order to reduce the costs, it is imperative to guide the farmers in need of loans to organize themselves and establish primary cooperative organizations undertaking the tasks of investigation and preliminary audit, credit building, risk regulation, so as to bring their role in daily management and supervision into full play. It is learned from the experience of the long-term spontaneous development of German cooperatives and the successful experience of America in establishing land bank cooperatives quickly in a top–down manner, so that as primary organizations of land financial system, these cooperatives are often indispensable in the normal functioning of the system.

Fifth, financial institutions with government support are suggested to be established as the long-term credit support to land financial system. Institutions with long-term credit such as land banks are an important part in the land financial system of a number of countries and regions. On the one hand, these financial institutions are "the last lenders" in promoting the sound operation of the overall land financial system; on the other hand, they provide credit enhancement or guarantee support to land retailing financial institutions, with a view to promote sound development of the land financial system.

5.4. Problems in the Marketization of Domestic Land Finance

5.4.1. *Problems in the development of urban land finance*

5.4.1.1. *Excessive reliance on indirect bank financing*

Currently, bank indirect financing occupies an absolute proportion in China's urban land financial system, as the financial structure of China has long been dominated by banks, and meanwhile, the development of capital market has always lagged behind economic and social development. The unbalanced land financial structure has led to low financial efficiency and the excessive accumulation of financial risks in banking system, which affects the healthy economy and social development. In terms of land reserve, to raise funds solely from commercial banks is defective. In the first place, the length of maturity and the operating cycle of land reserving do not fit to each other, as the period for commercial bank loans is short, usually ranging from six months to one year and can be reused, whereas, the operating cycle of land reserving is generally two to five years, some even longer; next, the source of commercial bank loans is not stable enough as they are greatly liable to the influences of financial policies and economic environment; moreover, the different operation targets make it impossible for all the justifiable requirements of land reserve institutions to be satisfied. In other words, after the adoption of uniform land acquisition policy, it was required objectively that the government purchased land needed to be activated in an open manner, so as to achieve the goals of economic development and social progress, whereas, for commercial banks, the operation target is to maximize profits. As a natural result, commercial banks are, more often than not, in favor of those land reserve institutions and projects yielding good profits, and stay far away from those institutions and projects which need funds but generate poor profits.

5.4.1.2. *A serious lack of financial innovation*

Due to system constraints and various obstacles, there is a serious lack of innovation in financial products both in direct and indirect banking financial activities, which is reflected by the lack of diversified financial products revolving around land development, circulation, possession and other links, thus no effective services are provided to promote the smooth functioning of land market.

5.4.1.3. *Hidden financial risks in land reserve*

First of all, the pressure to expand scale drive and reduce non-performing assets results in the serious concentration and convergence of bank loans; afterwards, some land development plans are not implemented and not taken into consideration in making supply plans, so the rights will not be legally safeguarded in case any problem occurs; in addition, despite the fact that the land reserve institutions nationwide are established with the full funding from the governments, some local governments invest little registered capital and some of the capital has yet to be allocated. The revenue and expenditure of such institutions are separated, i.e., nearly all of the revenue is turned in, while the expenditures basically rely on financial allocations, in case any local fiscal problem occurs, and the funds are not allocated in time, the operation of land reserve institutions will also encounter difficulties, which may lead to bank loan risks; in addition, quite a lot of land reserve institutions obtain loans from several commercial banks by taking advantage of the competitions among banks at the same time, in which case the banks can hardly understand the real operation of these institutions. That may lead to "paying off old debt with new debt". Once there is any operation risk, for instance, the fund chain breaks as follow-up funds are not in place, the land institutions will be confronted with difficulties that will threaten the security of bank funds; moreover, the risks also include dummy guarantee and collateral, as well as operational risks.

5.4.1.4. *Lack of multi-layered land financial market*

A multi-layered land financial market includes a primary and a secondary land financial market, especially a secondary mortgage loan market as well as a housing mortgage loan securitization market, and the latter two are crucial in facilitating the smooth transaction of financial assets and products generated from the land. At present,

China's land financial market is less developed, which seriously affects the land-use efficiency and is unfavorable to the wholesome operation of real estate market.

5.4.1.5. *Absence of security functions of land finance*

The construction of land financial system is to improve the efficiency of the land market as well as ensure the fair use of land. On the one hand, there is a long way to go before China realizes the heavy task of satisfying citizens' basic needs for housing, and on the other hand, people are now wrapped up in city building movement and have constructed many "ghost cities" with high residential vacancy rate, where the speed of building construction exceeds that of infrastructure construction and population centralization, such as Kangbashi New Town in Erdos, Inner Mongolia. This is a problem which merits great attention.

5.4.2. ***Problems in rural land financial development***

5.4.2.1. *The number of agricultural loans cannot meet the demand of land transfer*

Substantial investment and more funds are needed in expanding production scale through agricultural land circulation to purchase agricultural machinery and equipment and to build facilities, compared with traditional agricultural production. However, presently, there are no enough agricultural loans to support the large amount of investment needed in agricultural production. Besides, the rural financial institutions only grant limited credit to rural households, but allow a great deal of agricultural funds to flow out. The limited loans can only meet farmers' temporary living needs or the needs of simple reproduction, rather than satisfy the need to expand the production.

5.4.2.2. *The structure of loans cannot meet the demand of land transfer*

The loans needed in land transfer are mainly fixed investments used to expand production scale, which are generally of long term, large scale and concentrated investment directions. At present, the structure of China's agricultural loan is featured by: First, the loans are often short-term loans offered in spring and recovered in autumn; second, they are concentrated in daily production and operation with limited assets investment and scattered borrowers; and third, being small in size, the loans could not meet the needs of massive funds.

5.4.2.3. *Lack of strong policy-oriented financial support*

The positioning of policy-oriented finance is not clear: Policy-oriented finance is generalized and weakened alternatively. In fact, policy-oriented finance designed not exclusively to make profits is still needed in China's rural areas. Compared with the fiscal funds invested directly in rural areas, policy-oriented financial model boasts higher efficiency. Taking into account the long-term subsidies rural areas have made to urban areas, it is fair and reasonable to increase policy-based financial support for agriculture, rural areas, and farmers.

5.4.2.4. *Obstacles in mortgaging rural land-use rights*

It has always been an issue of great controversies that whether or not rural land-use rights and rural land contracted management rights can be mortgaged. Some experts believe that rural land-use rights are the basis for maintaining the production and living conditions of farmers, therefore, social problems like the emergence of a large number of farmers with little or no farmland will appear if the mortgage of these rights is allowed. Issues concerning the mortgage of rural land contracted management rights and homestead are not discussed in the communiqué and decision of the Central Committee of the CPC on several big issues on promoting the reform and development of rural areas (The decision passed at the Third Plenary Session of the 17th CPC Central Committee.). The decision on major issues concerning comprehensively deepening reforms adopted at the Third Plenary Session of the 18th CPC Central Committee, stressed that under the premise that it conforms to planning and the control of land-use, the sale, leasing and demutualization of rural, collectively owned construction land is allowed, and the land is granted the equal rights with state-owned land to come to the market and be priced with the same standards, which is not yet practical in the rural land and homestead is not collectively owned construction land.

5.4.2.5. *Supporting measures are to be improved*

The development of agricultural production has a significant bearing on ensuring national food safety given that it is of a kind of public goods production of low profits and high risks. Thus, preferential policies concerning agricultural production loans are to be adopted to promote agricultural development. But, the government's preferential policies to provide loans with discounted interests and tax incentives to businesses concerning agriculture production to credit agencies is not as favorable as expected, thus, it is hardly possible for commercial banks in pursuit of maximized profits to offer loans for the development of agriculture production. These deficiencies result in the dilemma for both farmers who have no easy access to bank loans, and credit institutions which find no eligible persons or enterprises to offer the loans; on the one hand, lack of assets in rural areas lead to the small amount of total agricultural loan, on the other hand, the saving deposits of credit institutions are rising unremittingly.

5.4.2.6. *Rural credit guarantee mechanism is yet to be established*

It is hard for land financial institutions to conduct business normally in rural areas due to a number of reasons, for instance, the weak profitability and risk-resisting ability of farmers of weak basic conditions, lack of corresponding risk management and guarantee mechanism, and slow development of rural insurance business.

5.4.2.7. *The distortion of cooperative finance and private finance*

For one thing, rural cooperative financial institutions in China, as the main body of rural land finance, are being reformed along a wrong path, i.e., the institutions are being transformed into commercial banks and developed in cities, which are neither in line with international practices, nor conform to China's rural areas financial development needs. For another, the majority of the financial system is formed on the initiatives of farmers, whereas, controversies lie in how to guide private finance to come under the "sunshine". It should be noted that rural land finance will suffer from capital shortage in the near future if the huge private financial resources are not utilized.

5.5. How to Build Chinese Financial Market Land

5.5.1. *To build an efficient and sound land financial market system*

Land financial market is a long-term financial market with enterprises engaging in land development and management, individuals, real estate consumers, as well as various financial institutions as the major participants, who mainly deal with activities closely related to real estate businesses, for instance, capital loan, capital financing, security issuance and trading, land trust investment, and land insurance. It is an integral part of the land market and financial market, and meanwhile the results of the combination of the land and financial markets and their penetration into the real estate market. It is suggested that China should establish a complete land financial market mainly composed of the land credit lending market, land mortgage market, land security market as well as the land trust market. Among them, the land credit lending market is where financial institutions provide loans to borrowers with borrowers' credits; the land mortgage market is a market where financial institutions provide loans to borrowers with land and relevant certificates as security guarantee; the land security market is a market where land securities are issued and traded; the land trust market is a market where land is trusted to banks, and the trust usufruct is transferred to investors after segmentation.

5.5.2. *To establish and improve land financial mechanism*

Faced with increasing difficulties in controlling the total amount of land, China is perplexed by ever growing loss of state-owned land assets in recent years, which indicate a lack of effective macro-control means and mechanisms to optimize land resources allocation and calls for the establishment of policy-oriented dedicated financial mechanism, so as to promote the China's economic reform and transformation of economic growth, activate the assets function of land, and further promote economic development in urban and rural areas.

5.5.2.1. *Basis for the policy-oriented land financial mechanism*

Policy-oriented land financial institutions make it possible for the establishment of an effective land property right system and promote the financing of land development funds *via* issuing land securities, which can accelerate the conversion of land assets to productive capital assets. State-owned urban land ownership and rural collective land ownership are public real rights. Land securitization is to transform land property rights from real rights to stock rights or obligatory rights, which is conducive for clearing land property rights. It is supposed to be conducted by policy-oriented land financial institutions to ensure the long-term interests of those in possession of public property rights. To turn land property rights into stock rights or obligatory rights is conducive for promoting land capitalization. The development of policy-oriented land financial institutions will facilitate the improvement of the land mortgage system. Presently, real estate projects are likely to obtain primary land mortgage loans from some commercial banks, but industrial projects and quality agricultural production projects with lower profits that cannot be generated in a short term are less fortunate as they still have no access to land mortgage loans. Policy-oriented land financial institutions can take advantage of the State's industrial policies to promote the financing of funds *via* issuing land securities, and provide preferential mortgage interest rates to industrial lands with the key support of the State. Besides, policy-oriented financial institutions can provide projects of development potential with secondary land mortgage loans in supplement to the primary land mortgage loans offered by commercial banks.

5.5.2.2. *Design and operation of policy-oriented land financial institutions*

Land financial institutions are generally non-profit institutions dominated by the government, who provide funds to land managers or other institutions engaging in land credit with favorable terms, for instance, the Federal Land Bank of America, the Land Credit Bank of France, as well as Land Financial Bank of Korea and so forth. It is suggested that most of China's policy-oriented banks should be non-profit institutions under the leadership of the government, which are expected to fulfill the following functions: To develop and implement national land financial policies, to provide funds, guidance and other conveniences to other land financial institutions, to supervise and administrate other financial institutions, to approve the mortgage applications regarding the land-use right, to provide land managers with long-term loans with low interests, as well as to issue land securities or commission other institutions to issue land securities and repay the capital and interests.

Currently, it is popularly practiced internationally that the cooperative land financial institutions function as the basic organizations of rural land finance. Given that China is not yet fully-fledged in many respects, it is unrealistic to expect farmers who are less qualified to develop land mortgage cooperatives on their own initiatives like what German farmers have done. It is thus suggested that land-use right mortgage office be set up in existing rural credit cooperatives to handle specific businesses. Specialized land financial institutions throughout China are supposed to help farmers to establish land mortgage cooperatives exclusively handling financial businesses when conditions permit, i.e., the overall system of policy-oriented land financial institutions are basically improved and farmers are greatly enhanced in quality. Coupled with the "low interests" operation mode, rural credit cooperatives, the non-profit and mutual cooperative public interest groups with mutual cooperation as its most prominent feature, greatly reduce farmers' burden to pay back interests, moreover, it is easy for these cooperatives to carry out their businesses in the branches of the cooperatives that are scattered in all townships and towns at present. As a natural result, these cooperatives are selected as the specific institutions to manage land financial businesses. It is proposed that the land-use right mortgage office that links the State's specialized land financial institutions with farmers, i.e., to handle mortgage businesses concerning land-use rights for farmers in line with the State's land financial policies.

5.5.3. *To innovate land financial products: Land securitization*

5.5.3.1. *The operation mode of land securitization*

There are two representative points of view on how to operate land security: The first is to develop land security operation mode with urban originators as the subjects, which was put forward on the basis of analyzing the meaning of land securitization and operation mode after referring to America's experience in real estate securitization. In this mode, rural land reserve institutions are expected to requisition purchase, exchange land, and then develop the land in centralization in line with urban land-use planning, afterwards, launch the developed lands in accordance with urban land transfer planning. The operational funds of land reserve institutions are required to be provided by specialized land financial institutions or commercial banks, and the funds are collected *via* issuing securities with future urban land income cash flows as guarantee. In comparison, land security operation mode with urban originators as the subjects is instructive for China in the process of urban land securitization as the mode is more reasonable in overall structure. As China is more developed in urban land market, it is an effective and prudent way to give priority to rural land securitization, whose experience can be afterwards applied to rural land market. The second mode is the securitization of urban land development. The basic idea goes that urban land State ownership, the development, investment and management rights over tracts of land in urban planning areas, as well as the right to the use of land and parcels of land be separated on the basis of the existing situation, i.e., land ownership and use rights are divided; urban governments are expected to act as the representatives of state-owned land ownership to set up urban land development limited liability companies in line with the regulations of the Company Law, raise public social funds to invest in urban land development *via* listed stocks or land consolidation securities.

The former scheme is analogous to land security, and the latter to land stock. It is not feasible for urban governments to set up limited liability companies engaging in urban land development on account of the current status at different places in China as well as the stringent requirements for issuing listed stocks. Certain adjustments are proposed to be made to the former mode in light of the experience of foreign counterparts. Firstly, in terms of the issuers, there is no doubt that financial support is needed in the operation of land reserve mechanisms, therefore, policy-oriented land financial institutions can play the role of both urban and rural land security issuers. Secondly, about the subject matters of land securitization, they can be either land assets or cash flow of future land incomes. Thirdly, with regard to securities underwriters, they are mainly investment banks. Fourthly, speaking of credit rating agencies, land securities evaluation experts with reliable experience should be selected from domestic and international intermediary agents to ensure the quality of credit ratings on land securities. Fifthly, when it comes to the supervision of land securitization, it is inclusive of the supervision over the issuance process and the operation of land funds, and the issuance of land securities is projected to be supervised by the Central Bank as well as securities regulatory institutions.

5.5.3.2. *Scope and procedures of land securitization*

In theory, land with development value nationwide can be securitized, including both state-owned land and rural collective land in terms of ownership. Therefore, land securitization is inclusive of urban land securitization and rural land securitization in scope.

First, speaking of urban land securitization, it consists of the securitization of land in the direct control of urban governments, and corporate land-use rights securitization. The basic operational procedures are: First, to obtain the authorization of urban governments; second, land-use right holders obtaining the rights *via* transfer or assignment for the purpose of financing shall allow specialized land financial institutions to manage the income cash flow during a certain period in the future, and specialized land financial institutions are expected to obtain financing through issuing land securities. In case the land-use rights are obtained in the form of allocation, holders of the rights are not necessarily the holders of land-use rights during the procedures of land securitization unless they pay the land transferring fees, re-sign the contract as well as obtain land-use certificates beforehand; third, specialized land financial institutions should hand over land securities to underwriters through bidding underwriting for sales, and get capitals from these underwriters; fourth, specialized land financial institutions turn over the capitals to the clients (those who are in need of financing).

When it comes to rural land securitization, its procedures include: First of all, rural collective organizations sign contracts with rural operating entities (including township enterprises, individual contractors, etc.) to contract the use rights of rural land to the entities in the form of management contract (land contract management right); then, rural operating entities shall allow specialized land financial institutions to manage the income cash flow during a certain period in the future for the purpose of financing, and specialized land financial institutions are expected to obtain financing through issuing land securities; afterwards, land financial institutions should hand over land securities to underwriters through bidding underwriting, and get capitals form these underwriters; and finally, the financial institutions turn over the capitals to the clients.

5.6. Establishment of National Land Regulation Fund

To establish a national land regulation fund is the breakthrough in the reform of the marketization of China's land finance. In order to promote the optimization of urban land financial markets and solve the deep-seated problems in the current land market, it is suggested to set up central and local land macro-control funds with incomes like land transferring fees, land-use fees for new construction land as well as social funds, and the funds are expected to play an active role in urban and rural land reserve and primary development, so as to enhance the government's ability in land reserve and market regulation, providing a reasonable guide to land investment and exploring channels for real estate investment, as well as effectively curbing asset price bubbles. It is expected that by taking advantage of state macro regulation funds, the dominant position of national land ownership be strengthened, so as to develop the operation and circulation system concerning national state ownership capital asset value in combination with financial innovation and promote the development of land financial market.

5.6.1. *Basic idea of the national land regulation fund*

The basic idea of the national land regulation fund is to incorporate part of the land revenue into the central land regulation fund and provincial and municipal land regulation fund respectively at a certain ratio before the land revenue enters into local fiscal revenue in line with the principle of "government guidance, market regulation, and expert management" and revolving around mechanism innovation and sustainable development, so as to develop national land regulation system (land fund for short). The capital of central land regulation fund comes from part of the revenue of national land development (land tax), and mainly used for the sustainable development and use of land, supporting the infrastructure construction in poor and remote areas, as well as ensuring the stable development of land market. Mainly derived from part of the revenue of local land development (land tax), the capital of local land regulation fund is mainly designed to strike a balance between regional development and support the development of local infrastructure. When conditions permit, the central, provincial and municipal land funds are expected to be the investment platform attracting social and other funds that be invested into national infrastructure projects, form a national land fund market operation system operated by professional management teams, as well as bring the exemplary and amplification effect of land funds in the control of government to support infrastructure development and balanced development into full play.

The land fund is a public welfare management and investment fund that the government who own the land authorizes specialized institutions to raise funds in an oriented and public way as initiators for the restructuring and operation of land assets, and promote urban and rural development. Land funds are expected to fulfill the following main tasks: To promote the optimal allocation of land resources and rational use of land, to raise funds *via* collecting transferring fees of state-owned land-use rights, land-use fees, land appreciation fees, land lease fees and other fees generated from the land, and invest the collected funds in land purchase and reserve, land development and consolidation, as well as the construction of public facilities in urban and rural areas. Land finance is a kind of non-profit governmental behavior that is closely associated with the land management system, fund management mode and operation mode adapted to the market economy system. Whereas, it is different from the current general domestic investment funds listed on securities market, the government's specialized fiscal accounts and some other public welfare funds, it has dramatic differences with some full-blown foreign funds.

5.6.2. *Overall structure of the national land regulation fund*

In light of China's actual conditions, land regulation fund shall include central land regulation fund and local land regulation fund. The central land regulation fund is to the market what the "Central Bank" is to land market. It is established initiatively by the specialized institutions with the authorization of the central government, aiming at assisting the central government to further promote the implementation of land control policies nationwide.

Established by local governments, local land regulation funds are designed to carry out land regulation in local areas, and provide support for urban and rural land purchase and reserve or primary market. Given that there is no corresponding legal basis for land finance at present, it is advised that land finance be operated with trust mechanism in areas with suitable conditions, and carry out financing pilots concerning the development and consolidation of tracts of land, meanwhile, financial products with land assets value or revenue as the guarantee should be designed in the form of trust, which is the first move in the attempt to establish new land financial systems. The operation mode of funds should be adopted when conditions permit. In consideration of the long-term development trend, the "land bank" mode integrating the characteristics of land resources and land assets value makes use of urban stock land and suburban reserve land with the throughput mechanism of reserve land, and it is conducive to stabilizing market prices, as well as regulating and stabilizing the market, therefore, it is where land finance is heading for. Figure 5.1 depicts the target, levels, methods, approaches, structures, and mechanisms of the construction of Chinese land financial system.

5.6.3. *Organizational form of land regulation fund*

The land fund is mainly concerned about investors, fund managers and fund trustees. The investors of land fund, i.e., the sponsors, can be the central government, local governments, financial institutions or other institutions boasting good credits and abundant capital, such as housing funds, social insurance funds and other public welfare funds. Specifically, the land fund includes: First, land transfer revenue, which mainly refers to the appreciated value in the process of land reserve, consolidation and development and serves as the main source of land regulation funds; second, fiscal appropriation, i.e., the start-up capital the government invests at the establishment of land fund; third, bank loans from both commercial and policy banks; fourth, other funds, including various insurance funds, pension funds and retirement funds.

Then, as the decision-making body of the funds, managers of land regulation funds are professional land assets management institutions who will be in charge of the investment and accounts management in a more transparent and effective way. In the long term, it is proposed that instant efforts be made in the development of Land Fund Law and construction of relevant systems in line with the future national circumstances, to promote the establishment of professional land fund management institutions. In the short term, it is recommended to refer to the management mode of fund companies to set up funds management companies.

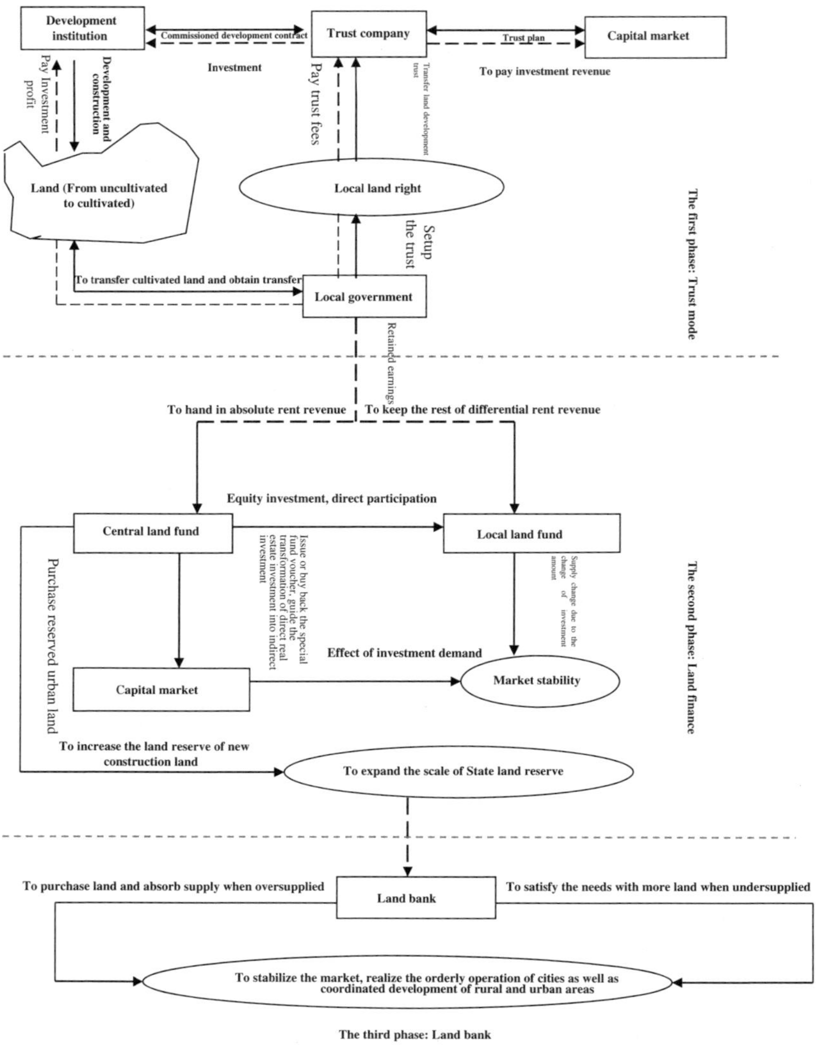

Figure 5.1: Diagrammatic sketch of the target, levels, methods, approaches, structures, and mechanisms of the construction of Chinese land financial system.

At last, the trustees of the funds are the nominal holders and keepers of funds' assets, the subject of fund supervision, the communication junction for land regulation funds investment companies and fund managers; and the trustees can be commercial banks, saving banks, specialized banks, as well as trust and investment companies.

5.7. Conclusion

Since China's adoption of land paid use system, both the values and the drawbacks of land assets are embodied to some extent. For instance, the adoption of urban land bidding, auction and quotation system results in problems like the soaring price of urban land, the low efficiency of urban land-use, loss of state-owned land assets as well as the ineffectiveness of national regulation policies, and so forth, which calls for the improvement of the existing land system. It is suggested to build Chinese land financial systems based on the analysis of the value of urban and rural land assets, break through the rigid constraints of the current land administration system *via* the interaction of the government and market, so as to build a market-oriented and flexible land assets management system in addition to the land assets management systems featured by planning, control, and administration, manifesting and strengthening the State's land ownership, enhance the government's ability to develop economy, give full play to the decisive role of market, realize the macro strategy to promote the balance between efficiency and equity, as well as sustainable development, and finally, bring out the superiority of socialist public ownership of land.

The establishment of a sound Chinese land financial system boasting interaction of the government and the market are projected to: First of all, manifest and strengthen the State's land ownership, that is, to substantiate and materialize the system; second, set up land assets and capital system on the basis of land assets value and future increment incomes to provide continuous and stable financing methods and channels for land development as well as urban management; to develop a kind of market regulation system with the involvement of land assets and value, with a view to enrich the land market regulation system mainly dealing with land planning, taxation, administration, and price.

The land financial system integrating land and finance attempts to establish a system revolving around manifesting and strengthening State-owned land ownership, which operates with the principle of "generating wealth from the land, investing the wealth into land development, and the appreciation goes to the public", capitalize the land value-added revenue equivalent to absolute rent and part of the differential rent, showcasing the economic benefits of State land ownership; capitalize part of the land value-added revenue of differential rent to realize the economic interests of local governments; capitalize the remainder of land value-added revenue to realize the economic interests of other market entities, such as investors. In accordance with different ways to realize the interests of different entities, it is advised to develop a land financial system reflecting the real contents of State land ownership and actual benefits of market entities through financial market and innovation, including a series of policy-oriented land financial instruments and commercial land financial instruments. Policy-oriented land financial instruments include land funds, land development funds, as well as municipal securities and so forth. And, land fund is the most significant policy-oriented land financial instruments, and meanwhile, the most essential content of the practice of land financial reform. Commercial land financial instruments are inclusive of the stocks and securities mainly issued by companies *via* making use of land assets evaluation, as well as the financing instrument designed with future land revenue as the guarantee or a series of financing certificates; the former includes land investment funds and land projects financing, and the latter is inclusive of LABS (land asset-backed securities), REITS (real estate investment trusts) as well as CMBS (commercial mortgage-backed securities), etc.

To establish State land regulation fund is the breakthrough in the reform of China's land financial system. In order to promote the optimization of urban land financial markets and solve the deep-seated problems in the current land market, it is proposed to set up land regulation funds (land funds) as the fiscal revenues like capital funds collecting land revenue with land transferring fees, land-use fees for new construction land as well as social funds. Land funds include central and local land funds. Central land funds refer to the capital pool, the land transferring fees collected equivalent to absolute rent; local land funds refer to the capital pool collecting differential rent. The central land funds can be associated with local land funds *via* direct participation or hold the securities issued by the latter, and *vice versa*. The central land funds are different from local land funds as the former are apt to promote market regulation and the latter are industry investment funds mainly invested in land development and the low-income housing of general residents in cities and towns.

The land fund links the policy-oriented financial system and commercial financial system, and serves as an important instrument the government uses to regulate the market. Land fund is supposed to stabilize market prices in two ways. The first is to form the smooth channels where social capital comes in and out, and stabilize market prices *via* guiding social forces to transform direct investment into the real estate industry to indirect investment through the capital transmission mechanism with the central land funds and local land funds. For example, the central land fund (index analysis through early warning systems, etc.) predicts that there will be abnormal rise in market prices in the future, then the central land fund should issue special land securities, to absorb social capitals to be invested in land or real estate industry, and reduce the investment demands of the society to land or real estate industry. Then, the fund is invested to local land funds, which enlarges the supply of general residential land, so as to meet the demand of general residents for housing, thus, promoting the stability of market prices in the weakening of investment demand and increasing of general housing residence. Secondly, to realize market price stability *via* the development of land reserve and use plan of the central government nationwide, in order to absorb planned urban land reserves. For instance, in line with the premises of land-use planning, urban planning and urban land reserve plans, the central land fund introduces some land to the market to expand land supply so as to absorb market demand and stabilize market prices. The innovation in this paper lies in the construction and design of the land financial system.

In short, to establish the land funds activating the interaction between the government and market is the breakthrough in innovating land financial system. Land finance is a kind of policy-oriented and open fund, and meanwhile, an important means of macro control. The establishment of a balanced interests mechanism with the participation of the central government, local governments as well as various market entities *via* the innovation of land financial system is conducive for guiding the rational development of market economy with economic and financial levers, realize land capitalization, assets capitalization, assets securitization, securities marketization as well as market standardization, so as to realize the targets of national coordinated operation, support, and the sustainable use of land resources. The operation and management of land fund elements should reflect the essence of marketization, and needs a set of effective marketization operational systems as carrier. The CDB realizes the government's goal *via* marketization, which is expected to play an important role in the design, operation and management of land finance. It is both necessary and possible to summarize the experience of development financing in promoting urbanization development, integrating relevant resources, and building the operation platform for basic housing and land finance to serve national strategy in accordance with the requirements of the basic function and structure of the central land regulation funds.

Gradual efforts are expected to be made to establish, develop and improve the land financial system, which serves as an important means of macro control, so as to achieve the intensive use of land resources, guide the orderly development of urbanization, stabilize land and real estate prices, coordinate the urban and rural development, improve the pattern of land development, create more favorable conditions for urbanization and agricultural modernization, and promote the harmonious development of man, land and economy *via* using land as a property and supporting land development and operation with cycling and rolling land revenue.

Given that the land financial system is a new thing that takes a long and complicated process from theoretical innovation to practice, it is proposed that unremitting efforts be made to deepen and develop the understanding and practice concerning land financial reforms, as well as strengthen the construction of supporting systems in-line with the requirement of emancipating minds and solving problems in a realistic manner.

CHAPTER 6

GAINS AND LOSSES IN ABOLISHING AGRICULTURAL TAX AND THE COUNTERMEASURES

The abolition of agricultural tax played a guiding role in alleviating the burden of peasants, but it could not fundamentally help get peasants out of poverty, nor was it helpful in cultivating the awareness of rights and obligations among the modern rural citizens. In the new era, the right direction should be firmly kept, tax system improved, security reinforced, education strengthened and awareness cultivated, so as to make steady progress, reconstruct the rights and obligations of the rural citizens and create conditions for the all-round modernization.

The State Council proclaimed the abolition of agricultural tax in 2005, changing the thousands-of-years-long agricultural tax system. The abolition of the agricultural tax played a guiding role in alleviating the burden of peasants, but it did not fundamentally help the vulnerable peasants shake off poverty.

6.1. Predicament after the Abolition of Agricultural Tax

6.1.1. *The rural cadres become governmental officials*

After the abolition of agricultural tax, rural cadres tend to be formal and professional, as they are partly paid by the public finance. Though alleviating some of the peasants' burdens, the abolition cut off natural connections between peasants and the rural cadres. It was even harder to restrict the rural cadres' behaviors with the public opinion, and they were more apathetic with the rural affairs. The rural bureaucracy was then easy to breed and the interests of the peasants would be ignored.

6.1.2. *Farmers were isolated*

The abolition of agricultural tax canceled the subsidies for the agricultural expenses shared by the rural collective in practice. Farmers were more isolated and estranged. "Everyone took his own route" and worked more single-handed. As a result, the rural areas were more like a heap of loose sand and the disintegration of the rural communities was speeding up. The necessary cooperation among the farmers was diluted and the conflicts concerning transportation and irrigation increased. The traditional antidotes against conflicts lost efficacy while the new ones did not start to take effect. Basic collective functions and public conditions for human settlements were difficult to maintain in some villages. Thus damages were caused to the normal society.

6.1.3. *The rural organizations are weakened*

Some of the rural organizations functioned even less effectively after the abolition of agricultural tax, and they were basically incapable of involving in the collective agricultural production. The rural collective was even incompetent for overall planning, which had a serious impact on the combination of centralization and decentralization and two-level management, the basic management system in rural areas. That has made problems that can be hard solved by a single household even more difficult. Peasants were confronted with more complicated irrigation problems, as the existing facilities were seriously damaged while the new ones were difficult to be available.

6.1.4. *The rural communities fell into disorder*

The abolition of agricultural tax has worsened the social disorder in some rural areas. Most peasants have bare awareness of ruling by law and of their rights, but the traditional bylaws of the rural communities have lost the legitimacy to solve internal conflicts in a forcible way. Some local governments were more out of line with the interests of farmers. No longer having to punctually collect the full agricultural tax, some governments at the basic level became less active to get involved in rural affairs. They usually adopt an indifferent and procrastinating attitude to smooth things over. The lack of principles makes it harder to maintain the basic social order, imposes challenges to basic social norms and bottom line, and accelerates the disintegration of the basic rural morality. The logic to avoid trouble would often lead to big troubles.

6.1.5. *Rural conflicts shift up to upper-level governments*

After the cancellation of the agricultural tax, the town and township governments have seen their functions weakened in the name of "reform", and thus are less capable of timely solving local conflicts. Therefore, peasants have to turn to governments at the county or upper-level, causing more petitioners and shifting up of rural conflicts.

6.2. In-depth Analysis of the Predicament Caused by the Abolition of the Agricultural Tax

Poverty of the peasants as well as the agricultural and rural problems root in many aspects and could be hardly solved simply by abolishing the taxes. Abolition of agricultural tax jurisprudentially violated the rights and obligations of Chinese citizens and brought about some new problems in economic construction and social management. Macroscopically, that may cause several bad political consequences. First, the vulnerable peasants seemed to be protected but actually they were alienated and lost their dignity. Second, peasants failed to have reciprocal rights and obligations and thus social contradictions could be fundamentally intensified and the construction of the harmonious society would be damaged. Third, widened peasants' income gap impedes macro control, rational allocation of resources and the social stability and development. Fourth, the public concern and support to the vulnerable peasants might be weakened and the basic rural security system was hard to construct. Finally, it did not help to educate peasants in cultivating their sense of duties and responsibilities as modern citizens. While the urban and rural integration was progressing, abolition of agricultural tax was in fact an inappropriate institutional barrier in cultivating the modern citizens' sense of duties and responsibilities, including the majority of peasants. According to the development of modern agriculture and modern society, it is the basic obligation and right of a citizen to pay taxes. Our purpose is to provide peasants and low-income groups with tax exemption and reduction and the basic security mechanism rather than simply abolishing the taxes. The problem is therefore very serious.

6.3. Solution

To protect the agriculture, developed countries do not level agricultural value added tax. However, like workers in other economic sectors, agricultural workers should declare their income tax every year according to the law, and the taxes are exempted or refunded based on their actual income. Some of them can even receive subsidies from the government according to related policies. In China where tax system is far from perfect, farmers, rich or poor, do not have to pay taxes after the agricultural tax was abolished, which does not help to cultivate the taxpaying obligation of every citizen and carry out the modern social construction.

A quite long buffering process is necessary to solve this problem with the general orientation as follows: The right direction should be firmly kept, tax system improved, security reinforced, education strengthened and awareness cultivated. Progress should be steadily achieved to reconstruct the rights and obligations of the rural citizens so as to create conditions for the all-round modernization. First of all, it is really necessary to give top priority to poverty alleviation for vulnerable peasants among policies concerning the rural area. Meanwhile, the constitutional spirit should be maintained, citizens' basic rights and obligations should be safeguarded and efforts should be made to enhance the peasants' intrinsic hematopoietic function. Agricultural tax, as an economic regulation, may be appropriately adjusted according to the actual situation. Secondly, the tax system and the basic security system in the rural areas should be further improved, subsidy policies should be made to exempt and refund the taxes of low-income groups, and the basic living conditions, health care, education and pension should be ensured so that the vulnerable peasants are assured of basic survival and development conditions. That is the basic right of the rural citizens. Thirdly, the rural household income tax system should be established upon discussion according to the actual situation of rural citizens so as to cultivate their awareness of paying tax. The system of tax substitution with volunteer work should be explored and established, under which rural citizens able to work can pay taxes by working for a certain number of days, to embody the basic obligations of the rural citizens. Finally, the legal education of the peasants should be strengthened. As Chairman Mao Zedong said, "The education of peasants is a serious issue." While in-depth research is carried out to learn from peasants, their civic and legal awareness should be vigorously cultivated. It is not only an important measure to implement the "*Organic Law of Villagers Committees*" and deepen the rural reform and development, but also a significant task of building the modern countryside.

CHAPTER 7

RURAL DEVELOPMENT STRATEGY ANALYSIS

The rich farmland in the countryside is the shared homeland of all human beings. The Chinese people, who have enjoyed a several-thousand-year-long farming civilization; have even more special feelings toward the countryside. Along the course of China's modernization, we need to handle correctly the relationship between urbanization and rural development and design a new development mechanism for the countryside with new ideas. We need to steer the rural development cause from the old "natural and passive" mode to the "planned and guided" mode, from a "blood transfusion" type to a "blood-making" one, and finally transform the "naturally scattered" housing mode into a "relatively intensive" one. And by doing so, we expect to propel the economic and social development of the countryside in an integral, comprehensive and internal way, and also accelerate the formation of the new pattern of urban–rural integration.

Rural development has been a major topic in China. Mao Zedong once pointed out in his well-known Investigation Report on Peasant Movement in Hunan Province, which was composed in 1927 after he had conducted an in-depth investigation about the peasants during the National Revolution period, that peasants are the vital force of revolution and pioneers of the resolution. At about the same time, Yan Yangchu, an eminent social activist who had been devoted to rural construction in Dingxian County, Hebei Province for a decade, created a mode called "peasant education — scientific rural development." And another well-known industrialist, Lu Zuofu, who had undertaken experiments about rural construction for two decades in Beibei Township of Baxian County, Chongqing Municipality, came out with a "people's livelihood industry — rural modernization" mode. Furthermore, between the years of 1931 and 1937, Liang Shuming had founded Shandong Research Institute of rural construction in Zouping County, Shandong Province, as well as a semi-monthly magazine named Rural Construction. He also did experiments about rural construction, and taught a course of "Introduction to Rural Construction," analyzing why and how to carry out rural construction under conditions at that time. In addition, since 1940s Fei Xiaotong, a great scholar, had devoted all his life to the in-depth research and study of the traditional rural social system, and written "From the Soil, Peasant Life in China, and Peasants in Lucun" as well as other investigation reports. Still more people have been committed to the study and promotion of rural development. Despite of the distinctiveness in their theories and proposals about the mission, steps and content of rural construction due to different historical backgrounds, their ideas of and achievements in rural construction are enlightening and inspirational for us to further address issues concerning agriculture, countryside and farmers and vigorously advance the construction of a new socialist countryside. Since the reform and opening up, both local and central governments have attached great importance to issues concerning agriculture, countryside and farmers. In this new era, such issues still remain a difficult part of reform and a weak point of development. Therefore, this article intends to probe into the rural development strategy from the perspective of development finance and offer relevant suggestions for reference in decision-making.

7.1. Implications, Features and Functions of Rural Areas

7.1.1. *Implications of the rural areas*

The term "rural areas" is a regional concept. It refers to rural communities comprised of market towns and many villages surrounding them with farmers and agriculture as the major players, and regional systems including rich contents such as economy, society and ecology. In terms of production, it generally refers to the areas with agriculture as its major way of production, and agricultural industry as the prerequisite to its existence and development. In terms of social composition, rural areas refer to the areas whose inhabitants are mainly engaged in agricultural production, material culture facilities are poorer than those in the cities while the power of customs, ethics and habits are stronger with families remaining the center of social life and interpersonal relationship is close. In terms of ecology, rural areas refer to areas with a small population in each settlement with large stretches of open greens between settlements.[1] In general, the scope of the rural areas, as a dynamic system, is conceptualized against the urban areas, including other areas other than cities, such as market towns and villages. Market towns are towns which are developed from market fairs where the People's Governments of townships or national townships locate, and are recognized by the county government. They are not within the administrative institution but they are the service center for economy, culture and life for a certain part of the rural areas. Rural areas exclude market towns. They include the areas where villagers live and are engaged in various productive activities, and those areas not included in the urban areas such as farms and forestry, etc. As a result, rural areas are different from villages. The former refers to a larger concept which includes the latter. Rural areas include villages and market towns outside the administrative institution. Putting the issues in the villages against the economic and social background of the rural areas can facilitate the design of policies in a systematic manner, and promote the economic and social development in the rural areas comprehensively and endogenously.

7.1.2. *Types of rural areas*

Rural areas can be divided into administrative villages and natural villages. The former are administrative entities with village

---

[1]Zhang Xiaolin (1998). On discrimination of rural definitions. *Acta Geographica Sinica*, 53(4), 79–85.

committees established. An administrative village may include several natural villages or village groups. The latter are village entities, naturally formed hubs of residents with varied scales.

Based on the classification of economic activities in the rural areas, there are agricultural villages (for crop production), forestry villages, poultry villages and fishing villages. There are also mixed villages engaged in crop and forestry, crop and poultry, and crop and fishing, etc. Agricultural villages are mainly engaged in crop production based on land resources; forestry village cultivation and cutting forests and woods, making use of the land resources; fishing villages aquaculture, based on the water area; and poultry villages animal husbandry, developed on land resources or grassland. Mixed villages develop agriculture, forestry, fishing, and animal husbandry, etc., making use of various land resources.

According to the distances between the villages and the cities, there are suburban villages and outer suburban villages. Suburban villages are adjacent to the cities or are relatively close to the cities. They share close connection with cities and are heavily influenced by various aspects in the cities, such as employment, consumption and culture, etc. Its development is obviously based on cities. Compared with general villages, suburban villages have more convenient transportation, better infrastructure and more developed economy. They keep traditional lifestyles of the villages and enjoy better natural environment and pastoral atmosphere. Outer suburban villages are relatively far from cities without urban features. They are mainly engaged in traditional agricultural economy with a weak basis for the second and third industries. Their transportation is under developed with poor infrastructure. With large areas of natural ecological system, they better preserve the traditional rural lifestyle and farming methods.

7.1.3. *Features of rural areas*

The development of rural areas can be roughly divided into six phases based on the various degrees of their economic development.

7.1.3.1. *Traditional and undeveloped rural areas*

They refer to the rural areas with peasant economy as their foundation and can on the whole be self-sufficient. Economy in those areas is extremely underdeveloped and their industrial structure is very simple: The first industry takes a major share in rural economy while the second and third industries are extremely underdeveloped. Farmers' income is very low with under 3,000 Yuan of annual net income per capita. As these rural areas are mostly located in remote and far away mountainous areas, their infrastructure is poorly equipped, transportation not convenient, information communication not smooth, and agriculture not mechanized or market-driven enough. All these lead to the fact that such areas are the slowest in economic development in China after the reform and opening up was launched. Rural areas of this category are weak in accumulating funds and lack the ability of self-development. Illiteracy among rural laborers is high. At the same time, however, because of their low development level, their ecological environment is fairly good, and agricultural resources are rich, especially water, grass, forest, etc., and they have significant potential for development.

7.1.3.2. *Underdeveloped rural areas*

The level of economic development in these areas is generally fairly low with agriculture as a major part of their structure. The first industry still takes a relatively large share in the economy, and non-agricultural industry started late with slow development. Recent years have witnessed certain development, yet non-agriculture level is still low with poorly equipped infrastructure and clearly-defined dual structure between the urban and rural areas. Farmers' income is relatively low with 3,000–10,000 Yuan of annual net income per capita. Meanwhile, as the contradiction between people and land is getting more intense and urbanization and industrialization is on fast track in these areas, a large amount of excess laborers, especially quite a few with relatively high level of education, became migrant workers and flew to the relatively developed coastal cities and regional hub cities, leaving the aged, women and children at home. Due to the outflow of rural talent, salaries from the engagement in the industrial sector becomes the major income source of the less developed rural areas, and the overall development in those areas is slow with relatively low rural economic development. The rural special structure is getting "hollow".

7.1.3.3. *Medium-developed rural areas based on agriculture*

With rich agricultural resources or regional advantages, these rural areas act on the national economic policies, adjusted industrial structure and develop the advantageous industries for rural areas such as vegetables, flowers, fruits and livestock and aquaculture, etc., with certain productive scale. Though the proportion of the first industry is relatively high, the marketization degree is getting higher. Farmers' income is relatively high with 15,000–30,000 Yuan of annual net income per capita. There is relatively large improvement in rural infrastructure and supporting facilities, and the urban–rural gap is narrowing down. As the government begins to strengthen the supervision and management of the environment and land resources in the villages and attach great importance to the governance of the rural environment, this category of rural areas has initiated the intensive development of the land within the villages as the outward expansion continues. The contradiction between the shortage of land and sufficiency of laborers is quite pronounced, yet the phenomenon of hollowed villages is eased.

7.1.3.4. *Medium-developed rural areas with fast development of non-agricultural industries*

The market economic system has rejuvenated the development of rural economy. Against the macro background of the structural adjustment and shift of rural industries, these areas rely on the rich agricultural resources or regional advantages and expedite the economic development. Rural enterprises emerge as a strong force, offering more employment opportunities and pulling more migrant workers back home. Changes begin to occur in the industrial structure: The proportion of the first industry drops and the development of the second and third is gaining speed and takes over 60% in proportion. Farmers' income is relatively high with 15,000–25,000 Yuan of annual net income per capita. Rural infrastructure and supporting facilities is relatively well equipped, the value of rural land is gaining value and the hollowed villages are getting less or even disappearing. At the same time, as land is more intensely used and buildings are densely mapped in the villages, the rural scenes are badly damaged or even disappear.

7.1.3.5. *Developed rural areas*

These areas mainly locate in the economically developed zones along the eastern coast. In general, the regional economic development is high with a reasonable regional economic structure. Social economic development in the rural areas is relatively high and the non-agricultural sector takes up a lion's share in rural economy. There are many township enterprises with the second and third industries taking up approximately 80%. Farmers' income is high with 25,000–35,000 Yuan of annual net income per capita. Market- and export-oriented agriculture is quite developed with well-equipped rural infrastructure and supporting facilities. Both the degree of urbanization and the unification of urban and rural areas are relatively high.

7.1.3.6. *Modernized rural areas*

The economic development in rural communities is advanced with fast growth. In terms of industrial structure, the first industry takes only a small proportion, and the second and third industries assume the absolute leading roles, taking up approximately over 95%. Rural infrastructure is developed, and farmers' income is high with over 35,000 Yuan of annual net income per capita. Their living conditions are good and living quality high. The difference between the urban and rural areas is basically erased. The way of production, way of living, and material, cultural and ecological civilization of the rural areas are developed in an all-round way. Social welfare such as education, health and culture are similar to those in the urban areas, and rural modernization has been basically realized.

Regionally speaking, the modernized and developed rural areas are mainly located in municipalities directly under the leadership of the central government, such as Shanghai, Beijing and Tianjin, etc., and around the hub cities in the economically developed areas in the eastern coastal areas. The medium-developed rural areas are mainly located in the central and northeastern areas with relatively good transportation and resources. Underdeveloped rural areas are expansively located, occupying the majority of the rural areas in China. Traditional and undeveloped rural areas are mainly located in the mountainous areas with occlusive transportation in the northwest, southwest and center of China.

In terms of the distance from the hub cities, the degree of rural economic development is diminishing along the transportation line as it is getting farther from the hub cities to remote cities. Modernized and developed rural areas are mainly located around the central cities in the economically developed areas, medium-developed rural areas are mainly in the suburbs of the regional hub cities, and underdeveloped rural areas are mostly far away from cities.

7.1.4. *Functions of rural areas*

7.1.4.1. *Safeguarding food security and supply of agricultural products*

"The base of a country is its people, and the people rely on the food". The arable land in the rural areas is the most important natural resource for food production, which is the top priority of China's rural development. To stabilize the sown area in the rural areas and improve the technological level is very important for securing food safety, supply of agricultural products and the transmission of industrial raw materials given the increasingly intense natural resource and the residents' improving consumption standards.

7.1.4.2. *Maintaining ecological balance and facilitating the development of ecological economy*

Rural areas have rich resources of arable land, forest land and grassland. The biomass produced by the forest per hectare is 100–400 tons, and that by arable land or flora per hectare is approximately 10–20 tons, which play an important role in sustaining water and land, conserving the water source, adjusting the climate, improving the environment and maintaining the ecological balance. The special environment in the rural areas well preserves the diversity of ecological species and at the same time improves the vegetation coverage, purifies the air and conserves water and soil, providing a natural ecological shield for the development of the cities. Rural area is the major player in the development of ecological economy. Driven by ecological economy, the nature-friendly low-carbon consumption and cultural consumption has become a new trend, providing a large market for the development of rural economy. The organic agricultural products in the rural areas can better meet people's consumption needs. Rural tours with rich local culture have become more and more popular each year, making the rural area a more energetic and more vibrant player. As a base for new energy revolution and ecological economy, rural areas serve as a new force in leading low-carbon economy and driving the development of ecological economy.

7.1.4.3. *Providing labor force for urban development and facilitating urbanization*

For a long time, with the development of mechanization in agricultural production, agricultural production needs less labor force, thus the surplus manpower in the rural areas increases to a large scale. The fast development of the cities calls for continuous labor input. Many rural laborers flow into the cities to work in all walks of life in all corners of the cities, making tremendous contribution to the urban development. Industrialization and urbanization absorbs a large amount of rural surplus laborers. Rural population moves to the cities, turning more areas into cities and towns and accelerates the urbanization.

7.1.4.4. *Bearing traditional culture and emotions*

Rural areas bear rich traditional cultural information and carry on the traditional farming culture passed down from long time ago. The ancient and profound rural culture gathers the essence of Chinese culture: Popular handcraft, music, art, dance, local plays and operas, mythologies and folklore, epics and ballads, traditional architecture, etc. Along the history, these cultural categories have taken roots in the broad land of the rural areas and become the spiritual blood vessel and genes in rural construction. Rural areas are less influenced by foreign culture. Some carriers of traditional culture (such as rural ancient architect, local folk songs, collective activities of local people, etc.) have been maintained, renovated, unearthed and improved for adaptability during the development. Thus Chinese traditional culture is well preserved and developed in the rural areas. The rural area is not only the source for food and farming civilization, but also the source for the human being. When the ape man stood on the ground, these ancestors of human being planted not only crops in the villages, but also the original emotion, the deepest memory and the support for survival. The profound rural land is regarded as the hometown of human beings. Chinese people with thousands of years of farming civilization attach special emotions to the rural areas, which carry their spirit.

7.2. Present Situation, Trend, Goals and Impetus of the Rural Areas

7.2.1. *Present situation of the rural areas*

7.2.1.1. *Rural construction lacks reasonable planning, and rural features are disappearing*

At present, the renovation and construction of most rural areas in China has not been systematically planned and designed. Rural construction is basically in anarchy, freely developed by the farmers themselves without order. No authentic design can be spoken of, and the irrational "keeping up with the Joneses" is pronounced with obvious arbitrariness. Some farmers' residences in new villages are similar to villas, but the surroundings are quite a mess. The residences of well-off farmers are unique in appearance with large building volume while the residences of those moderately well-off farmers are unified in appearance with simple exterior decoration or no decoration at all. The two kinds form a strong contrast visually. Some farmers, out of economic concerns and for their own convenience, usually build their home randomly by the main roads for external traffic of the village, which makes a messy layout of the village. On the other hand, quite a few farmers indiscriminately imitate modern building styles and build their new homes following their own wills. They copy the architectural models in the cities and try to keep up with the cities in every aspect. This lack of identity with the rural area has made the characteristics and value of the traditional residence fade gradually from people's memories. While large stretches of traditional rural residence have been re-built, some ancient architectures, old trees, wells and play stages which are witnesses to the vicissitudes of the rural area are gradually decayed or even destroyed because of lack of protection. Especially, during new rural construction, combining villages and pulling down the houses are often publicized as achievement during the officials' office. Architectural elements such as gray walls and black tiles are becoming the so-called features of rural architecture and farmers' actual needs are ignored, which lead to the gradual disappearance of rural landscape.

7.2.1.2. *Living conditions are improved yet infrastructure remains weak*

For example, the use of sanitary toilets in the rural areas of China was only 44.8% in 2000, and this figure was close to 70% in 2011.[2] Though the infrastructure in the rural areas is improved, the coverage is not wide enough to include all rural areas. There are also significant regional differences. Most rural infrastructure is still very weak, especially drinking water supply, sludge treatment, culture and health service facilities, etc., which hinder the economic development of the rural areas. In particular, the difficulties for farmers to visit the doctors are getting worse in the rural areas of China. According to *China Rural Statistical Yearbook of 2012*, from 1985 to 2011, the number of country doctors and hygienists for every 1,000 rural residents dropped from 1.55 to 1.27.

[2] *Source*: *China Rural Statistical Yearbook*, 2012.

7.2.1.3. *Industrial structure is changed and rural enterprises are developed to some extent*

Over recent years, rural industrial structure has been changing constantly. The primary sector is growing at a relatively slow speed with a shrinking proportion, while the development of the secondary and tertiary sectors is gaining speed. In some relatively developed rural areas, the rural enterprises are growing at a fast speed, formulating a new layout of leading enterprises driving up the development of rural industries. According to incomplete statistics, the number of agricultural gardens for leisure has exceeded 18,000, receiving over 400 million tourists every year. Their revenue of over 120 billion Yuan has benefited 15 million farmers.[3] Yet taking the whole country into consideration, the agriculture is still weak in foundation with insufficient potential. Difficulties remain in rural industries, and service industry in the rural areas cannot meet people's need. There are large discrepancies in distribution of labor force, yield and investment, etc., as the speed and level of development of various industries are different. The reasonable layout with harmonious development of the three industries in the rural areas has not yet been formed, and the shift of labor force between industries is hard to be realized. The level of industrialization is low, and the increase of farmers' income is slow.

7.2.1.4. *Conditions for agriculture are poor, and agricultural products are produced and operated in an extensive manner*

After three decades of reform and opening up, agriculture in China has gained tremendous progress. Yet there is a glaring gap between agriculture in China and that in the developed countries in the world. In China, medium- and low-yield land occupies two thirds of the total area, and the effective irrigation area is only 50%, and the effective utilization coefficient of the irrigation water is 0.53. The passive situation of living at the mercy of the elements has not been addressed from the root. Technological facilities for agriculture are not

[3] *Source*: *China Rural Statistical Yearbook*, 2012.

advanced, and the comprehensive mechanized cultivation and harvest takes only 52%, far below the ratio in the developed countries, which is 70–80%. The contribution rate of scientific and technological progress is only 53.5%. The organized agricultural production is at a low level, less than 0.5 hectare of arable land per household, and the ratio of farmers who participate agricultural industrialized operations and join specialized cooperatives are only 35% and 13% respectively. Moreover, the market system for agricultural products, the service system for socialized agriculture and the national supporting mechanism for agriculture are not sound, the contradiction between small-scale operation by individual families and the large market for agricultural products is still acute.[4] As the infrastructure for agriculture is lagging behind, it is hard to provide strong support and guarantee for modern agriculture and public services. During agricultural production, though the production bases for agricultural products are expanding, they are only growing in quantity, but not in quality. Much less do they know about the brand effect. Indiscriminate imitation happens from time to time. Farmers are mainly engaged in random and scattered cultivation, and there is no standard time for the products to hit the market. Processing capacity is poor and mostly is just primary production with little intensive processing. Agricultural products are low in technological content with little added value, which caused the weak competitiveness. The professional economic organization is weakly formed, hard to exert scale effect and intensive effect, which led to low industrialized operation level.

7.2.1.5. *Income of farmers has increased, yet their education remains low*

The net income of rural residents per capita in 2000 was only 2,253.4 Yuan, and that reached 6,977.3 Yuan in 2011. Farmers' income has increased by three times during the ten years, and is still on a steady rise. Yet the education level of farmers is still low as summarized in Table 7.1.

---

[4] *Source*: http://www.gov.cn/gzdt/2011-03/17/content_1826284.htm.

Table 7.1: Education level of farmers in China (%).

Year/ Education	Illiteracy or semi-illiteracy	Primary school	Junior high	Senior high and above
1990	20.73	38.86	32.84	7.48
1995	13.47	36.62	40.1	9.79
2000	8.09	32.22	48.07	11.62
2005	6.73	28.44	50.24	14.59
2010	5.47	23.51	52.97	17.39

Source: *China Rural Statistical Yearbook*, 2012.

7.2.1.6. *Villages are sparsely distributed, land is underdeveloped and "hollowing" phenomenon is pronounced*

Villages in China are sparsely distributed. Some villages are still in the remote mountainous areas or among the forests whose transportation is poor and economy lagging behind. Land in the rural areas is underdeveloped. Except for basic arable land and residential land, other land resources are less developed. Because of poor planning and management, part of the developed land is extensively used. Some land is even left barren. In the meantime, with the development of rural economy, the old residences in the villages are far from sufficient to meet the needs of farmers for production and living. For example, the alleys, doors and yards are small, the roofs low, the lighting poor, roads not flat, drainage not smooth, etc. Many villagers, therefore, construct their residences around the villages or along the roads. Farmers usually build new homes but do not pull down the old ones. Many houses are left to decay and collapse, which makes the villages "new in the outside yet old inside" and "expand outward yet hollow inward". As rural population have partially transformed to non-rural, a large number of villages became hollow as the villagers have left and their homes became empty. This has wasted the land and reduced the density of population. It has also increased the number of houses not for living and exacerbated the hollowness of villages, which affects the living condition of the farmers.

Taking Luojiadu village, Luohu town, Linchuan district, Fuzhou in Jiangxi Province as an example, most newly built residences in

Table 7.2: Uses of the homestead in Luojiadu Village.

Types of homestead		Number
Newly built homestead	Unoccupied newly built homestead	68
	Total pieces of newly built homestead	320
Old homestead	Abandoned old homestead	103
	Total pieces of old homestead	110
Total		430

Source: Field research by author.

Luojiadu village are randomly located without unified planning by the village committee, resulting in a messy layout. Meanwhile, the hollowed villages grow together with the expanding residential land along the roads, causing double waste of the land. According to field research, there are 103 abandoned old residences, 93.6% of the old residences and 23.9% of the total homestead (Table 7.2).

7.2.2. *Trend of rural development of the rural area*

7.2.2.1. *Industrial structure in the rural area is optimized and the production is professionalized*

In the 21st century, the industrial structural adjustment in the rural areas is the core task of the development of rural resources and rural economy. The major directions of industrial structural adjustment in the rural areas are as follows: First, to develop sustainable ecological and hazard-free agriculture with good quality and high efficiency, to increase food production, secure food supply and realize the general balance of need and supply of agricultural products; meanwhile, increasing the proportion of high-quality breeds and products and attach importance to the development of ecological agriculture. The second direction is to develop intensive, scale and professional agriculture which takes on the management mode of a factory and to promote the industrial development of agriculture. Thirdly, pivoting on the cities and towns and connected by the flow of resources and industrial interaction between the urban and rural areas, we should strive to develop internationalized modern agriculture with high efficiency and rural joint-equity enterprises, enhance the connection and flexibility of the economic systems of the urban and rural areas and lift the productivity and innovative ability in the rural areas through reasonable distribution of profit. Meanwhile, proper regional division of work and layout in agriculture and rural economy should be realized and specialized production patterns of various regions should be formulated. Based on the distinctive advantages of the rural areas in resources and the present economic foundation, high-quality and efficient agriculture should be the key area to develop. We should also cultivate rural enterprises and encourage the interactive development of the three "sub sectors", namely high-quality crop production, featured processing industry and tourism in the rural economic system. By extending the agricultural industrial chain, we can promote the development of the secondary and tertiary sectors and maximize the functions of the rural areas, and ensure the sustainable increase of rural productivity and farmers' income.

7.2.2.2. *Rural land should be used intensively and the layout of housing estate should be reasonable*

In the 21st century, the land resource allocation in the rural areas has been further optimized. Special attention will be paid to resource saving and environmental protection. Arable land will be protected and the intensive output effect of land will be enhanced. The layout of rural housing estate will be adjusted to a moderate scale and will become more standardized and rational. The relatively large housing estate with better basic conditions will be given priority for development. In particular, through "moving villages" and "combination of housing estates", etc., the integrated management of rural land and sustainable development of rural space will be initiated. The functions and cohesive power of central villages should be exercised to the full, and through the preferential policies such as economic compensation and employment training, population should be guided to flow to the central villages and urban areas. Villages will be established along traffic lines with convenient traffic networks between villages, which can not only raise the efficiency of production and facilitate the contacts between housing estates, but also make beautiful rural landscape.

7.2.2.3. *Rural architectures are standardized, and rural environment are scenic*

Influenced by urbanization, the messy layout of the traditional architects in the rural areas will be constantly improved. Ancient architecture will be renovated, and the construction of new buildings will be more standardized with increasingly unified exterior while maintaining the essence and features of rural traditional architectures. The modern elements in new rural buildings will bring in more modern styles which will gradually formulate new and modernized landscape in the rural areas. After indiscriminate development as if it were a blowout, the rural areas will pay more attention to if the landscapes are practical, scenery original, atmosphere simple and food ecological, and all these will contribute to the return to simplicity of the rural areas. The pattern of rural housing estate will be unique, rural buildings will be of antique flavor and the rural landscape will be natural and refreshing. Rural areas in the future will present more the landscapes of the nature, settlements, architectures, agricultural civilization and folk culture in a unique ensemble, which will grant high tourism value to the rural areas and formulate various tourist attractions to realize the coordinated development of the economic, social and ecological environment.

7.2.2.4. *Rural ecology and democratic management is improved*

The rural areas in the 21st century will be the habitat of modern material and spiritual civilization, integrating culture, education, leisure and entertainment. To improve the ecological civilization in the rural areas, China needs to make the environment clean and agreeable with increased afforested areas, more solid roads and more road lights to improve the living environment and to change the undesirable traditional living styles and habits. Development of rural resources will be more rational, regulated and sustainable, and efforts will be paid to realize ecological and harmless rural production. In the meantime, future rural development will stress more the expansion of rural democracy and self-governance of the villagers. An open mechanism of village affairs will be established, and popular legal education will be conducted to ensure the legal rights of farmers on the whole as masters of the country and to realize democratic management.

7.2.3. *General goal of rural development*

In the 21st century, the transformation in the rural areas of China will be one of the greatest events in the society. The general goal of the rural development is to develop the production and realize moderate prosperity with civilized atmosphere, clean environment and democratic management. Development of production provides material conditions for the development of the rural areas; well-off living is its ultimate goal; civilized atmosphere support rural development, clean environment offers it favorable conditions and democratic management political guarantee.

As modernization is carried forward with meticulous planning, innovative systems, creative ideas and integrated development, a landscape combining tradition and modernity will be gradually revealed in the rural areas of China. Rural economy will create and rely on its own brands by exercising local advantages in resources, developing and maintaining brand products and winning the market by its brands. Rural culture will be more characteristic by popularizing the fine historical and traditional elements and creating the characteristic cultural life which will not only entertain the farmers themselves but also will attract the outside world. Rural society will be more regulated as national laws will be deeply embedded in the rural society. Consciousness of citizenship and public ethics will be more manifest, and rural customs and habits not in opposition to the law will equally exert influence on the behavior and logic of the villagers. The villagers will not only follow local consensus, but will also follow national laws. The villages will have relatively balanced social information with the outside world. Rural environment will be more suitable for living with less rural population and more peaceful and natural environment. The hygiene will be improved fundamentally with more convenient living facilities for villagers.

At the end of this century, China may reach the level of a medium-developed country. Rural areas of China will be transformed from being historical and traditional to those combining tradition and modernity, Chinese farmers will be transformed to rural citizens with modern awareness, and Chinese agriculture will be transformed to an industry with 20–30 mu as the major category of scale and diversified operation with a certain level of modern technology. Though the degree of development of the rural areas of China cannot equal that of the rural areas of the present developed countries, fundamental changes will occur as compared with the traditional rural areas of China.

7.2.4. *Driving mechanism of the rural development*

7.2.4.1. *Exogenous driving mechanism*

7.2.4.1.1. Policy support

To expedite rural construction, the country has issued a series of policies which facilitates the development of rural construction. In 2003, the 3rd Plenary Session of the 16th Central Committee has raised five strategies coordinating the planning of urban and rural development, regional development, economic and social development, harmonious development of humans and nature, and domestic development and the demands of opening to the outside world, placing the coordinated planning of urban and rural development on top of the strategies. In October 2005, *Proposals of the Communist Party of China (CPC) Central Committee on the Formulation of the 11th Five-year Plan for National Economic and Social Development* proposed that "construction of socialist new countryside is a significant historic task in Chinese modernization", and made clear the goals for rural development that "the production developed, the life ample, the local custom civilized, the village accommodate, the management democratic". In 2008, the *Law of the People's Republic of China (PRC) on urban and rural planning* has implemented the philosophy and idea of coordinating the development of the urban and rural areas. The Report at the 18th CPC National Congress further stressed the task of enhancing the coordinated urban–rural development, injecting more momentum to the rural development, gradually narrowing the urban–rural gap and encouraging the mutual urban and rural prosperity. It is vital to insist on the industry nurturing agriculture, the cities supporting the villages and the policy of giving more, taking less and losing control, and to increase policy support to strengthen agriculture, benefit farmers, and enrich rural areas. It is also necessary to accelerate the development of modern agriculture and strengthen the integrated productivity of agriculture, and place the priorities of the national infrastructure construction and the development of social undertakings in the rural areas, and carry on the new rural construction and poverty relief and development so as to comprehensively improve the conditions for production and life in the rural areas.

7.2.4.1.2. Enterprises as models

The development of rural enterprises has driven a large number of rural laborers to shift to non-agricultural industries and encouraged the establishment and development of a number of small towns and opened a broad road for the industrialization of the rural areas. The urban industrial enterprises will participate in the rural economic construction through various operational models such as joint venture, cooperation and shareholding, expedite the re-organization, restructuring and technological progress, improve the quality of rural enterprises and facilitate the development and upgrading of agricultural industrialization. During the 11th Five-year Plan, the increased employment opportunities offered by rural enterprises amounted to 15.56 million with 3.11 million of annual increase, totaling 158 million and contributing over 35% of the income increase of the farmers. The accumulated capital for supporting the construction of rural areas and the subsidiary social expenditure reached over 140 billion Yuan.[5]

[5] *Source*: *China Rural Statistical Yearbook 2012.*

7.2.4.1.3. Promotion of urbanization

Besides the general urban functions, Chinese urban areas have another special function: To promote the dual urban–rural structure adjustment, encourage the structural adjustment in agriculture, increase farmers' income and coordinate the urban–rural relationship. As farmers increase their production and income, they urgently need assistance from the cities in terms of science and technology. This assistance from cities will help increase the income of farmers, be they individual farmers or farmers growing crops or raising livestock or handcraft producers for leading enterprises. The cities will drive up the intensified land use of the rural areas, which will greatly raise the utilization rate and economic benefit of land and increase its production value per unit. The industrialization and commercialization as accompanied by urbanization has offered opportunities for the development of the secondary and tertiary sectors, and also created a large employment market, which is conducive to the shift of excess labor force in the rural areas, and also provides opportunities to receive education and master modern technology and business information. Many farmers, after having worked for a while in the cities would go back to the rural areas and become rich making use of the technologies, information and capital they owned, and lead his fellow-villagers to become rich too, which contributed to the construction of a harmonious society in the rural areas.

7.2.4.1.4. Information technology as a driving force

The rural construction of China is in the Information Age. Driven by the tides of information technology, efficient and practical agricultural information service system and advanced agricultural technologies will be popularized and change the farmers' philosophy in agricultural production, shift the way of agricultural growth, innovate the growing model of agriculture and accelerate the economic development in the rural areas. Information technology will facilitate the development of rural social undertakings through on the one hand, multimedia education of information technology to realize the share of resources for rural areas and the development of rural education to cultivate new-type farmers; on the other, establishing an information system for disease control and intervention which can improve the level of medical treatment and public health in the rural areas to some extent and accelerate the integrated construction of the urban and rural areas.

7.2.4.2. *Intrinsic advantages*

7.2.4.2.1. Natural resources

The natural resources in the rural areas in China are less developed, and the ecological environment is relatively well preserved. Man-made environment and natural ecological environment is integrated as a kind of community which closely integrates human settlements and the nature in harmonious co-existence. The coordinated interaction of the lifestyles and production activities of the rural people and the natural ecological system constitutes integrated landscapes including natural scenery, rural settlement, agricultural and forestry scenes, etc., and a complex of local cultural landscapes integrating mountain and water-oriented, ecology-oriented and tradition-oriented sceneries, offering value both in nature and local culture and serving as the foundation of sightseeing agriculture, rural tourism, vacation and residence. The rural areas can exercise their advantages in natural sceneries and actively develop rural tourism such as "Leisure rural trip" based on local resources and natural sceneries to drive the development of relevant industries.

7.2.4.2.2. Differentiation of traditional agriculture

Driven by industrialization, the differentiation of traditional agriculture in the rural areas speeded up. Agricultural production has begun to shift from being traditional intensive cultivation to large-scale mechanized production. Using the scientific methods of cultivation and following the natural law of the growth of crops, the quantity and quality of local products have been raised to the maximum extent, scale of production expanded, and conditions for agricultural production improved, agricultural labor productivity raised to a large-scale, farmers' income increased, and the integrated development of agriculture, industry and the tertiary sector realized through constantly increasing the technological investment. Meanwhile, the traditional agriculture in the rural areas has evolved from the single crop-cultivation and livestock and aquaculture breeding to an industrial chain with rural features involving various industries and covering the phases before, during and after production. Large-scale rural enterprises have appeared. On the one hand, the production efficiency of agriculture has been greatly raised and agricultural and sideline products have been enriched; on the other, farmers are liberated from the land by engaging in non-agricultural industries, and the backward awareness of peasants is gradually replaced by "new culture". The well-off economic conditions of the farmers stimulate their urge for modern civilization, which is beneficial to mobilize the enthusiasm of the farmers in rural construction.

7.2.4.2.3. Strong urge of farmers for development

"Rural enterprises" and "tides of migrant rural workers" have broken the closed and tranquil state of the rural society under the influence of urbanization and industrialization. There are more and more people who routinely go to work in the morning and be home at dusk in the rural areas. Some farmers with better economic conditions have even moved to market towns or downtown area. The influence of urban culture has made the rural areas more and more diversified. Farmers have rid themselves of the traditional and conservative peasant awareness which is unwilling to change the status quo and cherishes blood relationship as core value. Instead, with innovative, ambitious, rational and open mind, they have new requirements for the rural environment and living conditions and urgently hope that they could change the present situation of the rural areas. This is the new appeal of farmers for rural development. Rural areas in China have good potential with relatively little competitive pressure and large room for development. The quality of rural laborers has been growing. Some farmers have received trainings in professional knowledge and skills and have mastered relatively advanced productive techniques and operational philosophy. They have modern awareness and certain innovative talents, and have become new type of farmers with knowledge, skills and business acumen. Relying on local characteristics and industrial resources in the rural areas, they have strong wishes to start their own business in an innovative fashion, thus emerged a group of leading characters with entrepreneurship. They are models for other farmers in growth of production, employment and income, etc. Self-employment of farmers has become a new highlight for rural development.

7.3. Relationship between Urbanization and Rural Areas

Urbanization is a historical process with constant flow of rural population to the urban areas and the continuous shift of the primary sector to the secondary and tertiary sectors. This process manifests itself in four aspects: First, urbanization is the process of the flow of rural population and labor force to the urban areas; second, it is the process that the secondary and tertiary sectors aggregate and develop in the urban areas; third, it is the process of the shift of rural landscape to urban landscape; fourth, it is the expansion and transmission of urban civilization, awareness and lifestyle. The core of urbanization is the change in employment structure, industrial structure and community structure in the rural and urban areas. Rural areas and urbanization is mutually affected and interpenetrated. During urbanization, it is not only the shift of rural areas to the urban areas that occurs, but also the counteraction of the rural areas to the urban areas. Their relationship is shown in the following four aspects.

7.3.1. *Population transformation*

The most obvious manifestation of urbanization is the transformation of rural population to urban population. Ray M. Northam, an American urban geographer summarized the transformation from rural population to urban population in 1979 as an "S" shaped curve (Fig. 7.1). He divided urbanization into three stages, namely the initial stage with under 30% of urbanization rate and relatively slow

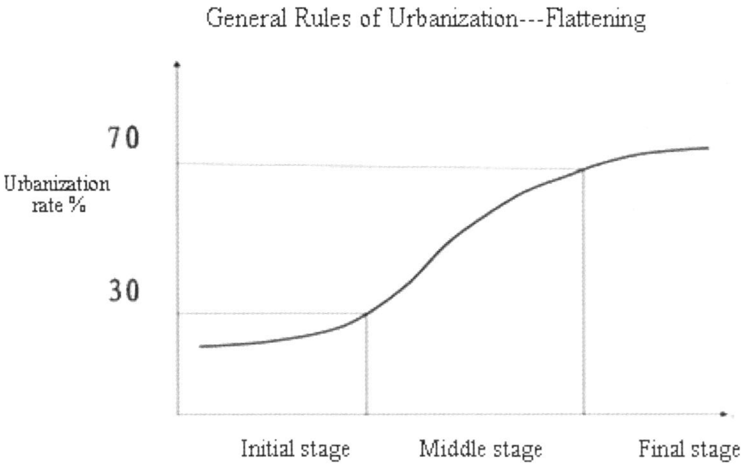

Figure 7.1: Urbanization rate of different stages.

development, the middle period with rapid growth of urbanization rate from 30% to 70%, and the final stage where the urbanization rate is high with stable development.[6]

At the initial stage with low level of urbanization and slow growth, the pulling power of the urban areas for rural population is relatively weak. The transformation from rural population to urban population takes a long time at a slow speed, just as urbanization of China took almost a century to rise from 10.64% in 1949 to 30.48% in 1996, 0.42% per year on an average, yet it only took 15 years to grow rapidly from 30.48% in 1996 to 51.27% in 2011, 1.39% annually on an average. China is currently in the middle stage with rapid urbanization rate. During this period, the significant difference in economy and income of the urban and rural areas is pushing the flow of rural labor force to the urban areas. The high level of public service facilities in medical treatment, public health and education also contributed to the flow. It is expected that by the mid-21st century, the urbanization rate in China will reach 70%, which means that China will enter the final stage with high level of urbanization and stable development by

[6]Wang Jianjun and Wu Zhiqiang (2009). Division of development phases [J]. *Acta Geographica Sinica*, 64(2), 177–188.

then. As the urbanization level is increasing, the urban areas will be consolidated and expanded and urban issues such as traffic jams, environmental pollution, housing shortages, etc., will occur. Meanwhile, the improving infrastructure and transportation network in the rural areas will cause backflow of a part of wealthy urban population from the cities to the rural areas, i.e., counter-urbanization, which will facilitate the mutual development and prosperity of the urban and rural areas and realize their integration.

7.3.2. *Transfer of industries*

During the industrialization, there was large difference in income between traditional agricultural industry and modern non-agricultural industries, which encouraged the change of the industrial structure of the rural areas from consisting of only the primary sector to consisting of three sub-sectors, but primary sector remains the major part. The good infrastructure and market service system in the urban areas have made it possible to share and concentrate the resources, information, technology and capital, etc., in order to provide sufficient room for the development of non-agricultural industries and to facilitate the communication and integration between the urban and rural areas, between industries and between production and circulation. Urbanization is the gathering process of non-agricultural industries to the urban areas; meanwhile, as the surplus rural labor is being transformed to non-agricultural labor after they entered the urban areas, the secondary and tertiary sectors have been upgraded and developed. As the non-rural industries are gathering in the urban areas, rural labor force is moving towards the urban areas, making the areas of transferred land expanding and expediting its circulation. Rural land is gradually concentrated, which facilitates the participation of foreign capital, especially urban investment to realize the mechanization and industrialization of rural agriculture.

7.3.3. *Shift of landscape*

Rural landscape consists of a variety of land mosaics in the rural areas, including ecological systems such as farmland, fruit garden, artificial forests, farms, pastures, waters and villages, etc. It mainly features agricultural characteristics, and is a complex comprising of natural ecological structure and artificial features based on natural landscape.[7] With distinctive pastoral features, it is not only restricted by the natural environment, but also is influenced by the operational activities and strategies of human beings. With the development of urbanization, society and economy, there has been obvious transformation with rural landscape. Some agricultural land in the suburban areas turned into non-agricultural land for industrial, commercial and residential uses. As buildings in the cities are dense and skyscrapers appear, the domicile of people in the outer suburbs turns from bungalows made of soil to buildings and villas. What's more, the individual rural villas are mainly located along the traffic lines outside the villages. Roads connecting the villages, counties and towns are smooth and covered with concrete, formulating convenient traffic networks in the rural areas. Some entertainment facilities in the cities gradually appear in the rural areas, which accelerates the integration of the urban and rural areas.

7.3.4. *Change in way of living*

The employment structure, income, consumption needs, cultural literacy, education, birth rate, mobility, sense of openness, values, way of life, etc., in the cities are quite different from those in the rural areas. During urbanization, urban civilization and urban way of life expand and permeate to the rural areas around the cities and towns. Especially, the gathered and expanded flow of people, goods, capital and information heavily influences the social psychology and social behavior of residents in the rural communities, pushing their way of thinking and behavior toward modern civilization and break through the habit of interaction linked by bloodline and location to establish modern way of interaction. Villagers are getting rid of the shackles of traditional customs of production and living and are enhancing their democratic and legal awareness and self-consciousness through

[7]Liu Liming (2004). Discussion on characteristics of Chinese rural landscape and its planning objectives and contents. *Ecology and Environment*, 13(3), 445–448.

acquiring new ideas and new skills to become the major players in the market and owners of fortune. At the same time, with the improvement of urban environment and the constant progress in material civilization, people are not only satisfied with having roofs over their heads and full stomachs, but have higher pursuits for spiritual enjoyment such as tours and vacation. Crowded and noisy artificial landscapes will not satisfy the need of urban residents for a quiet, fresh and comfortable environment and for nature. More and more urban residents choose rural tours combining viewing agricultural sceneries, agricultural production, farming activities, leisure and vacation. It has become a fashionable way of life of the urban residents.

7.4. Strategy for Sound Rural Development

7.4.1. *Careful formulation of rural development planning to depict a blueprint of modern rural development*

Planning goes ahead of construction, and the level of planning directly influences the rural development. Rural construction is a long-term historical task going through the whole process of modernization, which requires planning beforehand. The process of planning is also one that coordinates resources from various parties to reach a consensus, make joint efforts and for agglomerative effect to reduce and eliminate irrational investments.

First, the overall planning of county economic and social development should include rural construction planning. We should not only take into consideration the rural development, but also urbanization. Construction of infrastructure, featured industries and welfare undertakings should be carefully designed to promote new house construction, ancillary facilities and comprehensive environment treatment.

Second, the rural areas should be planned as a whole guided by a general blueprint, the specialized planning such as industry, agriculture, service sector, social undertakings and integrated land utilization should be improved, and the layout of farmland, gardens and development zones, agricultural structure and urbanization system should be decided. The credit evaluation of rural construction projects should be conducted comprehensively in order to prevent and address the credit risks of low returns, high risks and long periods of the public welfare projects, and to push forward the public construction of the rural areas on condition of general profitability. The guidance of planning, in terms of industries, will grant agriculture not only the economic value, but also ecological value; in terms of spatial distribution, it will make the market towns more like satellite towns and make villages more like the new type of villages. If the banks could keep risks under control, they may fund non-profit or partially for-profit projects such as health, education, roads, water supply and sewage, etc., and be paid back by the latter in the future. Thus, not only can we avoid problems such as the discontinuation of the pre-construction caused by insufficient fund of a certain region, but also be able to offer better public services to the people.

Third, planning for rural construction should follow the "four principles" and deal with the "six relationships". Four principles include enhancing industrial support to sustain the development, giving play to regional characteristics to showcase the diversity of the landscape, strengthening environmental impact valuation to integrate the architecture with the environment, and popularizing public facilities to share modern infrastructure with everyone. Six relationships to be dealt with include the relationship between environmental protection and utilization in selection of the construction site; the relationship between centralization and decentralization when planning about the layout, the relationship between local features and diversity in designing, the relationship between interaction and privacy in spatial design, the relationship between efficiency and fairness in public services, and the relationship between short-term and long-term development in designing administrative support.

Fourth, while highlighting the indices for material construction when planning for rural construction, we should also stress market construction. It should combine systematic financing planning with project construction proposals and solve the problems of "how to conduct" and "where to get money". Thus the implementation of the planning can be built upon a secure and steady basis with financial guarantee and kept in line with the overall planning and future profit.

7.4.2. *Properly handle the relationship between urbanization and rural development*

First, an equal and mutually beneficial operational mechanism for the urban and rural areas should be established. We should optimize resource allocation and allow the equal and reasonable flow of factors of production between urban and rural areas. The public services in urban and rural areas should be equally promoted to provide equal public services to rural residents as those provided to the urban residents. The supply of public services and products for urban and rural areas should be balanced to promote the infrastructure, public services and public finance in the rural areas to guarantee equal rights, opportunities and services for urban and rural residents. The fiscal expenditure structure should be adjusted to enhance investments in education, health, culture, ecological environment, infrastructure and social security, etc., in the rural areas so as to establish and perfect the rural social security mechanism step by step, and realize the full coverage of social welfare and social security including new rural cooperative medical system, the subsistence allowances and endowment insurance, etc.

Second, the urban–rural integration mechanism should be innovated. We should continue to adjust relations of production while improving the superstructure, conduct reforms in the cities and also in the villages, drive up the momentum of the rural areas while prioritizing the external environment, balance urban and rural reform with institutional innovation, and guard and promote the integrated development of the urban and rural areas with institutional construction. We should stabilize and improve the basic operational mechanism in the rural areas to ensure the stability of the land contract relationship in the long term. We should improve the agricultural support and protection mechanism to guarantee stable growth of agricultural investment and formulate protection mechanism on the price of agricultural products.

Third, we should make efforts to promote the integrated development of the urban and rural areas. The planning and layout should be integrated to balance the room for urban and rural developments. Division among industries should be considered on the whole to eliminate the alienation and opposition between the urban and rural areas. The service functions of the urban and rural areas should be integrated to encourage integration in all aspects including employment, education and health, etc., in the urban and rural areas. The urban and rural society should progress as a whole to balance the material, spiritual, political, cultural and ecological construction. Urban areas should lead rural areas, and rural areas can support urban areas. The combination and complementation of the advantages of the urban and rural areas can further drive up the rapid development of the integration of the urban and rural areas.

7.4.3. *Develop rural economy with special features by capitalizing on local advantages*

Featured industry in the rural areas is an important industry related to many fields such as agriculture, industry and communications. It is not only an important component of rural economy, but also the most vibrant element. Developing featured industry in the rural areas can heighten the overall quality of economy and competitiveness in the rural areas. Featured industry in the rural areas is the kind that is the most suitable for industrialization, commercialization and the market. Especially, the featured industry in the rural areas marked with rural geological features can help significantly increase the additional value of products. These products with distinctive design and packaging can lengthen the industrial chain of the products through logistics transportation, advertisement and marketing so as to win better economic profit. The development of rural featured industry can directly improve and change the situation that Chinese rural economy is in; "an inferior position in terms of division of labor on the industrial chain of international economy". Rural featured products are specific products rooted in their original birthplace. Local people are the best human resources with understanding of these products. Especially, many rural featured industries only require simple and repetitive skills. Its low requirement on the employees' education suits most farmers. Successful development of rural featured industries can effectively improve employment of local farmers, increase farmers' income, reduce poverty in rural population and social conflicts and improve social harmony.

7.4.4. *Building the school district to innovate the rural social management mechanism*

As the "county-centered" management mechanism is established, and the layout of middle schools and primary schools is adjusted in the rural areas, the original mechanism with the central school in the county or town as the first-tier management organ of the rural education can no longer meet the needs for balanced development of the compulsory education. It is, therefore, imperative that the central school in a school district instead of the central school in a county or town serve as management within a town. Taking counties as the major unit, a three-level management mechanism including the administrative organs in education on the town level, the central school in a school district should be established to promote the balance development of the compulsory education within the towns and counties.

First, division of school districts. Within a town, according to the administrative division, we can divide a school district based on elements such as population distribution, location of schools, economic and cultural foundation, development of education, coverage of high-quality educational resources and the prospective scale of local education, etc. A school district can be about 2 km by radius, covering 3–5 big administrative villages or 7–8 small administrative villages with a population of around 20,000 persons. Each school district can establish a central school, which can be a nine-year system school or a primary school; meanwhile, other schools which are also offering compulsory education will no longer assume the roles of legal persons. Instead, the rest schools and village primary schools will become affiliates or teaching branches to the central school of the school district.

Second, coordinated development. We should take into consideration the future changes in birth and improve the adjustment and planning for the distribution of local middle schools and primary schools. For the schools unsuitable for the construction of the school district and with an obvious small scale, we can make proper adjustments under the condition that students be enrolled properly.

Third, innovated and improved management mechanism of school districts. We should strengthen the interior management of school districts and the quality of the teaching staff and education. Without changing the present institution of primary schools and junior high schools and taking the service zone of rural junior high schools as a unit, we will establish a mechanism with primary schools and junior high schools link together within the service zone. We should appropriately deal with the relationship between the school district, the incumbent town government and village self-governance associations to fully exercise their duties in supporting schools and encouraging the smooth construction of school districts.

7.4.5. *Strengthen financial services to promote the rural land shareholding system*

The rural land shareholding system is a further division of contractual operational right of land from land ownership based on their division under household contract system. Pursuant to the basic principles of shareholding and cooperation, the farmers' contractual operational right of land will be turned into stock equity to establish cooperatives without changing the prerequisite of land contractual operational right of land. Farmers will entrust cooperatives to operate, and benefit from the returns according to their proportionate share of equity. This form of operation is conducive to expand the scale of land operation and raise the utilization rate of land.

First, the reform of land property right system should be enhanced. Land property right relationship should be regulated, and the property right relationship between the country, the community and farmers should be scientifically and rationally defined. We should further clarify the rights of farmers in land contracting, and separate land ownership from the right to occupy, use, benefit from and dispose of the land. Under the condition that the rural land ownership is owned by the farmers as a whole, we should grant more rights over the land contracted and operated by the farmers, such as pledge, transfer, lease and inheritance.

Second, the shareholding system should be regulated and improved. We should clearly define the economic nature, distribution of stock right, rights and obligations of members of the cooperatives, institutional structure and their functions, distribution of the revenue and the financial systems, etc. We should adhere to the market-oriented operation and clarify the rights and responsibilities to establish the modern corporate system. Democratic management should be strengthened and relevant mechanisms should be improved to ensure the security of the stock equity of farmers who become shareholders with their land so as to address any concerns of the members of the cooperatives.

Third, financial credit and loan support should be enhanced. Financial institutions should set reasonable prices in the principle of equality of risks and returns to set different rates to meet the need for loans on different risk levels and reasonably lengthen the term for loans. They should be creative in the kinds of credit and loans, and offer loans in forms of mortgage (such as the transferable operational right of the land and large-scale agricultural use production equipment), pledge (such as stock equity) and credit (such as block credit facility and entrepreneurial leader for cooperatives). The risk sharing mechanism for land transfer loans should be established, including improving agricultural insurance system and rural credit guarantee system to build up a shield against risks for financial support of land transfer.

7.4.6. *Significantly develop agricultural technology to support modern agriculture*

We should take scientific and technological progress as our fundamental drive and increase investment in agricultural science and technology so as to formulate a national agricultural scientific and technological innovation system with reasonable distribution, mature functions, efficient operation and powerful support. The leading role of science and technology in supporting agricultural development and improving people's livelihood should be fully exercised to improve the regional distribution of featured agricultural products and scale production. We should pay special attention to the promotion and application of advanced and suitable technology in land, water and other aspects of the environment, and develop sustainable agriculture with high yield, fine quality, and high efficiency. We should highlight the advantages and features of the agriculture as an industrial system, and encourage and support social capital to participate in the development of vegetable industry. We should improve our processing capability, build up brands, expand the market, and increase farmers' income through various channels.

7.4.7. *Strengthen rural infrastructure construction to enhance people's living and educational quality*

First, we should improve the rural traffic infrastructure and realize the full coverage of asphalt or concrete roads in rural areas as soon as possible. We should further our efforts in safeguarding the hygiene of drinking water in the rural areas with special attention to that in the remote and far away areas and areas in poverty.

Second, we should further establish the power grid construction in the rural areas to meet the needs of production and life in the rural areas. Information construction in the rural areas should be enhanced to fully utilize the modern network technology and integrate information resources related to agriculture for the construction of the comprehensive information service platform for agriculture. We should further the rural energy construction in the rural areas to lead the renovation with rings, toilets and stoves in the rural areas.

Third, we should improve the environmental construction of the living environment of the rural areas. We will focus on solving the prominent issues such as roads in the villages, water supply and sewage, garbage treatment, cohabitation of people and livestock and pollution in agricultural production, etc., to improve the living conditions of the farmers. We should make efforts to continue the renovation of dilapidated houses in the rural areas and construction of new-style residence for a tidier and cleaner environment and fine, healthy and harmonious living conditions for the rural residents.

Fourth, we should reinforce the infrastructure for education, cultural and public health in the rural areas to promote the development of social undertakings such as education, health care and culture, etc. Students should be educated, the aged supported, the sick treated, and there should be housing provided to everyone. The minimum standard of living, maintenance of households enjoying five guarantees, endowment insurance, public health system should be established and improved, and the residents' awareness of health and environmental protection should be enhanced. We should also meet the requirements of rural residents for education, health care and entertainment to enrich the spiritual life in the rural areas. We should improve skill trainings and develop vocational education in the rural areas.

7.4.8. *Advance the development of rural democracy to improve peasants' democratic and legal awareness*

We should lead the farmers to participate in the democratic election, decision-making, management and supervision so that the related knowledge and skills can be applied and experienced in the democratic practices and become a part of the life experience and habit of the farmers. We should improve the mechanisms such as "discussion on each single case", disclosure of village affairs and democratic supervision, etc., to guarantee the farmers exercise their democratic rights pursuant to the law, and allow farmers the right to manage their own affairs in the village.

7.5. Summary

Rural areas are rural communities comprised of market towns and many surrounding villages with farmers and agriculture as the major players, and a regional system including rich contents such as economy, society and ecology. The rural land is regarded as the hometown of human beings. Chinese people with thousands-of-years of farming civilization have special feelings toward the rural areas. Putting the issues in the villages against the economic and social background of the rural areas can facilitate the design of policies in a systematic manner, and promote the economic and social development in the rural areas comprehensively and endogenously.

In the 21st century, three major transformations will take place in the rural areas in China: First, the transformation from historical and traditional rural areas to those combining tradition and modernity; second, Chinese farmers will be transformed to rural citizens with modern awareness; third, Chinese agriculture will be transformed to an industry with 20–30 mu as the major category of scale and diversified operation with a certain level of modern technology.

Rural construction will remain a difficult and complex task of strategic significance in the long run. For a long time, the rural areas have made significant contribution to urbanization and industrialization. In the new era, it should not remain a slogan for the urban areas to feed the rural areas, and the rural areas to feed agriculture. Rather, it should be put into action. The government should play the leading role to coordinate and integrate the relationships between various parties, and make efforts to create the atmosphere in the whole society to care for, support and participate in the construction of the rural areas so as to open up a new scene where the urban and rural areas facilitate each other and become mutually prosperous. The government should provide necessary financial support for the rural construction by reforming the financial distribution system through shifting the target of concessions to the rural areas, including rural infrastructure investment and establishment of rural public service system. The government should enhance the management of the funds for assisting agriculture and increase the efficiency for using the capital. Various industries should give full play to the leading role of the cities in improving the rural development based on their distinctive features and enhance the influence of the urban economy on the rural areas. The measures include supporting modern agricultural development, assisting the development of farmers' specialized collective organizations, aiding the processing and sales of agricultural and sideline products, supporting tourism in the rural areas and promoting "One Village One Product", etc. At the same time, the government could facilitate the development of social welfare through assisting the rural areas building schools, clinics, recreational room and venues for physical activities, etc.

In order to implement the strategic deployment of the central government for new countryside construction and formulate the mechanism and philosophy of rural development, we need to probe into the financing model supporting rural development, and facilitate the transfer of rural area from the "historical and natural" development to "planned and guided" development, from "passive" development to "active" development, and to expedite the transfer of its development mode from "blood transfusion" to "making blood", and from "natural and scattered" development to "relatively concentrated community".

CHAPTER 8

NEW-TYPE HOUSEHOLD MANUFACTURING AND NEW-TYPE URBANIZATION

The new family of manufacturing industry is the product of new technology revolution. Conveniently seizing the opportunity of new technology revolution may provide important industry support for the healthy development of China's urbanization. Using digital tools, through the Internet, and logistics network will connect creative production and services, manufacturing a new type of family, likely to the traditional craft combined with modern technology, the innovation idea combined with the actual manufacturing, the large- and medium-sized cities combined with a distribution of a wide range of small towns, the construction of small towns and rural development, the combination of the local resources and the global market, will promote the coordinated development of industrialization, informatization, urbanization and agricultural modernization.

8.1. Proposal of the Topic

As the third Industrial Revolution is making breakthroughs, if China seizes the opportunity, it may provide important industrial support to healthy urbanization. Industries not only put up stages for population gathering, but also offer momentum for urban prosperity. Industries and urbanization are mutually supporting. During the process of industrial restructuring and upgrade, large-scope manufacturing featuring high consumption of land and resources is not necessarily the industrial development direction of urban areas; industries seriously polluting the environment and health do not comply with the requirements of healthy urbanization. A high-quality modernized urban area not only absorbs traditional industries in line with requirements of the area, but also needs new industries along with the development trend. New-type household manufacturing comes into shape under digitized, intelligent and network-based technologies. It may combine traditional techniques with modern technologies, innovative concepts with practical manufacturing, large- and medium-sized cities with widely distributed small villages and towns, development of small villages and towns with rural development, and local resources with global market, so as to provide industrial support for healthy development of new-type urbanization. The article analyzes the key content and features of new-type household manufacturing, studies its potential and trend, and discusses the development mode required by urbanization in China, and proposes policy measures to accelerate development of new-type household manufacturing.

8.2. Overview of New-Type Household Manufacturing

8.2.1. *Definition*

New-type household manufacturing, also named "desk factory", "mini manufacturing", "new-type household handicraft" and "new handicraft", refers to the new-type handicraft manufacturing that uses digital tools and connects innovative ideas, production and service through Internet and logistic network in the workshop of households. Handicraft here means using technologies such as three-dimensional (3D) printing to "customize" products so as to reflect proper changes and meet the demand of customers.

New-type household manufacturing uses 3D printers as the major tool. 3D printers are the important achievement of revolutionary breakthrough in science and technology. The 3D printing technology uses cohesible materials such as metal powder or plastics to construct objects through printing layer-by-layer on the basis of digital module files. It is being gradually applied in product manufacturing, such as jewelry, shoes, hip joint, tooth, accessories and parts of airplanes and automobiles. Back in 1989, S. Scott Crump in the US successfully developed the early-stage 3D printing technology, namely, the fused deposition modeling. In 1995, Jim Bredt and Tim Anderson, graduates of Massachusetts Institute of Technology (MIT), coined the term "3D Printing". In 2003, MIT professor Neil Gershenfeld opened the course of "mini manufacturing"; the British government established the world's first mini manufacturing laboratory in Manchester, the cradle of the first Industrial Revolution. In 2007, the first-generation desk 3D printers were invented in the Unites States, embarking on a brand-new future for desk factory, whose influence was no less than that of the first PC 30 years ago. PhD Adrian Bowyer from the University of Bath initiated the Replicating Rapid-prototyper (RepRap) open source project, which promoted the movement of 3D printers into households. On 25 January 2011, French sculptor Gael Langevin made a life-size robot by using a 3D printer at the cost of only USD800. In February 2011, the famous economics magazine "The Economist" published an article titled as "How Does 3D Printing Change the World". By the end of 2011, venture capitalists have injected USD10 million respectively in the 3D printer manufacturer MarkerBot, 3D printing service provider Shapeways and the "crowd funding" website Kichstarter. In 2012, the US under Obama administration formulated a new national policy, stipulating that mini manufacturing labs will be built in 1,000 universities and colleges in four years with digital manufacturing tools such as 3D printers and laser cutting machines furnished, and the new generation of manufacturing engineers will be cultivated. The 3D printers may "print" a new era, and the new-type household manufacturing is arousing world-wide attention.

8.2.2. *Features*

New-type household manufacturing is the important achievement of revolutionary breakthrough in science and technology, and is featured by digital tools, household workshop, shared use, delicacy production, network-based connection and socialized operation. Digital tools: Just by a slight click, you will be able to use digital tools to establish factories, control production tools, combine ideas and business, design on the screen and produce models and products with 3D printers. The real world and the virtual world can be switched anytime, and the process of manufacturing products takes more resemblance to making up figures. The process of drawing up 3D objects on the computer screen is indeed the process of writing mathematic formulas corresponding to the product design. The formulas describe not only the shape of the product, but also its physical performance and form, such as flexibility and hardness, electric conduction and heat insulation, and lubricity and coarseness. Symbol analysts become manufacturing engineers, and digital products are exerting more influence on physical manufacturing. Household workshop: Without a fat investment in factories and recruitment of labor force, you just need good ideas and a small number of equipments such as a credit card, a computer and a 3D printer to start up a manufacturing company in your bedroom or an empire in your dormitory. Shared use: People who startup businesses can easily find reference materials they need *via* the search engine, and the gains fully reflect the general trend of knowledge sharing. Such convenience is impossible to enjoy if all inventions are hidden. Delicacy production: Customized and small-batch production embodies individuality and reality. It usually focuses on the niche market. The focus of production is on products suitable for small-batch desk production and those not produced by large factories such as parts of vintage cars and fashionable stickers for Apple Mac computers by using computer-controlled CD burners. Network-based connection: Through network configuration, ideas, raw materials and services can be selected worldwide, and products can be manufactured either through desk factory or by other companies after forwarding requirements to them *via* design document standards. People who startup businesses do not need to wait for orders, compete with cheap labor force or provide products to dealers. They just need invent products and foster their own brand to become a seller at large-sized network platforms (e.g., Etsy) or directly sell products to global buyers *via* their own website. Socialized operation: Manufacturing new products is no longer the specialty of a small group of people, but an opportunity for most people. Therefore, everyone can have a try. Through connection and cooperation *via* Internet, more people can be drawn to participate in to generate more ideas and form the "maker movement". Such new-type household manufacturing can initiate the bottom–up innovative activities, and its way of distribution is not a traditional compound pattern of large industrial chains and industrial regions, but the physical geographic pattern that reflects ideas of people starting up business. This materializes new features of production socialization.

8.2.3. *Market*

New-type household manufacturing is the advanced form of specialized division in market economy. Adam Smith mentioned in Wealth of Nations that a society can develop better through specialized division. New-type household manufacturing enables resource allocation worldwide, delicacy production and customized sales, and symbolizes that specialized division of market economy comes into a new stage.

New-type household manufacturing complies with humanity and the advanced mode of organizational behaviors. The ultimate objective of production is not maximized profit but maximized value. While seeking basic life guarantee, people value products for which their ideas are adopted and individualized commodities to a greater degree. Engagement and participation makes people feel more satisfied and happier.

New-type household manufacturing better meets the market requirement for individualized delicacy development. Large-scale production of manufacturing enterprises is neither an inevitable road nor the ending point of product manufacturing reform. With new technologies, companies using handicraft and flexible equipments will play a bigger role in modern life. The new-type household manufacturing industry, based on high-tech digital manufacturing, effectively combines local resources (including ideas) with global market and traditional handicraft culture with Internet culture, and materializes real product digitally designed and printed with 3D printers. It endows ordinary people new opportunities, new approaches and new abilities, and is able to provide the market with more finer and better products and services.

New-type household manufacturing helps create more jobs. Traditional manufacturing generally requires large input at the initial stage and faces difficulty in development due to high labor cost. Take the US for instance. In a certain period of time, it had to transfer manufacturing largely to countries and regions with low labor cost. The manufacturing industry is the last choice for Americans when they try to get employed, and the absolute number of employees in the US manufacturing industry takes the smallest proportion in total labor population of the US in the world. The new opportunities for revitalization of new-type household manufacturing industry is flexible and elastic, helps create jobs, and brings it to the US manufacturing industry and also to China.

8.2.4. *Representatives of new-type and traditional household manufacturing*

The representative of traditional household manufacturing is Spinning Jenny invented by a British weaver James Hargreaves in the 1760s and named after his daughter. This is the earliest hand-powered multiple spinning machine, which can be easily made at low cost and takes up space only as large as a desk. Applicable at home, it is equipped with eight spindles and can weave multiple threads of yarn at the same time, boasting efficiency eight times that of old-fashioned weavers. In some sense, Spinning Jenny is the "desk manufacturing" at that time. It can be operated at home, brings higher income than outdoor work, consolidates the core family system, creates better living and work environment for children, and promotes the rapid growth of British population in history. Such household manufacturing frees more ordinary people from land, enables them to be more independent financially, terminates the agricultural age in the British history, and promotes the development of villages and towns. Such household handicraft not only is a form of industrial production, but also promotes the combination between tradition and fashion. Some valuable lace manufacturing techniques are carried forward and have become an important part of the first Industrial Revolution.

The representative of new-type household manufacturing in the world is the modern 3D printing company that two MIT graduates Jim Bredt and Tim Anderson founded in 1995 on the basis of renovating ink-jet printers. Such manufacturing only requires small investment and a small labor force, and you can record a best-selling album simply in bedroom. It enables people to control means of production again, and can easily translate ideas into reality.

Despite the many differences between new-type and traditional household manufacturing, both reserve the feature of "customer-tailored" service in nature. Customized service existed in the early market, and is and will be after by people at present and in the future. Though traditional and new-type household manufacturing appear in different historical stages, they both embody the power of the mass, which features the mass participation, satisfaction of demands by tools, evaluation of ideas, improvement of tools, unique power by making the best use of tools, creation of the most tasteful products and contribution to social progress.

8.2.5. *Historical foundations of new-type household manufacturing*

Traditional household manufacturing benefited from the historical conditions of the first Industrial Revolution. The Renaissance in Europe laid the cultural foundation for the Industrial Revolution and manufacturing development. A series of patents and policies & regulations not only stimulated the inventions of craftsmen, but also gave impetus to share the inventions with others. The strategic adjustment of Britain from resorting to military force to control the world, to monopolizing the world by relying on trade was the political foundation of the Industrial Revolution in Europe. The use of steam engines and Spinning Jenny as well as continuous input of cotton and other raw materials from India and Egypt offered technical and material conditions for the revolution. Relaxed regulations and sufficient land in

Britain and other European countries and convenient traffic provided necessary space and contact channels with the outside world for modern manufacturing in Europe. Manufacturing development not only requires efficient production but also requires outbound shipment of the finished products; an urban area with space for industrial expansion must have convenient transportation. Of course, what's more important is that household manufacturing provides social progress with more benefits than harms, which is the internal condition for its rapid development. Despite such bad outcomes of the Industrial Revolution as hard work and long work hours, for which the British poet William Blake in the 18th century called "Satanic Mills", achievements of the industrialization were dominant. People migrated from countryside to urban area and from thatched shacks to brick buildings; as health conditions were improved, from 1800 to now, the average life expectancy of male Caucasians in the West was doubled from 38 to 76.

Now, new-type household manufacturing benefits from wide application of the latest technological achievements in the social and economic progress besides the fruits of previous Industrial Revolutions. Along with the technological progress, new technologies keep changing traditional industries and cause traditional manufacturing toward decay, but also create conditions for return and revitalization of traditional manufacturing in the new age. For instance, in Manchester, the cradle of the first Industrial Revolution, people still recollect their past, when the city was the largest industrial city in the world, but now it is nothing but a decayed place. Some workshops stand there, waiting to molder, and give the city a tint of waste. Some buildings attracted investors' interest during the real estate bubble, but ended up in nothing due to lack of new manufacturing, and stand in embarrassment between the past and the future. Unemployed young people camp up in the empty old workshops, play music and put up labels of recordings, seeming to tell people the possible prospect of re-emerging industrial design and engineering. However, the long-hovering unemployment and despair among the youth are like the reprobation for the remnant industry. In order to resume the glory of Manchester, Britain took the opportunity of the third Industrial Revolution and set up the world's first "mini manufacturing lab" here.

8.2.6. *Prospect of new-type household manufacturing in China*

China enjoys a long history of household manufacturing. During the Spring and Autumn and Warring States Period, China already had treadle looms, which freed hands of weavers from lifting. With hands now used in picking and beating-up, each weaver can weave 0.3–1 meter of cloth each hour, greatly improving the productivity. In the Song and Yuan Dynasties, on the basis of various existing weaving machines, water-driven spinning machine was invented. It had dozens of spindles, and was a major invention of applying natural force into weaving machinery in ancient China. The invention was over four centuries ahead of the West. During the long development of the feudal economy, China's handicraft economy such as porcelain making, pottery, weaving, sculpture and painting reached the height of glory, and made important contribution to development of human civilization. The Chinese people, not short of originality and wisdom, can create more handicraft products to meet the demand of social progress when conditions allow. Facing global economic integration and Internet technology advance, China can fully use the latest scientific and technological achievements like other developed countries, build environment and conditions suitable for new-type household manufacturing through innovation and mechanism building, and promote progress of new-type household handicraft in China. It can not only provide jobs to youths in the countryside, but also explore new approaches for economic growth and accelerate urban modernization.

8.3. Development Mode of New-Type Household Manufacturing

8.3.1. *Technical operation mode*

The technical operation process of new-type household manufacturing is the process of information being translated into materials and also the process of materials being translated into information. Since the minimum unit of information measurement is byte and that of material constitution is atom, the translation process is also the switch

Table 8.1: Basic equipment and price.

Equipment	Price in 2013 (RMB10,000)	Evaluated price in 2015 (RMB10,000)	Evaluated price in 2020 (RMB10,000)
3D printer	0.3–3	0.2–2	0.15–2
Numerical control machine	2.2–100	2–100	1.2–100
Laser cutting machine	1.2–158	1–140	1–130
3D scanner	5.9–100	4.5–80	3–80

Source: Market investigation by author, 2012.

between byte and atom. Technicians adopt the concept of digital collaborative design to change the design procedure and improve manufacturing efficiency. Through "reality capture", or object scanning, point cloud consisting of points is generated, and then connected into polygon network structure through software design, and at last the 3D structure is designed and revised on the screen.

As Table 8.1 shows, currently several printers are available in the market. Other related equipment, such as numerical control machines, laser cutting machines and 3D scanners, is relatively mature in technology. As the equipment technology is further improved and widely applied, their market prices will gradually be accepted by ordinary startup households.

8.3.2. *Operational management mode*

8.3.2.1. *Spirit of "hybrid inventing"*

The most noticeable advantage and unique quality of the new-type household manufacturing industry are digital information. Original design doesn't necessarily start from scratch, but can draw inspiration from existing documents on the Internet or re-interpret existing products. Revision of existing ideas in combination of oneself and local conditions can yield products of "hybrid inventing" and embody the spirit of innovation. "Hybrid inventing" explores various possible changes of a certain product, keeps improving the product, and promotes it as soon as possible *via* the Internet. This is the key to the development of new-type household manufacturing. Given the variety of changeable elements in the world and the unlimited forms of changes, "hybrid inventing" enjoys boundless potential.

8.3.2.2. *Principle of "self-selection, self-modification, self-production and self-sales"*

In the process of scanning with 3D technology, revising with Computer-aided design (CAD) software, printing with 3D printers and selling *via* Internet, product design does not mean making drawings but the mathematic formula of the product. Each product has its corresponding algorithm. The more changes in the form, the higher quality of the product; the greater changes are, the more complicated the algorithm is.

8.3.2.3. *Basic quality of people involved*

First, entrepreneurship is required, which takes ideas, originality and patience. Second, certain knowledge on computer, network operation and software is needed. Third, understanding on local resources and preference for local handicraft are preferable. Fourth, some experience with the real economy is better. Fifth, understanding on traditional culture and network culture is required to improve the cultural taste of the new-type household manufacturing.

8.3.2.4. *Mode of market operation*

A relatively unique mode of market operation for the new-type household manufacturing is taking shape, which is "originality first to cater to the niche market; locally based operation and global configuration; supply–demand balance and winning with uniqueness".

"Originality first to cater to the niche market" means there must be original ideas for not the public but a specific niche market to meet special market demand.

"Local-based operation and global configuration" mean that full consideration of local elements is required to embody uniqueness. Meanwhile, large-sized free-of-charge classified websites (such as craigslist) can be resorted to in order to look for components at the reasonable price. If necessary, some components such as welding can be outsourced.

"Supply–demand balance and winning with uniqueness" refer to the fact that the new-type household manufacturing does not attract customers with low price, but maintains sustained development through reasonable price negotiation while providing satisfactory products to customers. Focused on the niche market for customized products, products themselves are the basis of relatively high price. Those customers who have unique taste and know exactly what they prefer usually are ready for higher price.

8.3.2.5. *Pricing of products*

Three factors should be considered for the reasonable pricing: First, cost, including labor cost, materials, and postage etc.; second, profit margin, usually 50% to make up for the unexpected extra cost during startup, including extra insurance cost; third, profit of retailers, generally a 50% profit margin reserved for third-party retailers. Therefore, new handicraft products are roughly priced 2.5 times costlier, which is still considerably cheaper than traditional product price because concentric acquisition and wholesale are omitted. Traditional product price is usually four times the cost.

8.3.3. *Organizational system*

As Fig. 8.1 shows, new-type household manufacturing needs key contact and necessary support system and requires community cooperatives compatible with urban development. It involves personnel training, provision of equipment maintenance service, filing of demand and services, encouragement of innovation, and incentive for role models.

8.3.3.1. *New-type household manufacturing lab center*

If conditions and demand allow, community manufacturing lab centers can be set up in urban areas, where some large-sized

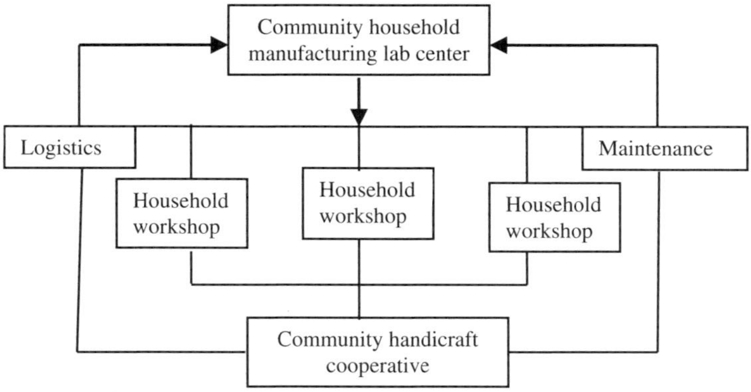

Figure 8.1: Organizational system of new-type household manufacturing.

manufacturing tools can be used to improve efficiency and elevate the innovation ability of communities. Complicated and large-scope processing can also be conducted here.

8.3.3.2. *New-type household manufacturing workshops*

Household workshops or desk factories can be set up in places where their features are suitable. These household workshops, free, energetic and joyful, allow entrepreneurs to tap fully into their potential and materialize their techniques and skills at most. The startups can be set at home, as long as they are covered by courier service network. Such new workshops are small in scale, unofficial and virtual in most cases, and most participants are not necessarily full-time workers of the companies. They are driven by ability and demand, rather than the subordinate relationship and responsibility. Therefore, such "loose combination of small units" is the free re-organization of powers for social development and a new type of industrial development mode. It greatly differs from traditional companies assumed by Ronald H. Coase. In such a new mode, various groups of people are not geographically limited, team up *via* Internet, and can make contributions anywhere in the world despite their educational background or employment status, as long as they have talent and ideas. Though trading cost is not minimized in such companies, people here truly work with others, who are of similar interest and vision. Such homogeneity of seeking people of similar interest *via* Internet is the new impetus of economic operation.

8.3.3.3. *Logistics support system*

Community manufacturing lab centers and the large number of household workshops are of globality at the first place since they usually provide services for cross-border customers and sell products online without being restricted by traditional distribution and regional layout. Therefore, a logistics support system needs to be established to support import and export of new-type household manufacturing products.

8.3.3.4. *Facility maintenance system*

Each urban community should be staffed with some full-time workers to provide facility maintenance services. This will be one of the responsibilities of the new-type urbanization management.

8.3.3.5. *New-type household manufacturing cooperatives*

These cooperatives are responsible for management of community household manufacturing, skill training, tutorial upgrade, web page update and evaluation and incentive.

8.3.3.6. *Eco-system of new-type household manufacturing*

The eco-system of new-type household manufacturing includes not only special customer groups but also other handicraft households and related entrepreneurs. They form different parts of the industrial chain, and the parts are mutually supporting and dependent to promote improvement of product quality. This will be the systematic support for success of the new-type household manufacturing and the true defensive advantage.

8.3.4. *"Crowd funding" mode*

"Crowd funding" refers to the process where the entrepreneurs post description of their project on websites to attract people who are interested and potential clients to fund the project.

8.3.4.1. *Features of "crowd funding"*

First, the investors are professional ones and also those interested in and the potential customers. Second, the ultimate objective of investment is not simply more capital but creation of a satisfactory new product. Third, amount of investment is not rigid, and therefore it's suitable for small private capital. Ways of crowd funding vary, such as donation, lease, and loans, etc. Investors not only fund a certain project, but may place orders for products when their investment exceeds a certain amount.

8.3.4.2. *Basic rules of "crowd funding"*

First, the lowest limit and deadline of project funding should be specified. If the lowest limit of capital cannot be raised by the deadline, the project funding plan should be abolished and the project cannot be launched. Second, compulsory implementation by the third party should be arranged. Project publicity and funding advertisement must be conducted on websites or the third party recognized by supervisors. If the project funding plan cannot be fulfilled, the fact that the investment cannot be embezzled before the deadline and validity period are met and that it is refunded to investors, must be ensured. Third, the system of incentive should be enacted. Incentives should be correspondingly granted to investors at different levels so that fund raisers can enjoy ownership and achievements of the project.

8.3.4.3. *Effects of "crowd funding"*

The "crowd funding" mode can address four problems for new-type household manufacturing. First, fund can be raised and available when it is needed. Second, fund-raising activities at designated time and in designated amount can solicit information on popularity of a product before it is developed and manufactured, which helps minimize risks. Third, specific customer groups are fostered. Fourth, concerning advertising and promotion, entrepreneurs and investors interact online, which helps mobilize more people to participate in product development.

8.4. Policy Measures

The CPC Central Committee and the State Council pay great attention to development of small and micro businesses, and have issued a series of fiscal, taxation and financial support policies. For instance, on 19 April 2012, the State Council issued Opinions concerning further supporting healthy development of small- and micro-businesses to guide development of the businesses. Given the differences between the new-type household manufacturing and traditional small and micro businesses, except for existing policies to be implemented such as national development fund for small and medium-sized enterprises, special funds and preferential taxation, it's necessary to formulate a set of targeted policy measures to support development of new-type household manufacturing.

8.4.1. *The state council issues guiding opinions to support development of the new-type household manufacturing*

First, to support new-type household manufacturing, it is included into national development strategy. The manufacturing's strategic position in the third Industrial Revolution and national development is confirmed, so as to reflect revolutionary breakthrough in science and technology, the industrial development and social transformation trend, support the development of the new-type household manufacturing, and promote economic growth toward delicacy development. Second, plans for new-type household manufacturing development, urban development and agricultural development are compiled to promote infrastructure building for the new-type industrialization, urbanization and agricultural modernization and enhance the supportive role of new-type industries for urban economic growth. Third, subjects of new-type household manufacturing and industrialization are greatly fostered. Efforts are made to tap into the role of government in organization and coordination, strengthen strategic design, deepen R&D of major technologies and materials, cultivate a group of leading enterprises with international competitiveness and micro manufacturing labs, and promote industrialization of key technologies such as 3D printing.

8.4.2. *National guide funds are established to support the development of the new-type household manufacturing*

Local investors, venture capital and other private capital are guided to support the new-type household manufacturing. Building of related financing service system and credit system is accelerated, and financing in a variety of forms such as intellectual property pledge, pledge by warehouse receipts, pledge by store operation right and pledge by commercial credit insurance policies is supported. The government arranges a certain proportion of annual procurement quota for the new-type household manufacturing. In combination with deepened taxation system reform, structural tax reduction policies are further improved and a supportive taxation system is established.

8.4.3. *The service system under which the entire society supports new-type household manufacturing is established*

First, the organization mechanism for international exhibitions for new-type household manufacturing is built to promote internationalized, market-based and specialized development of the industry. Second, the customs clearance system for the industry is established to increase customs clearance efficiency of new-type household manufacturing products and reduce clearance cost for logistics. Third, guide for brand building is strengthened and industrial standards and criteria are framed to fully tap into the supportive role of national quality inspectors and major labs and improve the quality assurance ability and specialized coordination level of new-type household manufacturing. Fourth, public platforms to serve the manufacturing are set up and improved to mobilize and optimize resource allocation, enhance service functions, further play the bridging role of industrial associations and improve industrial organization and self-discipline. Fifth, efforts are made to enhance guidance and policy evaluation and put into place and improve the systems of statistic surveys, monitoring and analysis and periodical issuance.

8.4.4. *The education and training mechanism for senior technicians is set up and improved*

First, the distribution structure of educational resources is adjusted. Technician college system is established on the basis of county-level economy to train people for the startup and provide educational support for new-type household manufacturing and urbanization. Second, new-type household manufacturing is guided to actively participate in highly-skilled talent rejuvenation plans to reinforce building of technician teams. Major talent projects such as the Professional and Technical Personnel Knowledge Update project should be tilted toward new-type household manufacturing. Third, technician training for the industry is unfolded, and social security policies for employees of the industry are improved.

8.4.5. *Intellectual property protection measures for the new-type household manufacturing are improved*

A set of incentive systems is established in full consideration of features of the new-type household manufacturing and network development. Reward is granted in corresponding amount with contribution to encourage more inventors to contribute their achievements.

8.4.6. *The role of development finance is played to support development of new-type household manufacturing*

First, efforts are made to coordinate with government departments to enhance policy study, draft national guide fund plans to support the new-type household manufacturing and provide reference for government decision-making. Second, in order to tap into the pioneering role of development finance, the systematic financing system and auxiliary input mechanism are established to enhance innovation in financing mode, develop financial products and support synergic development of the new-type household manufacturing and new-type urbanization.

8.5. Conclusion

The new-type household manufacturing is the result of wide application of new scientific and technological achievements in economic and social progress. It differs revolutionarily from traditional micro enterprises in terms of technical operation mode, operational management mode, fund raising mode and organizational system. This is a commercial Internet mode that creates market, and may form a new power in the grand environment of manufacturing to develop unique space for survival and prosperity. This emerging new power will break the industrial monopoly, change the pattern of manufacturing under a new era in industrial economy. China should seize the opportunity amid the current world trend and powerful strength of new technologies, fully tap into the role of latest scientific and technological achievements by considering the national conditions, especially the development requirement of new-type urbanization, and greatly support development of new-type household manufacturing. Such efforts can not only provide industrial support for new-type urbanization, but also boost employment, narrow down gaps between urban and rural areas and further tap into advantages of private resources. They play an important role in promoting economic growth and social stability and are of strategic significance for national economic and social development.

The next one or two decades will see robust development of new-type household manufacturing and also a key stage for urbanization in China. The country should take the opportunity to promote synergic development between new-type household manufacturing and urbanization. The prosperity of the new-type household manufacturing will undoubtedly lead to healthy urbanization.

CHAPTER 9

DEVELOPMENT-ORIENTED FINANCE BOOSTS SUSTAINABLE URBANIZATION

Urbanization is the history of agricultural civilization to industrial civilization process. Urbanization and industry need to cooperate beneficially; urban and rural areas need to develop coordinately; new and old towns need to support each other; reasonable layout should be formed between coastal areas and the eastern and western areas. The modern civilization should be realized by protection and development of traditions.

Urbanization is an inevitable trend of social and economic development, and a remarkable symbol of industrialization and modernization. For a long time, the CDB has been sticking in promoting China's urbanization through development finance and *via* market-based financing, made fruitful achievements, and played a significant role in optimizing the urban–rural layout. At present, China's urbanization meets the best opportunity ever. However, problems including irrational planning, resource and environment problems, inadequate public facilities, and unbalanced urban–rural development, still remain acute, which requires the guidance of the scientific outlook of development to appropriately deal with the relationship between tradition and modernity, urban and rural areas, coastal and western areas, and new and old towns, to further innovate systems and mechanisms, and to improve the mode of urbanization investment and fund-raising, for the sake of a urbanization mode featuring "rational layout, resource saving, coordinated development and advanced management".

9.1. International Urbanization Trend and China's Urbanization Development

9.1.1. *The trends and features of world urbanization*

Urbanization is a historical process in the transition from agriculture society and rural culture into industrial society and urban civilization. This process varies from stages in terms of timeliness and nations. Differences in national conditions, economic development and industrialization pace have resulted in great distinction in the urbanization mode of different countries.

In Britain, urban development and rural modernization took place basically at the same period. Driven by the Industrial Revolution in the late 18th century, the urban population in Britain jumped from 20% to 51% within nearly a century, making the country the first highly urbanized one in the world, and the first confronting "urban diseases" such as intensive growth of urban population, housing shortage, slum expansion, inadequacy of public sanitation facilities, environment pollution, and high crime rate. After that, the British government issued many regulations and took counter measures. Until the beginning of 20th century, "urban diseases" had been basically solved.

The United States was still a rural country after urbanization had been undertaken for a long time in Britain and other Western European countries. However, since 1860 urbanization in the US had been developing tremendously, rocketing to 51.2% in 1920. After the 1940s, due to the development of economy and popularity of automobiles, many urban population migrated towards suburbs, leading to the significant change of city layout in the US: It transformed from the original compact structure into multi-centered disperse structure, gradually forming a structure that city sprawled outward along the road lines with a low density. The low-density sprawl decreased the population density, bridged the gap among urban, suburb and rural areas. However, such "urbanization on wheels" also caused many problems, including: Large amount of forest and landing resources such as farmland had been wasted and the ecological environment had been harmed; individual housing was over-disperse, and the infrastructure in new residential areas were difficult to be set up; the development cost had been increased; old sectors in the city had been damaged and the infrastructure were not to be renewed, etc.

In Latin-America and Africa, many countries had been influenced by the notion of "prioritizing the development of big cities" advocated by Western scholars, believing that in order to alleviate one nation's poverty, the first step was to develop its large cities, and only large cities could provide adequate employment and foster agriculture modernization. Under such a background, a large number of rural population migrated into a few large cities. As a result of unemployment, slums sprouted and spread out largely, even accounting for 70% of the total landing for some cities. "Over-urbanization" grew worse and the quality of urbanization was low. Since the end of the 1990s, some Latin-American counties have started to solve over-urbanization problems, ranging from controlling the population growth, increasing the input to agriculture and rural areas, adjusting urban layout, and developing medium- and small-sized cities, etc.

Through the development of urbanization in varying countries and areas, we can see that the world urbanization develops with the following trends and shows following features:

First, sustainability becomes a significant subject of urbanization. It is unprecedented in the history of human development that at present there are over 50% of the population in the world living in urban areas. According to World Bank's prediction, the proportion will increase to 60% in 2020 and 80% in 2050. City consumes 75% of world energy resources and produces 80% of world greenhouse gas emission. Change in production and living style caused by urbanization leads to the sharp rise of per capita energy consumption and greenhouse gas emission, thus global climate change is becoming increasingly serious. It becomes a shared problem for nations to decrease the occupancy of natural resources as much as possible. The US and other countries with relatively high per capita resources are reflecting on their high land-occupancy and energy-consuming urbanization mode. In recent years, scholars have proposed "Smart Growth" and "Compact City" based on the principle of sustainable development and resource conservation. The concepts have gradually gained recognition from varying nations. At the World Economic Forum 2008 in Davos, mayors, regional directors, representatives in private enterprises from all over the world have advocated jointly the "Slim City Initiative", with the aim to build a platform for communication among cities and enterprises, support conservation of resources, energy and water, and focus on global topics such as sanitation and climate change.

Second, the coordinated development between town and country is the theme of urbanization. More than one hundred years ago, Ebenezer Howard, the British sociologist and founder of the modern urban planning, argued that town and country must be married, and out of this union would spring a new hope, a new life and a new civilization. This is the concept of the coordinated development between town and country. Town and country are essentially different and their complementary development requires the correspondingly differentiated planning and construction. In Latin-American countries, the "urban preference" in the investment policies has severely withered country and significantly enlarged the town–country gap. As a result, peasants swarm into towns, deteriorating the quality of urbanization and generating a large number of urban poor. On the contrary, Japan, Korea and other Asian countries with more population and less land take protective measures over agriculture, thus effectively avoiding the severe recession of country at the same time of the rapid development of urbanization. With the great improvement of living conditions, the rural areas show vigor and vitality. Most of the best resident environments recognized in the world recently are located in small towns and rural areas.

Third, the balanced development of cities and towns is the basic pattern of urbanization. According to the data from the relevant agencies of the United Nations, from the 1970s to 1990s, population of the towns with less than 500,000 population grew at the fastest rate (an average of 4.2%) while that of mega cities with more than 5 million population did at the slowest rate (an average of 2.3%). Of the world's urban citizens, 65% lived in small cities and towns. From the perspective of ecological economics, cities and towns, like trees, shrubs and herbs in a forest, will not comprehensively flourish unless they achieve the balanced development. Since the 1960s, counter-urbanization has occurred in the Western developed countries where a large number of population move from metropolises to suburbs, small cities, towns and rural areas. This shows that metropolises, although with concentrated energy incomparable to small cities and towns in terms of talent, information and capital, are finite in the carrying capacity of resources and environment, and the urban problems as a result of the unbridled development will inevitably move people outward. Without the balanced development of cities and towns, the "gradient" distribution of a range of socio-economic factors will not be achieved between urban and rural areas.

Fourth, combination of market-based and government-led development is the important condition for the health of urbanization. Most Western countries adopt the market-based urbanization with its scale, layout, function evolution and industrial division of cities resulting from the choice and action of the market. However, the urbanization totally boosted by market generates many problems. For example, the United States, a country with the most developed market economy, fails to offer effective guidance to urbanization. Excessive suburbanization, sparse outspread of cities, disordered urban construction and increasingly serious problems in spatial and social structure are attributed to the US government's insufficient guidance to the urbanization and urban development. On the contrary, the Western European countries, especially the United Kingdom, have solved the problems. While the rural labor force moves to cities and towns and alleviated the stress on employment and housing, a large population swarm in cities because the government regulates the urbanization by standardizing it with laws, controls its development with planning and accelerates the infrastructure construction, while the market mechanism plays its role.

9.1.2. *Achievements and challenges of China's urbanization*

In the past sixty years after the founding of the PRC, especially after the implementation of reform and opening up policies, China has undergone enormous changes in economy and society, highly reflected in the significant improvement of the urbanization. With the acceleration of industrialization, informatization and economic globalization, China is rapidly urbanized in a fast track of sustained high growth. It is reflected as follows.

9.1.2.1. *Rural labor force continues to move to cities, resulting in the unprecedented number of towns and urban population*

In the past 30 years after reform and opening up, China's urbanization rate has increased from 18% to 50%, with an average annual growth twice as much as that of the world in the same period (Fig. 9.1). There was a population of 666 million in cities and towns of China in 2010, with a net increase of 435 million. Considering the natural growth of cities and towns, at least 250 million people moved in and worked in industries, commerce and services, the secondary and tertiary industries. 653 cities are administratively designated, of which 111 are prefecture-level super-cities with more than 1 million population and 14 prefecture-level mega cities.

9.1.2.2. *The urban infrastructure is rapidly constructed, and the increasingly improved urban services are much more capable of supporting the economic development*

By the end of 2011, China's established cities had been 43,603.23 square kilometers in area, an increase of 4.86 times compared to 7,438 square kilometers in 1981. The per capita housing area in cities

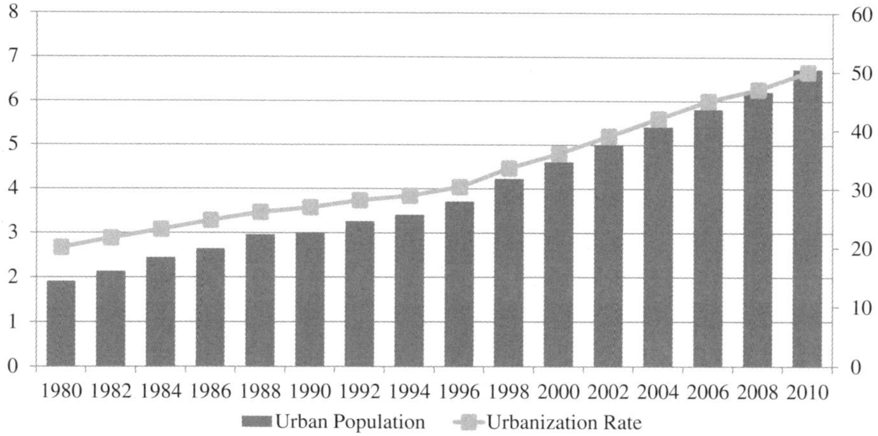

Figure 9.1: Urban population and urbanization rates of China, 1980 to 2010.

had soared from 6.7 square meters to 32.7 square meters, the urban roads had extended from 27,000 kilometers to 309,000 kilometers, and the urban infrastructure and public utilities such as water and gas supply, green space and sewage and waste disposal had been constantly upgraded. The investment environment had been further improved and comprehensive service function of the cities had been enhanced. Meanwhile, the urban infrastructure projects had been accomplished and put into use, which led to the development of relative industries and offered much greater support to the economic development.

9.1.2.3. *Urbanization has become the core force pushing forward the development of China's economy and society, and the quality of urban development has progressed steadily*

Cities and towns, as the carrier of China's economy and society, play an important role as the development center of national and regional society and economy. Today, 50% of the national industrial output, 70% of the gross domestic product (GDP), 80% of the national tax revenue, 85% of the added value of the tertiary industry and over

90% of higher education and scientific research institutions are concentrated in the administratively designated cities. The gross urban product and the per capita income keep growing at the rates of more than 10% for many years. When the denotation of cities and towns extends, great importance is also attached to the development of its connotation. The urban residents have enjoyed the greatly improved living conditions, educational opportunities and health care, unemployment and old-age security. With the growing economic and social effects, the quality of urban development improves steadily.

9.1.3. *Problems of China's urbanization*

Generally speaking, China's urbanization has made great achievements attracting the worldwide attention, but at the same time, we must recognize that some problems and contradictions still exist in the urbanization process. High attention should be paid to these problems and contradictions which restrict the healthy and sustainable development of urbanization.

9.1.3.1. *The urbanization is irrational in spatial layout, highlighting the shortage of resources and environmental problems*

The land is "urbanized" faster than population and the layout of spatial construction falls into disorder and even out of control. According to statistics, China's built-up urban area increased from 20,200 square kilometers in 1996 to 43,600 square kilometers in 2011 with an average annual growth rate of 7.7%, significantly higher than the growth rate (5.8%) of the urban population during the same period. Cities and towns have not fully drawn the population but the cake has been made too big. The low-density development pattern further deteriorates the shortage of land, and it is a tough situation to maintain 1.8 billion mu of arable land, a "red line" that must not be crossed. Moreover, excessive consumption of water, energy and other important resources causes pollution and deterioration of urban ecological environment, triggering serious social problems in some local areas. At present, 90% of urban waters and 65% of drinking water sources have been contaminated to different degrees. The centralized drinking water sources of half of key towns fail to meet the water intake standard and only 36% of the urban sewage undergoes treatment. The recurring blue-green algae incidents in Taihu Lake, Dianchi Lake and Chaohu Lake sound the alarm toward the disorderly expansion of urbanization.

9.1.3.2. *The urban constructions are not scientifically planned with insufficient infrastructure and urban development is lack of characteristics*

Many Chinese cities are formed by weaving several towns and the urban infrastructure construction, not holistically planned and coordinated with synthetic land utilization, cannot meet the need of economic and social development: The underground pipe network and infrastructure for environmental governance are time-worn and seriously overloaded in some cities; the backward road transport network of big cities results in the common failure of traffic congestion; the generally weak construction of comprehensive disaster prevention system and the imperfect urban public facilities of the emergency rescue mechanism impair the urban functions and increase the economic and social cost. Furthermore, the contradictions between construction and protection are increasingly highlighted in the vast and extensive urban construction. Many cities are similar in construction styles without unique features. Protection over natural, historical and cultural resources is neglected in some cities and towns. With "constructive" destructions frequently occurring, traditions of these cities are fading away.

9.1.3.3. *Cities are poorly managed and operated with imperfect social security systems*

The urban management and operational efficiency can hardly meet the needs of the citizens in utility services supplies such as water, gas, metro, public transport, in construction of social security systems in terms of education, employment and health care, and in building and supply of affordable houses for urban residents. Take housing for example; in recent years, the housing prices in major Chinese cities have generally risen sharply and the housing has become the primary problem confronted with urban low-income households. From 1998 to 2007, the area of China's newly built affordable houses accounted for only about 10% of the total new housing area in the country as a whole, showing an obviously inadequate investment and a serious imbalance between supply and demand. The imbalanced local finance impedes the development of low-rent housing system and the low-rent housing construction has just begun in the economically backward western regions.

9.1.3.4. *Uncoordinated urban–rural development widens the income gap*

The urban–rural income gap has been continuously enlarged in the country as a whole. According to statistics, from 1997 to 2011, the per capita net income of farmers of the whole country increased by only 4,887.2 Yuan, 29% of that of urban residents during the same period; the average annual per capita net income of the farmers of the whole country grew at a rate of 16.7%, 72.6% of that of the urban residents during the same period. The urban–rural income gap enlarged from 2.79 times in 2000 to 3.13 times in 2011. Considering some non-monetary factors in the income of urban residents such as housing, education, health care, social security and various other social welfares, the income gap between urban and rural residents was about four to six times. The then current consumption level of rural residents was just equivalent to that of the urban residents in the early 1990s, and that of many poverty-stricken areas was even lower.

9.2. Strategic Importance and Historic Mission of Urbanization

Constantly pushed forward by industrialization, China's urbanization will maintain the momentum of high speed in a long period of time. Provided the urbanization grows by one percentage point each year, it is expected that about 20 million rural people will move to cities and towns for living, education and employment. By 2020, China's population will have totaled 1.45 billion, of which the urban population will be 810 to 840 million, and the urbanization rate 56% to 58%. By then, China's society will have the majority of rural population qualitatively changed and the urban society will be gradually matured and shaped. By the middle of the 21st century, when China will become moderately developed modern country, the urbanization rate is expected to exceed 70% with more than one billion urban population, and China will become a highly urbanized country.

9.2.1. *Urbanization is the most important lever to achieve China's modernization and rejuvenation of the Chinese nation*

Now at the critical period of urbanization, China should coordinate the development of cities and towns and gradually upgrade urbanization, which are of great significance for expanding domestic demand, boosting the national economic growth, optimizing the urban and rural economic structure and promoting the virtuous cycle of national economy and coordinated social development. It can be said that urbanization is an inexhaustible impetus for China's economic growth and it is the most important lever to achieve China's modernization and rejuvenation of the Chinese nation. It was true in the past three decades, and so will it be in the next 50 years or the next century.

9.2.2. *Urbanization is the fundamental solution to issues concerning agriculture, countryside and peasants*

China is a large agricultural country with more than 800 million peasants. Issues concerning agriculture, countryside and peasants have always been the major problems perplexing China's economic development and social stability. Currently, there are about 300–400 million surplus rural labor force. Although the percentage of agriculture in GDP has fallen to 15%, the agricultural employment still accounts for as high as more than 50%. In the long run, problems about agriculture, countryside and peasants can only be solved by urbanization, which will significantly reduce the number of peasants and guide the rural surplus labor force to be non-agriculturally employed while realizing the large-scale agricultural operations, thus increasing the income of peasants. This is the road that all developed countries in the world took to realize the agricultural modernization. Marx pointed out that "the history of modernization is the one of rural urbanization." Urbanization is not only a carrier of industrialization and the impetus of social development, but the fundamental way out to solve issues concerning agriculture, countryside and peasants.

9.2.3. *Urbanization is the core strength to "expand the domestic consumption, guarantee the economic growth and implement the economic restructuring"*

Urbanization can effectively increase demand and stimulate consumption. It turns a lot of peasants into towns-folk and makes it possible to intensively manage the rural land on a large scale. The per capita income of peasants thus increases and they are enabled to enjoy city lives and modern civilization sooner. Peasants' traditional lifestyle is changed and the self-sufficient small-scale peasant economy is turned into the commercialized consumption-based economy, thus substantially catalyzing the domestic consumption. Meanwhile, the construction of infrastructure and real estate in many cities in the process of urbanization will boost the development of the upstream and downstream industries on the chain of manufacturing industry, and therefore the total of the social investment will increase, leading to a higher economic growth. With the increase of the total economy, urbanization changes human settlement patterns, continuously deepens the social division of labor and booms the urban and rural markets. It will surely accelerate the development of the service-oriented tertiary industry, further optimize the industrial structure, and balance the development of various categories of the national economy.

9.2.4. *Urbanization is an important source to boost independent innovation and improve the efficiency of economic growth*

Independent innovation is the soul of a country or a nation to achieve its progress. Significant modern technologies and management innovations often occur in cities because any of them must be supported by a large number of talents, certain technical accumulation and adequate social capital. With the deepening of China's urbanization, the city groups gathering a large number of senior professionals, cutting-edge technologies and abundant capital will necessarily become the cradle of China's independent innovation and greatly improve the efficiency of economic growth.

9.3. Treat Well Four Relationships in Urbanization

Joseph Eugene Stiglitz, the American economist and 2011 Nobel laureate in economics, pointed out that the development of urbanization of China, the world's largest developing country, and high-tech of the United States are the two key factors that will exert a profound impact on the human development of the world in the 21st century. It is of great practical significance for China to blaze a successful path of urbanization with Chinese characteristics, which will be another contribution China makes to the world civilization. For healthy urbanization, it is necessary to treat well the following four relationships.

9.3.1. *The relationship between tradition and modernity*

China, with a long history and profound humanistic foundation, has many cultural heritages. "Many well-known historical villages, towns and cities spread all over the country, silently passing down the everlasting vitality of the Chinese nation and witnessing the vicissitudes of history and the era". These well-known villages, towns and cities with typical Chinese traditional characteristics have become China's irreplaceable scarce resources and valuable treasures in the process of urbanization for they are unique and non-renewable. Currently, many Chinese cities regard building modern and international metropolis as the goal of urban development and they directly copy the Western model in the urban construction. Consequently, a lot of cities are identical and have no features in Chinese history, culture and landscape. The growth of a city needs a long period of time, which may even last for thousands of years. It has been proved by the urban development at home and abroad that it is an important way to achieve the modern urban civilization by attending to the essence of traditional culture, preserving unity and coherence of the urban history, and maintaining the natural and continuous cultural development. As the saying goes, "The more local characteristics a place reflects, the more attractive it is to the world." Modernity and tradition are not antithetic, and modernization does not mean to abandon the tradition. Instead, modernization should be achieved without destroying the tradition. A worldwide study shows that almost all the countries with ancient civilizations protect the overall ancient historic towns and villages because they are the glory of the country and the foundation of the national culture. Without strict protection of them, a nation will not continue in the world and the national culture cannot be international. The Chinese nation with ten thousand years of glorious civilization should do more to protect the ancient historic towns, villages and other historical and cultural heritages. The modern civilization should be achieved with protection and development of the tradition.

9.3.2. *The relationship between urban and rural areas*

The urban–rural development should be further coordinated and the past long-term urban–rural relationship of getting agriculture to support industry and countryside to support cities should be turned into the new relationship of getting industry to support agriculture and cities to support countryside, thus promoting the rational flow and efficient allocation of productive factors between urban and rural areas. It is a major strategic initiative to change the dualistic urban–rural structure and achieve harmonious development of relationship between Chinese urban and rural areas. China is a country with a large agricultural population, about 660 million in 2011. If urbanized at an annual rate of 1%, China will still have as many as 500 million rural people in 2020. Therefore, the rural development must not be ignored in urbanization. However, driven by the interests of market mechanism, rural resources such as labor forces, land and capital gather in cities, causing a serious loss of rural resources and a clear imbalance in the allocation of resources between urban and rural areas. The arable land problem is the most serious. China's rural household land contract system actually guarantees the peasants' necessities of life with the arable land which has been the protection, and in fact the last protection to the peasants when fairness and efficiency are coordinated through land policies. China is a country with considerable shortage in land resources per capita. The North American countries have land of 200 hectares per household, the EU 50 hectares, and the Asian countries one hectare, while China only half a hectare. Urbanization requires more construction land, but land resources should be protected to ensure the food security, especially arable land. Because of the wide gap in interests, when they come into conflict in reality, arable land is often appropriated at the price of the peasants' rights and interests; in particular, those at the periphery of cities has been used for non-agricultural purposes at a low price. It is a widespread phenomenon that peasants become "landless". We should be aware that the rural land provides the peasants with the most necessary basic means of subsistence and the most direct way of employment. It is a major long-term task to protect land, especially arable land in the process of urbanization. Only by effectively protecting the land resources, can the fundamental position of agriculture be consolidated, the national food security be ensured and the long-term social stability maintained. The countryside cannot achieve its development without the radiation and leadership of cities, while the urban development is inseparable from the promotion and support of the countryside. The holistic planning of the urban and rural development should be further improved, new ways to synthetically utilize the urban and rural land be explored and the integration of cities and countryside be accelerated. It is the only way to guide the orderly and healthy development of urban and rural areas.

9.3.3. *The relationship between the coastal region and the central and western regions*

China is a vast country with great differences in the development of productive forces, economy and technology as well as the foundation of social development in different places. The coastal region in the east and the central and western regions are urbanized at different levels. The eastern region, with an urban population accounting for over 50%, has entered the mid- and late-stage of urbanization with the pace slowed down, accentuating the connotation and quality of the urban development. The central and western regions, driven by the recent policies of developing the western region and promoting the rise of central region, have greatly improved their economic development and narrowed the gap with the eastern region in the growth rate of urbanization. Nevertheless, the central and the western regions have not been highly urbanized with an urbanization rate of only 34.56%, so increase in numbers and expansion in scale of cities and towns are the key points of their urbanization. Therefore, it is a realistic choice for the future of China's urbanization to take different paths in line with the characteristics of local development according to the differences of each place in economy, society, natural resources and ecological conditions. The coastal region in the east, especially Jiangsu and Zhejiang Provinces, enjoys the developed economy and high level of urbanization with reasonable structure of urban system and balanced spatial distribution. The surrounding economy and society are obviously radiated and impelled. In this area, the overall carrying capacity and competitiveness of the prime regional cities should be enhanced; mega cities should fully radiate and impel the development of smaller cities and towns and these smaller cities and towns should radiate and impel the countryside, thus realizing the coordinated development of cities and towns. The underdeveloped central and western regions should seize the opportunities that the state inclines economic construction focus to the central and western regions and the opportunity that the eastern region restructures the industries. The central and western regions should take full advantages of the resources and labor price, formulating preferential policies for investment and construction, and should develop new growth points. While the development of the provincial capitals and municipalities and other big and medium core cities are pushed forward, the structure of the urban system should be actively improved, the regional economic strength be enhanced, and the pace of urbanization sped up.

9.3.4. *The relationship between new and old cities*

China has more than 600 cities with an average population of 10,000 people per square kilometer and even higher population density in old cities. It has become the focus of Chinese urbanization to evacuate the overlapping functions and excessive population of old cities and improve the old public infrastructure. It is necessary to preserve old cities with local renovation, but the real way out is to build new cities at the periphery with comprehensive support facilities, concentrated industries and pleasant living and working conditions. However, in order to take in a large number of newly increased urban populations, many Chinese cities simply build houses in the construction of new cities, ignoring infrastructural construction and industrial development. As a result, new cities are featured by singularity of urban functions and weakness of core industries. The pendulum-style and tidal commuting between new and old cities are energy- and time-consuming. The population has not obviously moved to new cities while the old cities fail to be well protected. In the process of urban renovation, every bit of space is used to build incongruous high buildings, diluting and submerging the historical charm of the old cities. Meanwhile, some of the old streets and historic sites have even been forcibly removed, resulting in cities neither new nor old with obscure positioning. Protection and renovation of old cities must be carried out with meticulous research and elaborate planning and design. The scalpel-like approaches can be applied to achieve the micro-cycled local renovation. Instead, the bulldozer-like approaches which build large roads, squares and industrial parks by leveling off the old cities should be forbidden. Such an irrational renovation of old cities regardless of scale and laws stiffly imposes symbol of industrialization on cities, which will gradually lose their own characteristics and tastes. Detours of the Western countries offer us warning that large-scale renovations led by developers usually lead to negative consequences where the economic interests are given the prime priority, the public interest are ignored, the unity and coherence of the urban history are broken, and the cultural values of the cities are damaged. It is necessary to adhere to the principle that the government represents the public interests when renovating old cities. By formulating the development plans, establishing the policy system and supervising the implementation process, the government can well treat the relationships between the short-term renovation and the long-term construction, between the local renovation and the overall coordinated development. The upgrade of old cities and the development of new cities must be combined and the old and new cities must open and integrate to each other, thus fully complementing and sharing the resources.

9.4. Actively Explore New Ideas about Chinese Urbanization

9.4.1. *Make scientific plans before hand on the urbanization of the 21st century*

A nation or a country actually has only one chance for urbanization because the layout of cities and towns and the major infrastructure cannot be easily changed after urbanization. Therefore, scientific planning must be strengthened in the urban construction. The before-hand planning will ensure an overall, forward-looking and proactive urban development and prevent blind investment, repetitious construction and waste of resources. Without planning, the soul of urban development, cities and towns cannot be built well. Planning on urbanization is a policy-making, comprehensive, scientific and regional job. To constantly improve the planning system and lead the urban scientific development with scientific planning, attention must be paid to the work of the following aspects: First, investment must be increased to make high-standard planning of urbanization in the 21st century from the beginning. Planning must be made once for all but implemented step by step, which means we go to great lengths and do what we are capable to. It has been proved by the history that the level and quality of urban construction are directly determined by the formulation of planning and its implementation. We must make coordination based on the trend of economic and social development and the advantages of regional resources, proceed from reality, rationally arrange infrastructure and industrial development and keep a correct grip and treatment on relationships between planning of urban development and natural environment, national culture, geographical features and industrial nurturing. The planning of urban development must be linked to the overall land uses, coordinated with industrial development, adaptable to economic and social development, and united with urban and rural integration. Second, we must establish and improve the long-term and overall mechanism of urban planning and management. We should advocate "sunshine planning" to expand the scope of public participation and accept the supervision of the masses. Various key players in economy must be mobilized to positively take part in the urban construction, management and development. The leading role of planning in the urban construction must be constantly enhanced so as to improve the urban quality and grade. Third, planning must be strictly and consistently implemented and should not be changed under different leadership or due to personal likes and dislikes. We should act strictly according to laws and regulations and turn planning from a single improvement of spontaneous and disorderly construction into a significant guidance to command and lead the overall urban development.

9.4.2. *Build the low-carbon eco-city by giving priority to resource conservation and environmental protection*

Thanks to the development of urban civilization, cities have so far become not only the core areas where humans create both material and spiritual wealth, but the places with most environmental problems such as changes of ecological patterns, large consumption of resources and energy and occurrence of greenhouse effect. It is overridingly urgent for human society, including China, to find ways to coordinate the harmonious development between man and nature and actively respond to the change of global climate. According to statistics, the energy consumption of more than 200 Chinese cities at the prefectural level and above accounts for 55.48% of the total of the country and the carbon dioxide emissions 54.84%. China carries out the urbanization of 21% of the world's population with only 7% of arable land, 7% of freshwater resources, 4% of oil reserves and 2% of gas reserves in the world. Shortage of natural resources has already bottlenecked the urban development and the problems in ecological environment have become the substantial threat to the living quality of urban and rural residents. The extensive model of urban development with high energy consumption and serious pollution has been proved unsustainable, so we must seriously reflect on the building concept and development model of the city and actively pursue and explore a development path to build low-carbon eco-cities. The low-carbon eco-city proceeds from the maximum maintenance of ecological balance, highlights energy and land conservation and environmental protection in urban construction and development, and realizes combination and mutualism between human and ecological environment through low energy consumption, pollution and emissions. In the case of China, first, we should actively construct the sustainable urban transport system, giving priority to green transport such as walking and cycling as well as energy-saving public transport. Cities will be operated in an efficient and energy-saving way under the guidance of an overall and sustainable urban transport system. Second, we should vigorously promote technologies of green building and clean production and recycling economy, reduce energy consumption in construction and industry, improve resource recycling and boost energy saving and emission reduction of the cities. Third, we should strengthen the urban energy management, promote institutional innovation, reform tax and evaluation system, introduce the concept of green GDP and create a favorable institutional environment for the development of low-carbon eco-cities. Now in the process of rapid urbanization,

China as a country starting urbanization late, compared with developed countries, enjoys lower cost in construction and the advantage to build eco-cities on a large scale. We must seize this golden opportunity to develop low-carbon eco-cities, actively summarize the successful experience, courageously make innovation and practice, and blaze a new road for the healthy development of Chinese urbanization.

9.4.3. *Make intensive development and create distinctive city clusters and belts*

The city cluster is the product and mark of urbanization at its advanced stage. With colossal economy and dense population, the urban agglomeration is the significant hub of the urban system and gradually becomes the locomotive of the regional and even the national economic development. The GDP of the three major US urban agglomerations accounts for 67% of the total of the United States and that of the three major urban agglomerations makes up 70% of the total of Japan, while that of Chinese three major urban agglomerations, Pearl River Delta, Yangtze River Delta and Beijing, Tianjin and Bohai-rimurban agglomerations, account for only 38% of the total of China. In the future urbanization, the urban agglomerations and urban belts with central cities as the core will further develop and expand. These highly urbanized city clusters, with developed economy and complete urban support facilities, will become the important driving force for the growth of national economy and the strategic platform of a new round of national wealth accumulation. With the grand development of the western region, revitalization of the old industrial bases in the northeastern region and the implementation of other strategies, Sichuan and Chongqing city cluster, Mid-China city cluster, Mid-south Liaoning city cluster, Wuhan city cluster, Guanzhong city cluster and the urban belt along Yangtze River in Anhui are growing constantly. China is ushering in an unprecedented opportunity for the development of urban agglomerations. However, compared with those of developed countries, China's urban agglomerations are still in the stage of extensive economic growth. As the stereo urban network complementary among different levels, divisions of labor and functions need to be improved and the effects in scale, intensiveness, radiation and interaction have not reached their maxima. According to statistics, the energy consumption for one US dollar worth of economic value created by China's urban agglomeration is 5.9 times that of the seven Western industrial countries, and the average labor productivity is only 8,900 US dollars, only 1/7th that of the United States and 1/5th that of European countries. In order to speed up the growth of China's emerging urban agglomerations into the newpoint of economic growth, promote the coordinated development of urban and rural economy, and acquire the "development dividend" as high as possible, we should break the limitation of the administrative division, go beyond the administrative economy, innovate the system of regional development and turn from the original expansion of a single city into the group-style cultivation of urban agglomeration. We should also strengthen the regional industrial division and complementary advantage and promote the resource sharing and the free flow of productive factors. Moreover, we should enhance coordination of common products, integration of infrastructure and protection of the ecological environment among different cities, improve the complementary urban functions, promote the intensive and characteristic development of the city cluster and prevent the lack of emphasis on the traditional urban development, thus achieving the goal of real sustainable development of regional integration.

9.4.4. *Put people first and build cities and towns into the cultural, educational and leisure space*

The urban residents are the key players of cities, so adhering to the people-oriented scientific outlook on development is the fundamental guarantee to healthy urbanization and construction of the harmonious society. However, some places take materials as the foremost instead in the urban construction. Rather than being committed in increasing investment in human capital, offering more job opportunities, providing better social security and creating the more comfortable living space, they equate urbanization with building architectures, roads or bridges and ignore the people-oriented concept of development as well as the development of social undertakings. Modern cities should not be the piled cements of buildings and roads, but the harmony and unity between people and cities, between economy and society, and between man and nature. In the process of urbanization, we must firmly grasp the fundamental purpose of "putting people first, serving the people and bringing benefit for the people". We should put the cities' social development indicators at the important position and attach great importance to the coordination of social and economic development so as to achieve the ultimate goal of human's overall development. While improving the hardware facilities of the cities, we should also improve the construction of social and cultural facilities such as educational institutions, health care, museums, cultural centers, stadiums, and public gardens, etc. We should not only provide people with necessities of life including food, clothing, housing, transportation and education, but also meet their spiritual needs for culture and leisure, thus improving the level of residents' life and their overall quality. We should be committed to create a good environment for production and living, balance the economic and infrastructural construction with the ecological construction and social development, make an overall improvement of material and spiritual civilization, build cities and towns into advanced cultural, educational and leisure space, and enable all the people share in the fruits of urban development.

9.4.5. *Make innovation and build a financing mechanism to support sustainable urbanization*

As an important process in the economic and social integration between urban and rural areas, urbanization needs to be guaranteed with huge capital investment. It is estimated that the transfer of every rural person requires an average urban construction fee of 60,000 Yuan. Given an annual increase of population urbanization rate by one percentage point, the five-year investment in urban construction will total more than 4.2 trillion Yuan. It is impossible for the public finance to independently meet such a huge demand for funds. The shortage of funding more seriously constrains the urbanization in the backward areas. In order to speed up urbanization, we must broaden the financing channels and establish a rational, efficient and sustainable financing mechanism for urbanization. We must adhere to the market-oriented reforms, give full play to the guiding role of the public finance at all levels, and gradually diversify the investors of urban construction. We must reasonably define the scope of governmental investment and increase the investment in public welfare infrastructure and public facilities. We must reform and improve the urban taxation system and gradually establish the security system of urban construction funds. We must deepen the reform of investment and financing system of urban infrastructure, encourage all kinds of social investment (including foreign investment) in the construction and operation of urban infrastructure, and explore franchising, Build–Operate–Transfer (BOT), Transfer–Operate–Transfer (TOT) and other project financing models. We must reform the urban pricing mechanism for water supply, gas supply, heating, sanitation and public transport and promote a virtuous cycle of investment, operation and recycling.

9.5. Give a Further Play to the Role of Development Finance and Promote the Scientific Development of China's Urbanization

9.5.1. *Introduction to support of development finance to China's urbanization*

Since its establishment in 1994, the CDB clings to the concept and method of development financing, integrates the CDB's strengths in large loans and medium-and long-term financing with the organizational advantages of the government, and actively promotes the market, credit and institutional construction in the field of urbanization, thus forming a complete set of business operation model and risk prevention mechanism supporting the urban infrastructural construction, which has played an important role in accelerating China's urbanization. The CDB adheres to making plans beforehand, cooperates with the local governments on planning in the long run, and assists them in preparation of regional, industrial and urban development planning through technical assistance loans, thus ensuring that the urban infrastructure development is adaptable to the requirements of the future economic and social development, and to the carrying capacity of resources and environment. Meanwhile, the CDB actively consults with the local governments, enters into agreements as to development financing cooperation, makes use of its advantages as "the experts' bank", and actively gives counsel to the urban development through ways of providing financial support and consultation in development and finance.

By the end of 2012, the CDB had cooperated with 119 cities of 30 provinces, municipalities and autonomous regions in the country and cumulatively promised 186 urban infrastructural projects involving many areas such as construction of development zones, urban roads and rail transportation, sewage governance, tap water, gas supply, etc. Its loan balance had been more than 1.3 trillion Yuan with the balance of urban construction loans accounting for more than 20% of the total of the bank in the long period of time (as shown in Figs. 9.2 and 9.3). The overall assets of the urban construction loans are good in quality with only 0.6% of non-performing loans. With

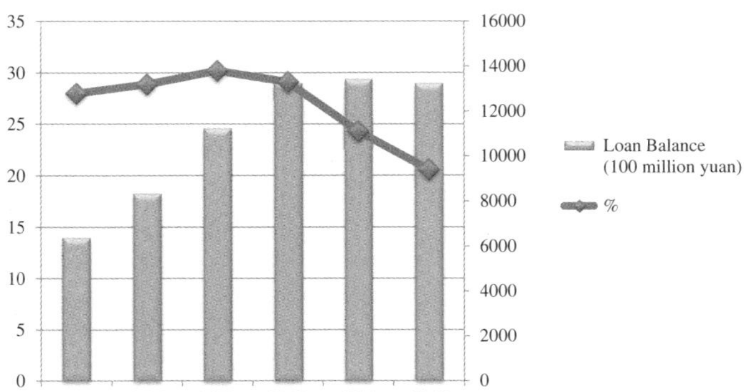

Figure 9.2: CDB's balance and percentage of urban construction loans, 2007–2012.

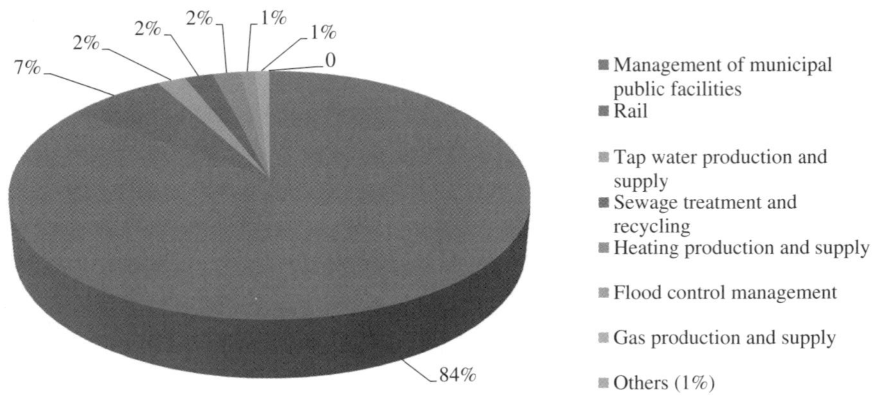

Figure 9.3: Distribution of CDB's urban construction loans in 2008.

the strong support of the CDB, China's urban infrastructural construction has gradually entered a virtuous cycle and become a new bright spot of China's economic growth in the 21st century.

9.5.2. *The development financing plays a role of innovation in promoting the reform of investment and financing system for urbanization*

In support of urbanization, the CDB advocates making plans beforehand, actively promotes the local governments at all levels to prepare planning on regional, urban, industrial and social development, and scientifically designs the basic functions, industrial divisions and infrastructural layout of the cities according to their carrying capacity of population, resources and environment. Meanwhile, systematic financing for these plans is arranged to successfully integrate development and project planning.

In light of the backwardness of infrastructural construction, shortage of funds, simplicity of investment channel and absence of key financing operators, the CDB supports the local governments to take advantage of their capability in organization and coordination, integrate administrative resources, excavate the urban potential in management, establish a number of urban construction investment corporations for the governmental financing and create conditions for the market-based financing of urban construction projects. At the same time, the CDB cultivates and incubates the credits of the platform enterprises, gradually turning itself from relying on governmental subsidies to an operator capable of sustainable market financing through its own credits. With the gradual introduction of market-oriented operation, the development financing plays a pioneering, leading and progressive role in the administratively monopolized construction and operation of infrastructure, and promotes the reform and development of investment and financing system for urbanization.

9.5.3. *The development financing plays a basic role in speeding up the infrastructural construction of urbanization*

Using soft loans as the initial working capital, the CDB settles the shortage of capital in urban construction projects and the problem of cash flow which is low at first and high later. By a financing combination, it balances the cash flow of different urban construction projects and improves the hematopoietic mechanism of these projects. It cooperates with commercial banks, insurance companies, trust companies and other financial institutions, plays the leading role of seed funds by means of syndicated loans, securitization and money management, and leads the investment of other financial institutions and social money in the urban infrastructural construction, especially in the less developed central and western regions. For example, in March 2009, the CDB issued 1.5 billion Yuan of 2009 Lanzhou City Investment Bond for the infrastructural construction of Lanzhou City, effectively relieving the tension of funds on urban construction in the western region.

Since the commercialization reform, the CDB has integrated the businesses of its subordinate CDB Leasing and CDB Capital, actively explored new models of financing for urban development, and vigorously expanded the synergies of investment, loans, bonds and leasing, thus providing overall and synthetic financial services for urban development. In November 2009, CDB Capital established China's first urban development funds in Xi'an, focusing on providing support to the local urban construction and the key projects of regional development. In February 2010, CDB Capital cooperated with the government of Nanchang city and established China's first low-carbon and urban development funds, putting forth efforts to promote construction of regional infrastructure, public service facilities and ecological environment in the key regions of Nanchang. By establishing the urban development funds, the CDB extensively attracts social capital, amplifies the amount of money, drives the investment of other capitals several times the size of these funds, and effectively alleviates the shortage of money for the local economic development.

9.5.4. *The development financing plays a role in effectively surmounting social difficulties in urbanization*

The rapidly developing urbanization inevitably generates some social problems such as unemployment, rising prices of real estate, widening wealth gap and shortage of skilled workers, etc. To resolve these conflicts and contradictions, the CDB offers great support for urban infrastructural construction. Meanwhile, it targets its services at the difficulties and hot issues in the relationship between the government and the people and gradually expands its successful market-oriented experience in the urban infrastructural construction from supporting the national key constructions in areas of infrastructure, basic industries and pillar industries to education, health care, housing for low-income families, energy conservation, carbon emission reduction, environmental protection and other more extensive areas benefiting people's livelihood. Both financial socialization and social financialization can be achieved in this way and the mission to strengthen the national power and improve the people's livelihood can be reflected. The CDB also offers microfinance schemes for re-employment and youth entrepreneurship to help solve problems in employment, provides the small and medium enterprise (SME) loans to solve the financing difficulties of SMEs, supports construction of low-rent housing and affordable housing to control the soaring prices of real estate and overcome housing difficulties of low-income population in cities, and supports the training of off-farm workers to improve their labor skills and provide a large number of qualified workers for urbanization and industrialization.

9.6. Conclusion

Urbanization is a historical process in which the agricultural society and rural civilization change into the industrial society and urban civilization respectively. Different countries take very different paths of urbanization due to the difference in their national conditions, economic development and industrialization. However, the development of international urbanization shows conspicuous trends and characteristics. First, sustainable development is the major subject of urbanization; second, coordinated development between town and country is the theme of urbanization; third, balanced development of cities and towns is the basic pattern of urbanization; and fourth, combination of market-based and government-led development is the important condition for the health of urbanization.

China's urbanization is of strategic importance and has its historic missions: It is the most important lever to achieve China's modernization and rejuvenation of the Chinese nation, the fundamental way out to solve the problems about agriculture, countryside and peasants, the core strength to "expand the domestic consumption, guarantee the economic growth and implement the economic restructuring" and an important source to boost the independent innovation and improve the efficiency of economic growth. Four relationships must be treated well to ensure the healthy development of China's urbanization. The first one is the relationship between tradition and modernity, and the modern civilization should be achieved with protection and development of the tradition. The second one is the relationship between town and countryside, and the development of urban and rural areas should be coordinated, thus promoting the rational flow and efficient allocation of productive factors between urban and rural areas. The third one is the relationship between the coastal region and the central and western regions, and China's urbanization should take different and characteristic paths according to the different conditions of each place in economy, society and natural resources. The fourth one is the relationship between new and old cities, and the upgrade of old cities and the development of new cities must be combined, thus fully complementing and sharing the resources.

China should actively explore new ideas about Chinese urbanization. China should make scientific plans beforehand on the urbanization of the 21st century and give priority to resource conservation and environmental protection. China should put people first and build cities and towns into the cultural, educational and leisure space. China should make intensive development and create distinctive urban agglomerations and urban belts. China should make innovation, give full play to the strategic financing function of the development finance, and promote the healthy development of China's urbanization.

CHAPTER 10

THE DEVELOPMENT-ORIENTED FINANCE SUPPORTS ECOLOGICAL GOVERNANCE OF THE SOUTHWEST ROCKY DESERTIFICATION*

Rocky desertification is a serious obstacle to China's rural development in karst regions. The karst mountain areas in Southwest China are also the ecological environment deteriorating and poor population concentrating regions because of the expansion of rocks instead of trees. This chapter analyses the promotion of rocky desertification governing by the strategy of finance and intelligence coordination and the mode of "Company + Finance + Technology + Rural Household".

10.1. Southwest Rocky Desertification

Rocky desertification means that land degrades and turns to stone in the subtropical and tropical moist karst regions, due to severe soil loss and severe exposure of bedrocks. Provinces and regions affected in

*This chapter was written in May 2006 and was revised a little recently.

China are mainly in Yunnan, Guizhou, Guangxi, Sichuan, Hunan, Hubei, Chongqing and Guangdong, especially Guizhou, Yunnan and Guangxi provinces, covering an area of 105,100 square kilometers and involving 65 million people. Carbonate and clastic rocks are crosswise and interbeddedly distributed and rock and earthhills appear at intervals in these areas. The local people depict this region as the place where "stones rather than trees grow". Ecologically deteriorating, these regions are densely populated by poor people. The areas of desertification are seriously deforested and incapable of water retention; severe water and soil loss exerts a serious impact on the downstream, leading to frequent natural disasters; and local poverty alleviation and sustainable economic development are restricted. The rocky desertification has become a severe obstacle for the new rural construction in Southwest China.

In 1980, Comrade Deng Xiaoping ordered the air force to improve the prairie by aerial seeding in the southwest regions. Since then, a group of scientists under the leadership of Mr. Ren Jizhou persist in their studies on the prairie and animal husbandry in the karst mountains in Southwest China. They have achieved important results with a certain development of artificial grass and grassland animal husbandry in the southwest areas. In recent years, cultivated land is converted into forests and pasture into prairie, enlarging the area of artificial grass. However, without grazing and mowing, the weeds are widespread and the artificial grass degrades quickly. Currently, the imbalance between grass and livestock gradually desolates most part of the artificial grass. Furthermore, the excessive reclamation and woodcutting and the backward farming system exacerbated the water and soil loss, and enlarged the rocky desertification area of the grass land. Especially in Guizhou and Yunnan provinces, the area of rocky desertification has reached 100 million mu, accounting for 34.43% of the total grassland. Among them, the grassland is 60 million mu in size with rocky area of 48.72 million mu in Guizhou, and the grassland 230 million mu with rocky area of 52.16 million mu in Yunnan. It has become a very urgent task to speed up the governance of rocky desertification in karst regions.

It was proposed in *several proposals of the Communist Party of China (CPC) Central Committee and the State Council on pushing forward the New Socialist Rural Construction* (ZF No. [2006] 1) to "actively implement the project of comprehensive prevention and control of water and soil loss in rocky desertification regions and black soil areas in Northeast China". Academicians Ren Jizhou, Zhang Ziyi and Liu Gengling of Chinese Academy of Engineering submitted a report to the General Secretary on 7 November 2005, which received high attention from the central leadership. On 23 November 2005, President Hu Jintao wrote the instruction: "Transferred to comrades Jiabao and Liangyu to read". On the same day Premier Wen Jiabao wrote his instruction: "Transferred to the National Development and Reform Commission (NDRC) to research". The next day, Vice Premier Hui Liangyu wrote the instruction: "Transferred to comrades Qinglin and Shengxian, who are expected to take initiative to research it with the NDRC". The Ministry of Agriculture and the NDRC are now developing the special governance program, and the hardwork is underway to prepare a large-scale grassland governance program in the area of rocky desertification, which has a very important strategic significance for pushing forward the new socialist rural construction, improving the local production and living conditions, eradicating poverty, protecting the successful implementation of the western development strategy and promoting the national unity.

In the Southwest China where it rains a lot, it accords with the laws of nature and the objective reality to grow the perennial pasture. With cattle, sheep and other grazing livestock and poultry, the perennial pasture can be used to further develop the livestock and poultry processing industry. In this way, the over-ground productive forces of the pasture can be rationally converted into the livestock products. The rocky desertification can thus be controlled and the income of the peasants will increase as well. Meanwhile, the animal manure can generate biogases, which can be used for fire and lighting, providing a relief from vegetation destruction caused by felling trees and plants. Currently, animal husbandry is the main source of income for peasants in the southwest mountains. The grassland governance and grazing livestock by growing pasture can effectively improve the local ecological environment, put the rocky desertification under control, and optimize the industrial structure in rural mountains. It is the major route for the poverty-stricken mountains to shake off poverty and strive for the moderate prosperity. Grass growth and cattle and sheep raising in Qinglong County, Qianxinan Autonomous Prefecture in Guizhou province allow every household in the project area to earn an annual income of 15,000 Yuan, more than twice that of the non-project households, showing a good result.

On 4 April 2006, I chaired the Symposium of Development Finance Supporting Development of Grassland Animal Husbandry in the Southwest Karst Mountains at the Investment Bureau of National Development Bank. Academicians Ren Jizhou and Zhang Ziyi of Chinese Academy of Engineering and leading officials of Animal Husbandry Division of Ministry of Agriculture, Yunnan Animal Husbandry Bureau, Guizhou Forage Workstation, Headquarters of West China Prataculture Corporation, Yunnan Lvsheng Meidi Science and Technology Industry Co. Ltd., Shanghai Jiaotong University Group, Wuhan University Innovation Investment Company, China International Engineering Consulting Corporation participated in the conference. Academicians Ren Jizhou and Zhang Ziyi said emotionally at the meeting that they were delighted to see that the CDB was the first bank caring and ready to participate in this project and they believed it would succeed this time. Academician Liu Gengling did not attend the conference for his poor health but he sent a letter specifically expressing his concern. Comrade Huang Qian, former director of the Social Affairs Division of Research Office of the State Council, made a profound analysis on the current grassland governance in the areas of rocky desertification, the lessons learned and the thresholds that must be crossed. Leaders of the companies agreed that the great support from the CPC Central Committee and the CDB was another great opportunity for the governance of the southwest rocky desertification in China. Comrades from the Animal Husbandry Bureau of Ministry of Agriculture hoped to promote the project by strengthening the bank-governance cooperation.

10.2. Idea of Development Finance Supporting Ecological Governance of the Rocky Desertification in the Southwest Region

Over the years, little progress has been achieved in the governance of the southwest rocky desertification for an important reason that production, education and research were disjoint so that a virtuous cycle of industrial operation system failed to be formed. It is a great program to bring the development financing into play to actively support the governance of the southwest rocky desertification, help build industrial operation system, support poverty alleviation with science and technology and promote the new rural construction.

10.2.1. *Objective, principles and ideas*

10.2.1.1. *Objective*

The objective of development finance supporting the governance of the southwest rocky desertification is: Under the guidance of the scientific outlook on development, promoted by both financing and intelligence coordination, using development financial instruments, combining production, education and research, alleviating poverty with science and technology, integrating credit resources, helping construct the industrial operation system, establishing a reasonable business model, speeding up the governance of rocky desertification and development of the grassland animal husbandry in southwest region, and promoting the new rural construction.

10.2.1.2. *Principles*

(1) The governance must rely on the national governance planning of rocky desertification, integrated with that of the local governments.
(2) The governance must be organized by the government, promoted by financing, combining production, education and research, and oriented by marketing operation.

(3) Various anti-poverty projects must cooperate with one another.
(4) The construction of credit system must be integrated with the industrial development.

10.2.1.3. *Overall idea*

The overall idea is: The government organizes the formulation and implementation of the governance planning of rocky desertification; the CDB helps construct the industrial operation system combining production, education and research; implementation plans will be holistically taken into account; resources from all aspects will be integrated; the credit structure will be further improved; company-style operation management platform will be established; farmers' participation will be actively organized; experts will offer technological guidance; important issues should be highlighted; pilot programs should be made well; and experience will be summarized in time and gradually extended.

10.2.2. *Operation model*

The governance of the southwest rocky desertification adopts the "company + CDB + technology + rural household" operation model.

10.2.2.1. *The provincial technological and financial services platform will be established*

The competent provincial governmental department organizes the company of technological and financial service for the governance of rocky desertification. The websites of pasture and animal husbandry workstation can be brought into play, and the institutions can be managed as enterprises (It is learned that grassland animal husbandry financial service companies are to be established in Yunnan and Guizhou). To ensure the success of the governance, the provincial animal husbandry technological and financial service companies integrate resources of all aspects, formulate specific governance planning of rocky desertification within the province, organize guarantee for loans, carry out technical training and establish the cultivation insurance system.

10.2.2.2. *Industrial platforms will be established at the city (prefecture) or county level to support the leading enterprises*

The city (prefectural) government organizes the regional leading grassland animal husbandry companies, attracts venture capitals from different aspects and adopts the limited liability partnership which allows the important experts and managers to participate as general partners. Taking the modern enterprise system, the leading companies carry the special governmental funds and the CDB funds, organize peasants to grow grass and breed livestock so as to enter the industrial chains, and organize and implement the grassland governance in the areas of rocky desertification.

The local government and the leading companies jointly push forward the establishment of the "company + rural household" industrial mechanism as well as the professional associations, cooperatives and other cooperative organizations to enhance the organization of peasants and raise their dominant position in the market. Centering on advanced varieties and farming techniques as well as storage, processing, trade and other economic activities, leading enterprises, specialized processing and marketing households, brokers and cooperative organizations help peasants to get rid of poverty and strive for prosperity.

10.2.2.3. *The CDB provides support in the form of financing and intelligence coordination*

Within the framework of development financial cooperation and with the support of the local governments, the CDB provides necessary soft loans and long- and middle-term loans, which, coordinated with various special governmental funds, promote the grassland governance in areas of rocky desertification. Meanwhile, the CDB provides financial advisory services, combines financing and intelligence coordination, amplifies the limited governmental resources, and pushes forward the governance structure construction, legal person construction, cash flow construction and credit system construction of the leading companies.

10.2.2.4. *Experts provide technological guidance*

The modern grassland animal husbandry in the southwest requires people to grow grass and form the grassland, select superior studs in the contracted fenced pastures to mate with the basic local female animals, and graze the animals in turns on the regional basis. This is a typical anti-poverty projects with science and technology, requiring long-term and exquisite guidance of experts in related fields. In order to better bring the role of experts into play, expert database and working mechanism need to be established to carry out feasibility studies, planning and design, tracking and monitoring, mid-term evaluation and post-review, and assessment of the experts' performance.

10.2.2.5. *The position of farmers as the key player should be strengthened to perform their functions*

Farmers are one of the key factors for the success of this project, so their training should be strengthened to change their extensive breeding and cultivation into scientific grass growth and animal grazing. With market-orientation and credit concepts established, peasants must have a clear understanding of the principle that "loans must be repaid by the borrower". Farmers' credit associations should be established and improved to create an investment and financing environment based on trust and honesty, where micro-credits are available to farmers.

Farmers take and repay the loans in kind which will increase spirally. The county and township grassland animal husbandry centers give farmers grass seeds, ewes and other in-kind supports, offer them micro-loans as the necessary startup capital, and organize them to grow grass and raise sheep and cattle. The county and township grassland animal husbandry centers unify the acquisition of the animals after their growth. The leading companies organize the export or further process the animals to increase their value. The in-kind materials are purchased with proportional distribution and spiral increment.

The experience of the World Bank can be drawn on for reference for the management of the peasants' micro-loans. The application is submitted by the township grassland animal husbandry centers and assessed by the expert groups; after granted, the grassland animal husbandry centers purchase the grass seeds, breeding sheep and cattle according to the budget for the farmers; after technically, financially and administratively reviewed, the accounts are rendered to the agencies delegated by the CDB for the loans; the government is responsible for guidance and supervision and subsidizes the peasants with certain interests of the loan.

10.2.3. *Marketing operation flow*

As Fig. 10.1 shows, commercial operation model reflects the characteristics of corporate operation, technical guidance, rural household as the major player, small groups of production and large-scale industrial clusters. It is a feasible and effective path to develop the grassland animal husbandry, control rocky desertification and help farmers out of poverty.

10.2.4. *Measures*

(1) The steering group for the development finance supporting the governance of the southwest rocky desertification will be set in the CDB and the executive teams in its branches.
(2) The CDB should actively track and involve in the formulation of the "12th Five-year Plan" concerning the governance of the southwest rocky desertification by the NDRC and the Ministry of Agriculture.
(3) The CDB, mainly its branches, provides appropriate financial advisory services, integrates finance and intelligence coordination, offers the necessary Class A technical assistance loans, helps build provincial and municipal platforms and develops industrial implementation planning, and promotes the pilot programs.
(4) The CDB takes the governance of rocky desertification as the specific work to support the new rural construction, incorporates it in the development financial cooperation, and launches the Working Plan of Development Finance supporting Ecological Governance of the Southwest Rocky Desertification as soon as possible. The CDB branches in Guizhou, Yunnan, Guangxi and Guangdong further improve their specific implementation plan according to their own circumstances, determine one or two pilot

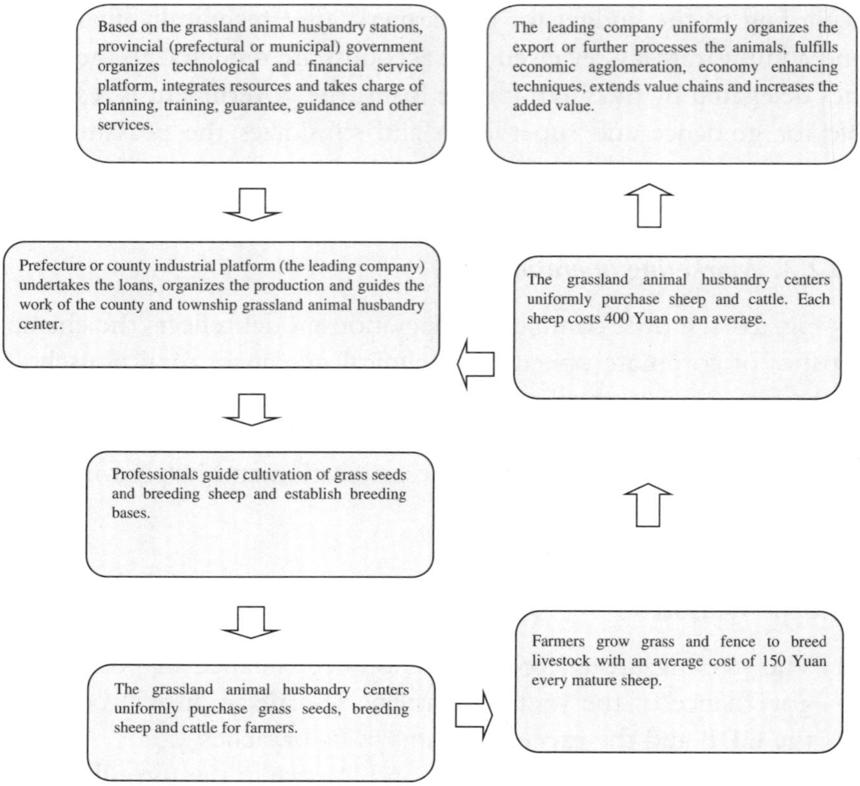

Figure 10.1: Marketing operation flow of ecological governance of rocky desertification.

units and establish platform companies responsible for the related work. The experience in the pilot programs should be summarized in time and spread on the regional basis.

10.3. Pilot Project at Qinglong County[1]

Qinglong County of Guizhou Province, a place suffering the most serious rocky desertification, is also one of the poorest counties in

[1] *Data source*: The on-site research in July 2006. Researchers: Zou Lixing, Xue Baojun and Zhou Ting of the CDB and Huang Qian of the Research Office of the State Council. The report was written by Zou Lixing.

China. With the support of development finance, Qinglong County uses scientific and technological means to vigorously develop grassland animal husbandry, innovates the anti-poverty development mechanism and has effectively controlled the rocky desertification. As an effective path to adjust the agricultural structure and help farmers out of poverty, it is valuable for demonstration and promotion.

10.3.1. *Introduction*

Qinglong County is located in the area suffering the worst rocky desertification in the west of Guizhou Province. Hillsides above 15 degrees account for 65% of the total in the county with most rocks exposed in the air. With the fragile ecosystem and the serious soil erosion, the contradiction between men and land becomes very severe. The county has a population of 274,200 with agricultural population of 252,900, making up 92.2%, and minority population 146,400, accounting for 53.4%. In 2005, the gross national product (GNP) of the county was 780 million Yuan with only 86 million Yuan of the local fiscal revenue. Among 181 villages across the country, 122 were the key anti-poverty and development villages. So far 34,300 absolutely poor people have not yet solved the problem of food and clothing. Some villagers still live with livestock in the low dilapidated huts with leaks on four side-walls. Some farmers in many a few villages live by selling blood plasma. It was a poverty-stricken county, hard to shake off poverty.

Over the years, the government has tried various means such as issuance of anti-poverty funds, intelligence poverty alleviation and suitable poverty alleviation to help peasants out of poverty. But in general they are means of "blood transfusion", unable to fundamentally help peasants shake off poverty. Because of the poor efficiency of grain plantation, the county government led peasants to develop fruit industry only with the same poor results.

In 2002, the CPC Qinglong County Committee and the county government decided to establish the Grassland Animal Husbandry Development Limited Liability Company on the basis of Qinglong County Grassland Animal Husbandry Center. In Jiangman Village where the natural conditions are extremely harsh, the scientific and technological anti-poverty project was implemented to grow grass and raise sheep, guiding the villagers to collectively plant high-quality pasture and breed Boer goats and hybrid mutton sheep on the farmland inappropriate to grow grain as well as on barren hills. In 2005, the per capita net income of the village reached 3,100 Yuan with the highest household annual income of 35,000 Yuan. Water, electricity, roads, television and telephone have already been accessible in the village. Some of the farmers who moved out have returned seeing the tremendous changes of the villages. When we visited the village, we witnessed the green artificial grass with sheep spreading all over the hillside; we personally perceived the deep identification of peasants with grass growth and sheep breeding. We learned from the leader of the county that among 14 towns and 68 villages of the county, there were more than 9600 poor households. Over 40,000 people grew grass and bred livestock with 100,000 mu of pasture and 105,000 herds of livestock on hand. The agricultural production went into the virtuous cycle of "growing grass and breeding livestock — protecting soil and water — increasing income". The grass growth and livestock breeding raised the net income of poor farmers from 631 Yuan per capita in 2000 to 1,647 Yuan per capita in 2005. The exploration of Qinglong County has changed the status quo of the poverty-stricken areas where "people are unable to live on the local soil and water". It is a feasible approach integrating poverty alleviation and development with governance of rocky desertification, encouraging us to enhance the confidence to pull more people out of poverty.

10.3.2. *Major approaches*

The successful experience and practices of Qinglong County can be summarized as: Governmental guidance, company-style operation, technical support and association's organization.

10.3.2.1. *Governmental guidance is fundamental*

The governments have played a leading role in the successful exploration in Qinglong County. Governments at all levels attach it with great importance and relevant departments actively cooperate and support it in terms of planning, policies and funding. Qinglong government integrates various resources and collects 2.35 million Yuan of project funds by organizing and coordinating sections of transportation, water conservancy, agriculture and forestry to develop grassland animal husbandry centers, holistically carry out infrastructural construction, and ensure grass growth and livestock breeding and the poverty alleviation with science and technology. Without governmental guidance, it is impossible to achieve success in the scientific and technological anti-poverty projects in poverty-stricken rural areas where peasants are poorly educated and informed. The governmental guidance is the basis for peasants' poverty elimination with Chinese characteristics, and the CDB has to rely on the government forces in its support to the grassland animal husbandry.

10.3.2.2. *Corporate operation is the key*

Qinglong Grassland Animal Husbandry Development Limited Liability Company provides peasants with services in four areas. First, it organizes the industrial production, provides support services for the important productive links, offers farmers with high-quality breeding sheep and guides them how to raise the sheep. Second, it facilitates the sales. With its stable sales channels, the company purchases the commercial sheep from the home of the farmers in accordance with the protected price. Peasants are paid in cash on the spot, relieved of the difficulty in sales. Third, it provides funds for farmers. As the farmers are short of funds, the company provides guarantee for their loans as well as grass seeds and pharmaceuticals. Fourth, it helps the farmers develop the market of commercial sheep. While boosting the prosperity of the peasants, the company has achieved its own rapid development. Starting from 100,000 Yuan in 2002, the company had 17 million Yuan of fixed assets with 14.25 million Yuan of sales revenue and 2,432,900 Yuan of after-tax profit at the end of 2005.

10.3.2.3. *Technical support is the guarantee*

The grasses are cultivated to grow in the subtropical climate and feed livestock; overseas Boer goats are introduced to mate with the local black goats to improve breeds and reduce costs; and the technical management is innovated. Academician Ren Jizhou and many other experts in grassland animal husbandry have repeatedly given technical guidance on the spot. The county has now established four technical service systems: First, the breeds are improved with the long-term technological cooperation with countries with developed animal husbandry such as New Zealand and Australia. A total of 18 origins of original Boer goats have been introduced from three countries for pure-bred reproduction, and the breeds suitable for mating with the local goats will be selected. Second, the "center — township — association — rural household" epidemic prevention system has been established and the herbal epidemic prevention technologies have been creatively developed. Third, the grass-livestock homeostatic technology has been adopted for scientific farming and rational development and utilization of the artificial grassland. Fourth, the technical training system has to be established to offer technical training for peasants.

10.3.2.4. *Association's organization is the basis*

Farmers are organized to establish the mutual aid credit associations, through which the scattered farmers are further organized for active participation and mutual help, creating favorable conditions for the cluster production and large-scale development.

10.3.3. *Innovation mechanism*

Qinglong model is most characterized by innovation mechanism. An ecological governance mechanism of rocky desertification which is practical, effective and warmly welcomed by peasants has been formed. It rationalizes the interests among the market, government, company, and farmers, mainly reflected as follows.

10.3.3.1. *Qinglong mechanism is a market-oriented industrial mechanism*

The pilot villages in the county formed a new "planting grass — breeding livestock — selling products" production system. Each sheep shares 200 Yuan of cost in the growth process. A little lamb takes eight months to grow to the standard 40 kilograms. A sheep is entirely sold at the price of 800 Yuan and the wholesaling price is 500 Yuan on an average with a considerable profit. The deep processed livestock products will generate even higher profits. Moreover, sheep adapt to group breeding without dangers of fatal diseases, which greatly relieves the peasants from the intensive labor. They are delighted to find they can earn more with easier jobs. The most important is that the commercial sheep has a huge market where the price has been in a steady increase. As a project with lower risk but higher return, the grass growth and sheep breeding is therefore the important direction to restructure the agricultural industry. "Growing grass and breeding livestock — ecological governance — increasing income" can be regarded as a gold industry.

10.3.3.2. *Qinglong mechanism is an interest linkage mechanism between the company and the farmers*

Qinglong Grassland Animal Husbandry Development Limited Liability Company organically makes itself and farmers as a community of interests through six ways. First, according to the relevant state policies and regulations, the Department of Land and Resources grades and evaluates the land by which farmers buy shares and involve in the production and operation of the base, drawing dividends by shares. Second, the graded land of the farmers is compensated once for all by areas. Farmers, over 60% of whose land has been appropriated take priority to be delegated as graziers after technical training, with 5,000 Yuan of annual income ensured. The third is the in-kind loan. The company organizes and establishes sheep breeding association in the poverty-stricken villages where grasses are planted and sheep are bred. Farmers are provided with free grass seeds, breeding rams and basic ewes in the form of "sheep" loan. The company also provides supporting technical services and sells the commercial sheep for farmers. Under the guidance of the company, farmers plant their own pasture, graze animals and manage the grassland. The increased sheep are distributed between the company and the farmers at the rate of 4:6 with the company taking 40% and the farmers 60%. Fourth, the company stands guarantee for the loans of low-income households to plant grass and breed sheep, provides technical training and the supporting technical services and sells the commercial sheep for the peasants. Interests are divided at the rate of 2:8 with the company taking 20% and farmers 80%. Fifth, technical services and product sales are focused on the non-poverty-stricken households which have developed relatively well. The company helps farmers change the breeding rams every eight months, provides them with free spring and autumn vaccines, offers technical services and sells commercial sheep for them. The profits are distributed at the rate of 1:9 with the company taking 10% and farmers 90%. Sixth, the absolutely poverty-stricken households are provided with free breeding rams and basic ewes. Profits are surrendered to them as much as possible and the sheep reclamation is appropriately prolonged. The company purchases the basic sheep for peasants with anti-poverty funds, and several years later the sheep are reclaimed for recycles. The anti-poverty funds can thus play better guiding role and expand effects.

10.3.3.3. *Qinglong mechanism can help to arouse the enthusiasm of the company's employees*

The company now has 186 employees, 151 of whom are the graziers converted from peasants. The economic responsibility system combining rewards according to work and according to effects is implemented. The public finance of the county continues to appropriate the salaries and benefits for the 25 managerial and technical staff members whose promotion, transfer, examination and assessment of professional titles are equal to those of serving staff in the similar institutions. Bonuses are offered based on individual performance and corporate effectiveness. In the poor mountainous areas at the exploratory stage, such a mechanism can retain the technical backbones, a practical situation in building a modern agricultural enterprise system with Chinese characteristics.

10.3.4. *Problems*

10.3.4.1. *The governance of rocky desertification is still an arduous task*

The "11th Five-Year" plan of Qinglong County proposed that 200,000 mu of grass should be planted and 250,000 sheep bred by 2010. The artificial pasture would increase by 20,000 mu and sheep by 30,000 herds every year. There are 1 million mu of developable grassland suffering rocky desertification in Qinglong, but only 1 out of 10 has so far been developed. The total area of rocky desertification has been over 30,000 square kilometers in Guizhou province, involving a population of nearly 20 million, of whom 2.66 million are absolutely poor, 4.65 million earn low income. It is a very arduous task to control rocky desertification and alleviate poverty here.

10.3.4.2. *The governance structure and management system of the company need to be further improved*

Qinglong Grassland Animal Husbandry Company has achieved an initial success in the industrial operation of grass growth and sheep breeding, but there is still much room for improvement in terms of the development planning, legal person structure and management system of the company, absorption and innovation of advanced technology in animal husbandry, construction of processing and distribution system, market development, and relations with the agricultural associations. Business can be made bigger and faster only by further strengthening the foundation of the company.

10.3.4.3. *There is a large gap in funding*

Each household needs about 6,600 Yuan of startup capital to purchase grass seeds and basic ewes.[2] A total investment of 171.2 million

---

[2] Each household needs 6,600 Yuan of infrastructural fund to start up grass growth and sheep breeding, covering 10 mu of grass seeds and fertilizers with grass seeds at the price of 40 Yuan per mu and fertilizers 20 Yuan per mu; 20 basic ewes, with 20 Yuan each; and a Boer bill goat at the price of 2,000 Yuan; it does not include peasants' reclamation of grassland and construction of sheep huts with their own labor.

Yuan is designed in the Qinglong "11th Five-Year Plan for Governance of Rocky Desertification", but various anti-poverty funds of the county are altogether only eight million Yuan every year, a total of 40 million Yuan in five years. A one-time five million Yuan may be invested in the county as the national pilot county to control rocky desertification. Qinglong County plans to borrow 80 million Yuan of bank loans and applies for another 80 million Yuan of national funds for special governance. The Grassland Animal Husbandry Company raised 11.2 million Yuan on its own. Leaders of the CPC Guizhou Provincial Committee hope the CDB to provide more financial support for the governance of rocky desertification in Guizhou Province.

10.3.4.4. *Some people wait and see with inconsistent cognitions*

Some provincial, prefectural, and county leaders have little knowledge of the Qinglong model and its value; Some people are entirely dependent on the state; some leaders rely on companies out of Guizhou provinces in governance of rocky desertification; as relevant policies and planning of the NDRC, Ministry of Agriculture, and Forestry Bureau and other departments are being developed, most of the local governmental departments wait and see without taking proactive actions.

10.4. Summary

Rocky desertification is a major obstacle for the new rural construction in the vast southwest areas, involving 65 million peasants in eight provinces (autonomous regions or municipalities). The ecological governance of the southwest rocky desertification is a large-scale strategy. Qinglong experience has changed the status quo, blazed a successful path of ecological governance of rocky desertification and peasants' prosperity out of poverty, and explored the effective forms of agricultural industrialization and the development of its economic organization. It has widespread the practical technology and become the successful practice of new rural construction in poor southwest areas. Qinglong model and the operation mechanism are not only the guidance for the development of grassland animal husbandry in the southwest region, but also an important reference for solving the problems about agriculture, rural areas and peasants in the entire poverty-stricken region. It is also an important implication to support the new rural construction with the development finance and the combination of production, education and research.

10.4.1. *The pilot ecological governance of rocky desertification at Qinglong County will continue to be implemented*

First, the advantage of the CDB in intelligence coordination should be brought into play. The CDB Guizhou Branch will help Qinglong County further improve the "12th Five-Year Plan" and scientifically formulate the development strategy of governance of rocky desertification and grassland animal husbandry. Second, experts will be organized to further diagnose the governance structure and operating conditions of Qinglong Grassland Animal Husbandry Company and help the company restructure according to the modern enterprise system, thus building it as the regional leading enterprise in agricultural industrialization. Third, more efforts will be made to promote financing. The CDB headquarters and branches jointly negotiated with the authorities of Guizhou Province and concluded that according to CDB medium-and small-size enterprise loan model, Hongsheng Capital Operating Company of Qianxinan Prefecture can serve as the borrower, thus unifying the borrowing and repayment; Qinglong Grassland Animal Husbandry Development Limited Liability Company acts as the user of the loan, handing out small anti-poverty loans to beneficial peasants and establishing the reclamation mechanism; Shijin Credit Guarantee Center of Qianxinan Prefecture takes joint and several liabilities and provides guarantee and Qinglong Grassland Animal Husbandry Company provides valid counter-guarantee for Shijin Credit Guarantee Center. The CDB branches are proposed to speed up the relevant reviews, try to issue 30 million yuan of loans, and expand the coverage of Qinglong model in the local area as soon as possible. The expansion will go beyond Qinglong County to southwest Guizhou Province.

10.4.2. *Qinglong experience should be actively promoted*

The "government + CDB + company + rural household" operation model is proposed to bring development financing into play after summarizing Qinglong experience. The CDB should further improve the operation model according to the actual situation so as to actively push forward the establishment of the provincial technological and financial services platform in Guizhou Province, integrate credit resources and technological advantages of governments at all levels, spread Qinglong experience, expand the pilot scope, and boost the governance of rocky desertification in Guizhou, Yunnan, Guangxi, Sichuan, Hunan, Hubei, Chongqing and Guangdong Provinces (autonomous region and municipality).

10.4.3. *The CDB should strengthen its connection*

The CDB should strengthen its connection with the State Council Leading Group Office of Poverty Alleviation and Development, NDRC, Ministry of Agriculture, Forestry Bureau and other relevant departments, actively participate in and assist the formulation of the special national governance planning of rocky desertification and related policies, better cooperate with the government to carry out the pilot programs and the national governance, and strive to bind the NDRC special governance funds, various government anti-poverty funds and the development financial capitals so as to achieve good economic and social effects through the operation of the company.

CHAPTER 11

NEW IDEAS FOR THE AGRICULTURAL COOPERATION BETWEEN CHINA AND SOUTH AMERICAN COUNTRIES

Strengthening the agricultural cooperation and development between China and South America is of important implications for both global grain security and China's grain security. Actively promoting the new channels in South American grain logistics, focusing on improving and building infrastructure in warehousing, logistics, port, agro-processing and other aspects features a new idea to strengthen the agricultural strategic cooperation between China and South American countries. The construction of new grain logistics channels, exploring the grain production capacity in areas covered by the channels and developing new farmlands not only helps to expand the local production capacity, but also helps to increase the grain supply for the international market. Besides, it also establishes the necessary security base for China's grain supplement.

11.1. Common Choice

11.1.1. *Food security as a global issue*

According to World Bank statistics, the global grain output has reached a record high of 2.59 billion tons in 2011, representing an increase of 2.9 times compared with 1961. Yet for all that, the global grain supply and demand situation is not optimistic. During 2010–2011, the rising grain cost has put nearly 70 million people into extreme poverty and the population suffering from hunger worldwide has reached 925 million. According to UN Statistics, as of the end of 2011, the global population has reached 7 billion, and calculating according to the current fertility rate, by 2050, the world population will exceed 9 billion. Rigid consumption resulted from the rapid growth of the world's population, the need of an upgraded food structure and biomass energy development will certainly bring enormous demand for food. The Food and Agriculture Organization (FAO) predicts that by 2050, the grain volume must be increased more than 70% from the current level in order to meet the global grain needs. If considering biomass energy development needs, the grain needs will be more substantial.

However, limited arable land and fresh water resources impose great constraints on the growth of global agricultural production, while the growth brought by technological advances is becoming increasingly slow. Comparing in a decade cycle as in the past 50 years, the average annual growth rate of the total arable land has decreased from 0.4% in the first decade to 0.2% in the fifth decade; meanwhile, the average annual growth rate of grain yield per unit area has decreased from 3.4% in the first decade to around 1.6% in the fifth decade. The difficulty faced by the growth of total grain output is becoming bigger and bigger (see Fig. 11.1).

In addition to the impact of supply and demand, international trade channels of staple food are narrow, the food source for international trade is concentrated in a few multinational grain merchants; grain is employed in speculation as a financial derivative and has exacerbated the abnormal fluctuations in international grain prices; besides, individual countries use food as a means to control oil prices and political and economic diplomacy and have made the global food

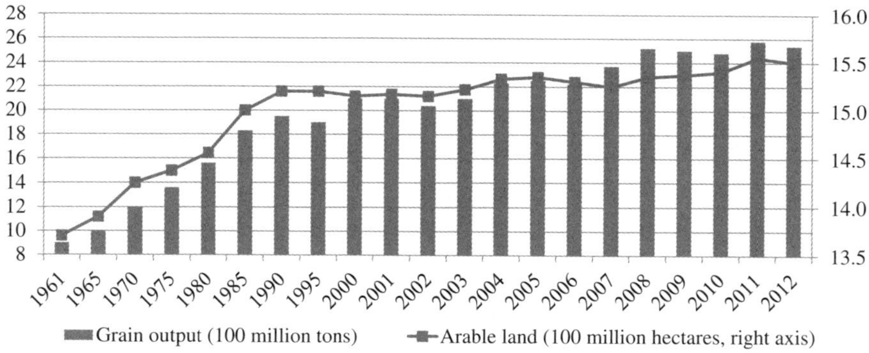

Figure 11.1: Changes in global grain production and arable land area, 1961–2012.

Note: The area of arable land in 2012 is estimated.
Source: UN FAO database.

problem more complicated. After the outbreak of the world food crisis in 2006 and 2007 resulting in the worldwide chaos and political instability in more than 20 countries, several countries in the world began to re-examine their agricultural policy, pay close attention to food production, and find ways to jointly cope with future food crises. The agricultural cooperation between China and South America helps to increase agricultural output and will finally make an important contribution to the global supply of agricultural products.

11.1.2. *Broad prospects for China–South America agricultural cooperation*

(1) South America is one of the most promising agricultural production areas. Development of land resources is one of the most basic approaches to meet global food needs. According to FAO Statistics, the theoretical amount of the world's arable land available for development is 1.32 billion hectares, mainly in South America and sub-Saharan Africa, accounting for 41% and 43% respectively of global arable land suitable for development and utilization. In comparison, South America enjoys better water, soil, light and heat conditions, and relatively sound infrastructure and is with no war distress.

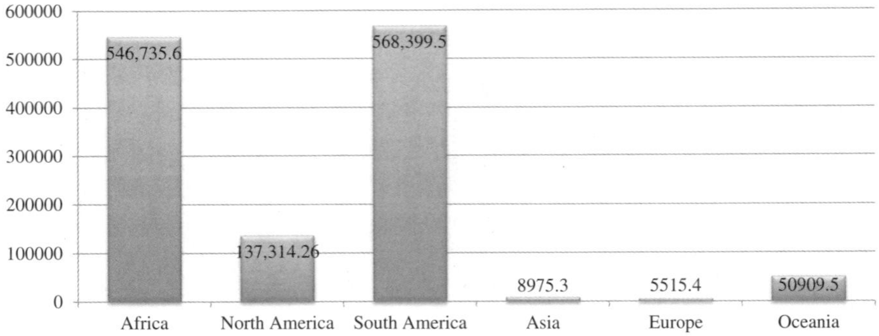

Figure 11.2: Actual potential arable land of each continent.
Source: UN FAO database.

Besides, this area is with relatively stable social security and features high degree of agricultural commercialization. For all these reasons, South America will naturally occupy an extremely important position in the future development of global agriculture and become the most competitive region for global agricultural resources. (see Fig. 11.2).

The arable land of 12 South American countries totals 144.538 million hectares, accounting for 8.4% of the land area. The arable land per capita is 0.36 hectares, much higher than the world's average level of 0.22 hectares and 0.09 hectares per capita in China. It's a region with great resource potential. Chile is the country that has developed the highest degree of its arable land with a ratio reaching 88.6%, followed by Argentina and Paraguay, 54.9% and 30.1% respectively.

South America has a rich reserve of arable land resources and is with 536.611 million hectares of arable land available for development. From the perspective of arable area, Brazil boasts the greatest development potential with an area of 314.772 million hectares, accounting for 58.7% of arable land available for development in South America, followed by Colombia, Bolivia, Argentina and Venezuela. The potential for the development of farmland is 43.692 million hectares, 42.012 million hectares, 32.113 million hectares and 35.161 million hectares respectively, accounting for 28.5% of total arable land available for development in South America (see Table 11.1).

Table 11.1: Arable land in South America (2011).

Item	Land area (1,000 hectares)	Arable land (1,000 hectares)	Ratio of arable land in total land area (%)	Cultivated area (1,000 hectares)	Ratio of cultivated land in arable land (%)	Cultivated land available for development (1,000 hectares)
South America	1,73,018.6	68,114.9	39.37	14,453.8	21.22	53,661.1
Argentina	27,366.9	7,116.1	26.00	3,904.8	54.87	3,211.3
Bolivia	10,833.0	4,606.7	42.52	405.5	8.80	4,201.2
Brazil	84,594.2	39,380.2	46.55	7,903.0	20.07	31,477.2
Chile	7,435.3	200.3	2.69	177.4	88.57	22.9
Columbia	11,095.0	4,769.0	42.98	399.8	8.38	4,369.2
Ecuador	822.0	919.4	111.85	253.5	27.57	665.9
Guyana	1,968.5	973.9	49.47	44.7	4.59	929.2
Paraguay	3,973.0	1,325.7	33.37	399.0	30.10	926.7
Peru	12,800.0	3,056.7	23.88	450.0	14.72	2,606.7
Surinam	1,560.0	673.6	43.18	6.5	0.96	667.1
Uruguay	1,750.2	1,252.2	71.55	184.6	14.74	1,067.6
Venezuela	8,820.5	3,841.1	43.55	325.0	8.46	3,516.1

Note: Arable land is the sum of temporary crop land, temporary grassland, fallow land and perennial crop land.
Source: UN FAO database.

(2) China is one of the world's largest and most dynamic markets. With the rapid growth of China's population, the escalation of the consumption structure of agriculture, and as the agricultural demand continues to grow rigid and with the constraints of domestic water and soil resources, China's dependence on foreign agricultural products has increased gradually. Since 2004, China has become a net importer of agricultural products; and by the end of 2012, food imports (including soybeans) from the international market has exceeded 80 million tons with import dependence up to 13%. Specifically, more than 80% of soybean is imported; rice, wheat, corn and other staple foods while still maintaining 97–98% self-sufficiency, are also subject to a gradually rising trend in imports. Besides, among China's imports of staple agricultural products, the import volume of cotton fluctuates within 25% to 45% in different years while sugar fluctuates within 10% to 30%. Calculating based on the current bulk imports of agricultural products, more than 900 million mu (67 million hectares) of overseas arable land is used to satisfy China's demand for agricultural products. It's predicted that by 2020, China's grain (including the soybean) imports will be between 95 and 123 million tons (soybean shortage between 70 to 93 million tons, and grain shortage between 25 to 30 million tons), a growth of 20% on the current basis. It is urgent to formulate plans ahead, make full use of the resources on the two markets, and accelerate the construction of China's overseas agricultural products safeguarding system. South America is the source of Chinese soybean, sugar and other agricultural commodities, and is also the region with the greatest agricultural development potential and the ability to export bulk products. Strengthening agricultural cooperation with South American countries is helpful to improve China's security of agricultural products.

11.1.3. *China and South America to jointly maximize the benefits*

China and South America belong to northern and southern hemisphere respectively, so the agricultural products come into season alternately. This helps to reduce inventory pressure for the agricultural producers in the place of origin and the agro-processing enterprises of the sales market, and also helps to improve cash flow speed. China and South American countries are highly complementary in terms of agricultural technology, capital and markets etc. Thus, capitalizing on the comparative advantage and jointly promoting agricultural development is conducive to maximize benefits.

South America enjoys a great potential for natural resources development; however, the development is not sufficient due to shortage of funds and other factors. The storage and food transport capacity is badly behind the growth of food production; in particular, the new grain production areas are faced with a serious shortage of storage capacity. Over 70% of grain transfer depends on road transport, making the proportion of logistics cost account for about 25% to 30% of the food price. This partly offsets the cost advantage of South American grain. The roads leading to main grain producing areas are not enough and are seriously damaged, the handling capacity of railways and major grain ports is far from adequate, and the food convoy congestion and port overstock during food sales seasons are quite serious. Inadequate infrastructure not only affects the efficiency of agricultural logistics in South America, it increases transportation costs, while also restricts the development of other resources in South America. South American infrastructure construction, subject to funding shortage and constraints of Environmental Investigation Agency (EIA), land and other limiting factors, progresses rather slowly.

China boasts strong economic force and technological strength, which could help to improve the infrastructure of the South American countries, increase agricultural production capacity, promote the economic development in cooperative regions, and promote local labor employment and increase revenue. China's agricultural cooperation with South America provides chances for both parties to learn from each other and achieve complementary advantages, which will not only bring stability to the world and China's agricultural supply, but also offer opportunities for China and South American countries to maximize the benefits.

The cooperative relationship between China and South America has also entered into a new era of rapid development in the new century, showing a good momentum of comprehensive, extensive and multi-level development. In agriculture, South America, the area with most potential for development, and China, the world's largest and most dynamic market, enjoy ever-closer exchanges; and the agricultural cooperation has further expanded to investment cooperation, technical cooperation and to other agricultural fields.

In recent years, China has signed the memorandum of understanding on agricultural cooperation with Brazil, Argentina and other countries, established the joint committees on agriculture and working groups with Brazil, Argentina, Chile and other countries, and has formed a fixed cooperation and communication mechanism. China and Venezuela signed the Quartet (Ministry of Agriculture and development bank of both countries) Memorandum of Understanding on Agricultural Cooperation, introducing for the first time the agricultural financial institutions into bilateral cooperation. Besides, China and Chile established a Sino–Chile demonstration farm in Tianjin. Chinese Academy of Agricultural Sciences and the Brazilian Academy of Agricultural Sciences jointly established a laboratory for cooperative research, etc. In 2008, China formulated China's Policy Paper on Latin America and the Caribbean and proposed to strengthen comprehensive cooperation with Latin American and Caribbean countries in agriculture, investment, poverty reduction and other areas. The formulation of the above mechanism and policy has laid a solid foundation for the further agricultural cooperation between China and major South American countries.

In June 2012, Chinese Premier visited four Latin American countries, to further clarify the direction of the agricultural cooperation between China and Latin America, and put forward specific initiatives: Advocated the establishment of Sino–Latin American Agriculture Ministers Forum; recommended the establishment of a Sino–Latin American emergency food reserve mechanism of 500,000 tons to respond to natural disasters and humanitarian emergencies; Chinese government would invest 50 million US dollars to establish a special fund for the development of Sino–Latin American agricultural cooperation; planned to set up in Latin America, five to eight agricultural technology research and development centers, agro-processing demonstration gardens and agricultural investment zones etc.; committed that China State Development Bank would take the lead to establish a special loan of 10 billion US dollars to promote the infrastructure construction cooperation between China and Latin American countries in production and areas important to people's livelihood. In 2013, China State Development Bank also organized the preparation of the Strategic Planning on the Agricultural Cooperation between China and South America. These initiatives are of great practical significance in promoting the strategic agricultural cooperation between China and South America, jointly coping with the rigid demand in growth of global agricultural products, the narrow international agricultural trade channels and agricultural price monopoly.

11.1.4. *Problems*

China and South America cooperate in agriculture by means of trade cooperation, technical cooperation and investment cooperation. The total trade amounted to $30.6 billion in 2012. But overall, trade cooperation is still the main approach with technical and investment cooperation still in its infancy. According to the statistics by the Chinese Ministry of Commerce, as of the end of 2011, Chinese investment overseas in terms of animal husbandry and fishery totaled 3.42 billion US dollars, accounting for about 1% of China's total overseas investments. The investment mainly focuses on China's neighboring countries, and the investment in South America is still in its initial stage. The total investment is less than 100 million US dollars, and companies involved in the investment cooperation and agricultural engineering contracting are less than 15. Agricultural investment is about purchasing or leasing land to directly engage in agricultural production and operation, with the main industries including soybean, palm and olive cultivation, forest products processing and fisheries cooperation etc.

The investment cooperation between China and South America is still at its start. The enterprises participating is small in quantity, the scale of investment is small, the investment methods are limited and the cooperation is faced with substantial difficulties.

Although the total amount of Chinese enterprises in South America is very small, it's still unfair that some international media defame Chinese enterprises' settlement in South America as "land occupation" and "colonization". Some countries have introduced bills to limit the total size of land purchase by foreign capital, and have reduced the investment enthusiasm of Chinese investors. Chinese enterprises, in serious lack of international business experience, need to take the long view and come up with a feasible strategic thinking.

11.2. Jointly Establish a New Channel of Direct Production and Sales

11.2.1. *Background*

In the past century, especially since the 1990s, international capital, mainly US and Japanese capital, has gradually realized the control over bulk agricultural commodities of major grain-producing countries in South America, *via* issuing production loans to agricultural producers and covering loans by food recovery, *via* establishing grain storage systems to increase the storage options of the place of production, *via* setting up (acquisition) storage and transportation docks in the main shipping ports to control multinational food logistics, and *via* promoting the control mode of genetically modified (GM) varieties patents. Currently, areas under the actual control of the four major multinational grain merchants have almost covered all core grain producing areas in Brazil, Argentina, Uruguay, and Paraguay; and the control is now further expanding toward food-producing areas newly opened in recent years, as well as Bolivia and other countries. Supplemented by the global and South American "agricultural condition prediction" and "yield revision" reports timely released by the US Department of Agriculture, such a control will directly affect the international future market prices and the transaction of spot goods. So far, Brazil, Argentina and other major agricultural exporters in the agricultural sector have gradually lost their say on decisions ranging from grain varieties to acquisition criteria, from pricing to trade quantity, which shall have a huge impact on income of farmers and national interests.

Similarly, although China is the world's largest buyer of agricultural products, it has little say due to the fact that it purchases from international grain companies. When China intends to purchase certain kinds of agricultural products, its price will increase. Lack of import channels and pricing power subject Chinese consumers to international grain dealers' price control. China's soybean oil processing industry suffers from greater loss with acute fluctuation of forward price.

Strengthening agricultural cooperation with South American countries and establishing channels between places of production and consumption can promote agricultural cooperation of the two sides, and it serves as a significant approach to protect people's benefit on the two sides and promote mutual development.

In consideration of existing international competition patterns, and after comparison and research, it is concluded that South American logistics channel is still a weak link. Four international grain companies also express their wishes to improve South American logistics channel. Therefore, to enhance strategic agricultural cooperation between China and South America, we should jointly establish new channels for direct production and marketing trade, improve infrastructure such as warehousing, logistics, ports and agriculture products processing, build international circulation system connecting production areas to form direct channel between China and South America, so as to reduce logistics cost of staple products like grain and promote the development of potential production areas.

11.2.2. *Current status of the channel*

There are three large international logistics channels between South American grain production area and China: First, going north through the main ports of Brazil, Argentina and Uruguay, and through Atlantic Ocean, Panama Canal and Pacific Ocean to China, Japan, Taiwan, Indonesia and other Asian countries and regions; second, to EU and Africa through Brazil and Argentina eastern ports and Atlantic Ocean; third, to China, Japan, and other Asian countries and regions through Atlantic Ocean, Indian Ocean and Malacca Strait. These three logistics channels for international grain are mainly controlled by four major grain companies.

Grain logistics direction inside South America: South America has a small population, and a majority of countries cultivate tropical crops, featuring similar agricultural product mix. With competition from North America in grain export, internal trade volume is small. South American countries have few traffic lines between each other due to the block of Andes and Amazon rainforest. With no coastal ports, Bolivia and Paraguay conduct international trade through land transportation, while other countries through their convenient harbors. Internal large quantity grain trade: Argentina exports flour, wheat, corn and other grains to Brazil, Chile and Bolivia through coastal ports and international shipping channels; Brazil exports beef and other animal products to Venezuela, Guyana and other countries.

The population of South America is mainly distributed in coastal regions, or cool highlands and mountain areas, while large scale grain production areas are distributed in mild inland plain or highland areas. Internal grain export is moving from inland to major coastal cities and ports, while that of major grain exporters such as Brazil and Argentina is from inland production areas to coastal cities close to Atlantic ports and from road, railway and water channels to major grain shipping ports. With the increase of grain yield, together with one-way flow and seasonal features, grain logistics channels are crowded and ports suffer from overstock.

11.2.3. *Establish a new channel for grain logistics*

Under the present logistics pattern, any single company will have to pay high prices to enter South American grain market and compete with international grain companies directly. Chinese companies must improve present logistics model and establish a new logistics channel free from international grain companies (e.g., the fourth grain channel). Based on the newly established fourth grain channel, Chinese companies can compete and cooperate with international grain companies.

The goal of the fourth grain channel is to combine with transport infrastructure planning of South American countries and to accommodate to their development strategy (for example, 85% of Brazil's soybean is produced in the south and 15% in the north. The strategic plan for future is that both south and north produce 50%): (1) Establishing seamless logistics channel in Brazil and other major grain exporters; (2) Expanding water shipping capacity of Amazon River, its branches and Parana, improve logistics infrastructure and substantially reduce logistics costs; (3) Build railway in Bolivia no-railway areas based on the existing railway system of Brazil, Bolivia and Peru, to open up Atlantic–Pacific railway grain transport channel; (4) Develop Parana water shipping capacity and improve logistics infrastructure system, as well as the substantially low logistics capacity.

The following three grain logistics passages are to be established, considering the distribution of potential grain production area and areas under the control of international grain companies.

11.2.3.1. *New passage of Amazon golden waterway*

Transport grains from Brazilian newly-developed grain production areas through Amazon branches Rio Madeira, Tapajos River and Xingu River, and enter international market *via* Santarem, Almeirim and other northern ports through Amazon River main channel and coastal grain harbors. The construction programs include ports infrastructure construction, bulk grain wharf construction and others.

Main advantages of this channel are: First, less transportation cost than road transportation, fit for grain transportation in central and northeastern Brazil (it's estimated that logistics cost per ton reduces by 40 dollars to ship export soybean from the north compared with that of the south); second, the Amazon River and its branches are not fully used and there are more investment opportunities in northern ports and roads. However, early stage investment will be great, since the channel goes through Amazon Rainforest Reserve and there are many environmental obstacles.

11.2.3.2. *Further develop Parana River grain transportation passage*

Further develop water shipping capacity of Parana River and its branches, as well as freight transport capacity of eastern Bolivia, central Brazil, Paraguay, and central and western Argentina. The focus of construction plan is on inland grain ports, and necessary river dredging near the ports, such as Encarnacion Port, Reconquista Port and Santa Fe Port. The grain will be delivered to international market through Rosario Port.

Main advantages of this channel include: First, in core grain production areas, with shorter water shipping distance and lower logistics costs; and second, exert comprehensive advantage of the channel and facilitate ore resources transportation from central Brazil and eastern Bolivia. The disadvantages are that ships need to transfer from inland water transportation to sea transportation, and that there is great difficulty to participate in the construction and operation of large scale harbors.

11.2.3.3. *New railway passage between Atlantic and Pacific for grain transportation*

Make full use of the favorable opportunity of Latin American regional economic integration, and the existing railway system in Brazil, Bolivia and Peru, to construct railway in Bolivian no-railway area and form a new freight railway connecting Atlantic Ocean and Pacific Ocean, forming a new logistics channel to transport grain from central Brazil to Asia through Bolivia, Peru and the Pacific Ocean.

Connecting port in the east of the channel is Brazil's Santos Harbor, which is connected with Antofagasta port of Peru or Iquiqueport of Chile through Columbia, Brazil and Santa Cruz, Bolivia. Main construction content is railway infrastructure construction and grain strategic loading point construction (regional entrepot storage).

This channel features four advantages over the previous channels: First, substantially reduce freight transportation distance between South America and China, reduce logistics costs; second, form a

China-based operational channel; third, give full play to the comprehensive benefits of iron ore transportation, salt mine transportation and grain transportation; fourth, in line with Latin American economic integration requirements, promote international circulation of internal mechanical equipment, project and service and relieve the problem of no departing channel in Bolivia. Its disadvantages are: First, different countries hold different view to this railway channel, and project line design and construction sequence are not unified, causing great difficulty in carrying out the construction; and second, large investment amount, while rail capacity might not be adequate, leading to large risks of operating loss.

11.2.3.4. *Intensify infrastructure construction and operation of important points*

The following infrastructures at two important points will be constructed through combining construction of new grain logistics channel and features of grain logistics.

11.2.3.4.1. Port grain wharf and logistics park

Search for suitable ports in northern or western Brazil, and conduct long-term lease or Build–operate–transfer (BOT), to control specialized bulk freight wharf and establish a logistics park integrating soybean processing, storage and logistics so as to guarantee the logistics operation and avoid long time demurrage of cargo or vessel.

11.2.3.4.2. Strategic loading point (regional entrepot storage)

After careful research and investigation, and in new grain production area (equipped with inland waterway, rail transportation or road transportation, and close to main production area of soybean), search for strategic loading point, build inland waterway or railway central terminal station, realize multi-model transport through inland port logistics park or railway logistics park, connect new grain production area with new ports, so as to increase traffic volume of inland waterway and railway as much as possible and reduce road transport and logistics costs.

11.2.3.4.3. New purchasing and storage system

Driven by the international market, South America witnesses a rapid increase in grain yield, while its storage capacity remains poor. With high investment demands for storage and drying facilities, farmers always sell grain to regional warehouses after storing for a short time upon harvest. Owning warehouses means owning control over grain from a certain number of farms nearby.

Chinese grain companies can make plans to establish independent grain purchasing and storage system in major grain production areas, newly emerged production areas in particular, or increase storage capacity through long-term lease to increase their say on grain prices.

11.3. Cooperation Mode and Policy

11.3.1. *Business mode*

Joint ventures and capital contribution are the main business modes at the initial stage. As for cooperative manners, it features great diversity. At the start of cooperation, joint ventures, cooperatives, shareholdings, China-funded enterprises and stock sharing with the host countries etc. are the main modes of cooperation to engage in local business and profit distribution. Areas of cooperation include technical cooperation, co-branding, project cooperation and product cooperation etc. The goal is mainly to become familiar with resources, markets, channels, humanities and laws, and to establish a good social relationship. When conditions are ripe, Chinese enterprises shall buy back shares or develop the markets as individual proprietorship enterprises. Partners are mainly local companies of host countries, with a special goal to strengthen the cooperation with Chinese immigrants or Chinese enterprises of certain economic powers in South America. During the joint venture process, Chinese enterprises should take more advantage of the local production, technical and managerial talents, focusing on the development of tangible assets, on the use and promotion of Chinese varieties, supporting production technology, production and processing patents and proprietary technology and brand etc.

Efforts should be made to timely carry out overseas mergers and acquisitions. Mergers and acquisitions of companies, enterprises of host countries or international agricultural trade companies is the most efficient and effective way to promote agricultural cooperation between China and South America. Mergers and acquisitions can take place *via* overall acquisition, restructuring holdings, holdings, shareholdings *via* capital increment, stock acquisition and other means. Mergers and acquisitions focus on the core enterprises or companies at the key links in the agricultural industry chain, with quickly capturing the market, expanding the scale of operation, avoiding horizontal competition and using the original brand to create profits for Chinese-funded enterprises as the basic goal.

We should follow-up with a complete industrial chain. Efforts should be made to follow the industrial chain operation ideas to strengthen the planning of key cooperative areas and key construction projects, attract upstream and downstream enterprises into mutual improvement and joint development, so as to form industrial composition and maximize the value of industrial chain.

11.3.2. *Policy base*

The strategic Sino–South America agricultural cooperation is based on the following basic points.

11.3.2.1. *An international perspective*

Against the backdrop of economic globalization and regional economic integration, a country's economic development, including the settlement of food and other strategic resource problems, need to be placed on an international level and on the basis of the large system of global food supply and demand balance. In the international market environment, while developing policies governing the Sino–South America strategic agricultural cooperation, besides considering the economic development of both parties, we should also consider multiple dimensions of global politics, diplomacy, trade and society etc. Agricultural strategic cooperation involves not only China and South America, but will also concern more and more countries and regions, even the global economy and trade. To this end, special attention should be paid to countries and regions outside China and South America, in particular, the economic trend and trend of cooperation of Europe, US, Japan and other developed countries, as well as the resulting impact on global food trade. In the Sino–South America agricultural strategic cooperation, we should properly handle the relationship between regional development and the global economy, consider the settlement of China's food problem from the perspective of global food market, try to avoid triggering or expand possible regional and even global sensitive issues, and try to avoid the consequential multi-stakeholder conflicts.

11.3.2.2. *A holistic perspective*

The policies formulated for Sino–South America agricultural strategic cooperation, besides reflecting the main role of the Chinese government, must also reflect the important role of professional sectors and enterprise groups. In addition to obtaining major agricultural products to meet domestic demand, it shall also include agriculture-related industrial policy support and the potential policy support areas that may attract successful cooperation. The purpose is to introduce Chinese agriculture to South American countries, achieve stable access to major agricultural products, and ensure national food security, backed by the joint attention, support and participation from the central government, relevant departments and business groups. Another goal is to achieve a coordinated policy support among decision-making sectors, financial sectors and enterprise groups in the expansion toward South American countries and agricultural cooperation.

11.3.2.3. *Industrial chain perspective*

The formulation of Sino–South America agricultural strategic cooperation policies should be conducive to derive maximum benefit for both parties and establish an extensive cooperation throughout the whole agriculture industry chain, including various sectors of production, processing, logistics, warehousing and sales etc. On the basis of establishing a stable access channel to agricultural products, the cooperation should extend further to related fields of agricultural production to help South American countries strengthen their self-development capacity; extend to the agricultural processing sector, to achieve value increment of agricultural products and provide the South American countries with more employment space; extend to the area of product sales. More marketing channels and sales terminals should be established to meet the livelihood needs of the South American countries; extend to the field of transport of agricultural products, to improve the transportation network and improve the inland shipping capacity of South American countries.

11.3.2.4. *Differentiation perspective*

While formulating the policies for Sino–South America agricultural strategic cooperation, different policy support must be chosen for each South American country according to their varied agricultural resources, production and development prospects, product trade patterns, and different agricultural development policies as well as Chinese and foreign cultural differences, combined with China's domestic demand expectation for agricultural products. Policy support for traditional agricultural exporting countries with abundant agricultural resources, policy support should focus on raising agricultural resources utilization and improving agricultural production conditions etc., so as to improve the production and export capacity of these countries; while for agricultural resource-rich countries incapable of self-sufficiency, policy support should focus on the improvement of land productivity to meet the need of self-sufficiency and a moderate amount of export; finally for economically backward countries with inadequate agricultural resources, policy support should focus on helping these countries toward resource efficiency, improve people's livelihood and wipe out poverty.

11.3.2.5. *Cooperation perspective*

Policy-making of Sino–South America agricultural strategic cooperation should be based on the needs of South American agriculture and food security, apart from China's strategic demands and economic interests of Chinese enterprises. Policies should be made with clear targets and focus, and adjustments shall be made in accordance with political change, social conditions and various risks, appeals and wishes of South American countries. We should pay attention to policy trend, implementation scope and effect, and solve the problems and conflicts facing South American countries in agricultural development through cooperation and help them to develop. China's agriculture should go global on the basis of mutual benefits to realize sustained win–win results.

11.4. Conclusion

South America is blessed with particularly favorable conditions for agricultural production and development. China, as a long-term and stable export market of South American agricultural products, is highly complementary with South America in the field of agriculture. Strengthening agricultural strategic cooperation is in line with the interest appeal of each party, and is of vital importance in safeguarding global food security and food security in China.

The basic ideas of China's agricultural investment in South America are: First, continue to strengthen the agricultural strategic cooperation between China and South America, make efforts to increase food output in South America to jointly cope with the challenges of global food security, while taking into account China's future demand for bulk agricultural commodities; second, take participation in the agricultural infrastructure construction in South America as an important breakthrough. Cooperation should focus on resource-rich South American countries with poor agricultural infrastructure and projects in favor of infrastructure integration in South America; third, create a new agricultural storage and logistics system, establish and improve a safety network of agricultural products supply; fourth, encourage strong and reputable Chinese enterprises to make investment in agriculture in South America, and also encourage them to explore the establishment of industrial cooperation mechanism to promote the deepening of industrial connection and integration with South America; and fifth, continue to enhance the level of national agricultural cooperation between China and South America, and build a comprehensive agricultural chain integrating agricultural technology R&D center, agro-processing demonstration garden and agricultural investment and development zone, etc.

Main points of Sino–South America agricultural strategic cooperation policies include: First, we need an international perspective, strategic height and sustained depth. The policies should be able to help and support China and South American countries to establish a mutually beneficial and win–win cooperation pattern, taking into account the relevant interests of other countries in South American countries; Second, we need to control risk, remain robust and prudent, and pay close attention to and follow the international political developments, political situation changes in partner countries, international trade trends, as well as risks such as exchange rate fluctuations. It shall include the assumption and management of risk that can bring investment benefits, placing control of various risks into an important position of policy formulation and execution. High attention should be given to risk control; and we should pursue a long-term, stable and sustainable operation from the perspective of policy formulation and operation.

Important starting points in Sino–South America agricultural strategic cooperation: Step up efforts to improve and build infrastructure facilities in warehousing, logistics, port, agro-processing and other sectors, focus on the construction of the New Logistics Passage of Amazon Golden Waterway, Parana River Grain Transportation Passage and New Grain Transportation Railway Passage between Atlantic and Pacific, build in South America a new grain logistics channel with China as the main player, improve the efficiency of logistics in South America, and promote local food production and market development.

BIBLIOGRAPHY

Chen Yuan (2010). *Study on the Establishment and Improvement of Social Security System Covering Rural and Urban Areas.* Beijing: Yanjiu Publishing House.

Chinese Society for Urban Studies (2008). *Report on the Development of Industries in Chinese Urban Planning 2007–2008.* Beijing: China Building Industry Press.

Dai Yingma (2008). *Theoretical Economics.* Zhejiang: Zhejiang University Press.

Deng Yingtao (2011). *New Energy Revolution and the Development Mode Transitions.* Hong Kong: Strongwind Publishing House.

Ding Chengri (2005). *Urban Planning and Spatial Structure: Sustainable Urban Development.* Beijing: China Building Industry Press.

Eric Anderson (2011). *China Restored: The Middle Kingdom Looks to 2020 and Beyond.* Beijing: Xinhua Publishing House.

Fang Qiyun and Yao Zhu (2008). *Development Economics.* Dalian: Dongbei University of Finance and Economics.

Fei Xiaotong (1984). *Chinese Native Society.* Beijing: People's Publishing House.

Ge Zhihua (2004). *Seek to Solve the Issue of Agriculture, Rural Areas and Peasants in China: The Rural Society in Transition.* Nanjing: Jiangsu People's Publishing House.

Gu Hailiang and Yan Pengfei (2009). *Review of History of Economic Thought.* Beijing: Economic Science Press.

He Xuefeng (2013). *Smallholder Stance.* Beijing: China University of Political Science and Law Press.

Hu Angang (2005). The four new features in social transformation in China. *China Revolution Newspaper*, 15 August.

Jenny Clegg (2010). *China's Global Strategy: Toward a Multipolar World.* Beijing: Xinhua Publishing House.

Jiang Hong (2012). *An Outline of World Economy: Research on Typical and Atypical Path of Development.* Beijing: China Renmin University Press.

Joint Research Topic Group of China Development Bank and China Renmin University (2006). *Development Finance in China.* Beijing: China Renmin University Press.

Keith Thomas (2008). *Man and the Natural World: Changing Attitudes in England 1500–1800.* Nanjing: Pheonix Publishing & Media Group Publishing House.

Liang Shuanglu (2009). *Borderland Economics: International Regional Economic Integration and Development of China Borderland Economics.* Beijing: China Renmin University Press.

Liang Suming (1989). *The Collected Works of Liang Suming.* Beijing: People's Publishing House.

Lin Shangli (2009). *The Community Party of China and the State-Building in China.* Tianjin: Tianjin People's Publishing House.

Liu Junjie (2005). *County Economic Development and Construction of Small Towns.* Beijing: Social Sciences Academic Press.

Mao Zedong (1975). *The Selected Works of Mao Zedong.* Beijing: People's Publishing House.

Nie Hualin, Lu Di and Li Quan (2009). *General Theory of Modern Regional Economy.* Beijing: China Social Sciences Publishing House.

Qin Qingwu and Xu Jinying (2004). *Issues concerning Agriculture, Rural Areas and Peasants: Problems and Solutions.* Jinan: Shandong People's Publishing House.

Ren Jizhou and Huang Qian (2011). *The Green Pastoral Prospects for the Karst Mountainous Areas: A Consulting Project on Agro-Grassland System in Karst Areas of Southwest China.* Beijing: Science Press.

Su Baozhong (2009). *A Study of the Old-Age Pension Problem in Rural China.* Beijing: Tsinghua University Press.

The Book Writing Group (2012). *Rainbow after the Rain: Explorations and Practices of Township Institutional Reform in the New Period.* Beijing: China Social Sciences Publishing House.

Wei Liqun (2008). *Policy Study and Policy Decision Reference.* Beijing: China Yanshi Publishing House.

Yang Jisheng (2006). *Analysis of Chinese Contemporary Social Strata*. Lanzhou: Gansu People's Publishing House.

Zhang Liang (1996). On the true nature of social transformation. *Journal of Jiaxing University* (*Social Sciences Ed.*). Volume 3, pp. 6–11.

Zhang Luxiong (2011). *Land to the Tiller: Reality and Logics of the Chinese Farmland System*. Beijing: China University of Political Science and Law Press.

Zhang Zhenghe, Tan Xiangyong and Xu Jun (2005). *County Rural Industrial Restructuring and the Allocation of Resources*. Beijing: Science Press.

Zhang Zhenghe (2006). Imbalanced urban and rural development in China. *People's Daily* (*Overseas Ed.*), 21 November.

Zheng Bingwen (2012). *Middle Income Trap: Case Studies from Latin America & Caribbean*. Beijing: The Contemporary World Press.

Zhong Xiangcai (2006). *Treatise on the Economic Thoughts in China in the 20th Century*. Beijing: China Publishing Group Oriental Publishing Center.

Zou Lixing (2006). *Financial Development and Structure in China*. Changsha: Hunan University Press.

POSTSCRIPT

It is my sincere wish to do something for rural economic and social development. Though the views may not necessarily be correct, this book, a result of independent thinking and emancipating mind on the basis of study, was written with care. I believe my book has some reference value for researchers and practitioners. The long accumulated Chinese rural problems require long time of development to resolve, and new problems will appear in the process of the development. Some of my designs and policy ideas in the book such as "enhance the overall, comprehensive and endogenous dynamics of the county economy and coordinate the urban and rural economic and social development" are suitable for the present tasks and completely consistent with the spirit of the third Plenary Session of the 18th CPC Central Committee; some of them such as "optimize the national land management structures and institutions" may enlighten the future generations. For a long time, I have been concerned about the rural affairs, engaged in research on economic policies, comparing the domestic and international markets and working in the bank. Such experience and background offers me a certain vision in the studies which focus on strategy and operability. My parents, brothers and sisters, wife and children have already left the countryside, but my feelings toward the countryside will be never gone.

I am first grateful to my wife and my son for the warmth of family and support they give to me.

I am grateful to my grandparents, who are simple and industrious peasants. They saved their own rice to feed me when I was young and taught me at every important stage of my growth.

I am grateful to my parents and brothers and sisters for their considerate care and assistance.

I am grateful to the commune leaders Gong Zhangfu and Yan Yousheng as well as all the fellow countrymen for their help and care when I went to the countryside.

I am also grateful to my mentors when I studied abroad; they are: Professor David Bloom, Professor Bhagwati Jagdish, Professor Miller Ronald, Professor Kenneth C. Kusterer, Professor K. Siegentheler, Professor Ngan-Ling Chow, and Professor Gong Yang.

I am also grateful to many friends, some of the leaders and colleagues (not mentioned here) for many of their assistances they gave to me.

I am especially grateful to Mr. Jiang Zhenhua, former vice chairman of the Standing Committee of the National People's Congress, who wrote a preface after going through the draft.

Finally, I am grateful to the readers, and any advice from you is welcome.

Author

INDEX